J. Z. (John Zephaniah) Holwell

A Review of the Original Principles, Religious and Moral

Of the Ancient Bramins

J. Z. (John Zephaniah) Holwell

A Review of the Original Principles, Religious and Moral
Of the Ancient Bramins

ISBN/EAN: 9783337184414

Printed in Europe, USA, Canada, Australia, Japan

Cover: Foto ©Thomas Meinert / pixelio.de

More available books at **www.hansebooks.com**

A REVIEW OF THE

ORIGINAL PRINCIPLES,

RELIGIOUS AND MORAL,

OF THE *Sam.ᵗ Miller's*

ANCIENT BRAMINS:

Comprehending an Account of the

MYTHOLOGY, COSMOGONY,
FASTS, AND FESTIVALS,

OF THE

G E N T O O S,

Followers of the SHASTAH.

WITH A

DISSERTATION on the METEMPSYCHOSIS,
commonly, though erroneoufly, called the
PYTHAGOREAN Doctrine.

By J. Z. H O L W E L L, Efq.

ILLUSTRATED WITH PLATES.

L O N D O N:
Printed for T. VERNOR, at his Shops, in MICHAEL's-ALLEY,
CORNHILL, and in FORE-STREET.
M.DCC.LXXIX.

INTERESTING

HISTORICAL EVENTS,

Relative to the

PROVINCES of BENGAL;

AND THE

EMPIRE of INDOSTAN.

PART II.

TO THE MOST NOBLE

H U G H,

DUKE AND EARL OF NORTHUMBERLAND;

EARL PERCY;

BARON WARKWORTH OF WARKWORTH CASTLE;

LORD LIEUTENANT AND CUSTOS RO-
TULORUM OF THE COUNTIES OF MIDDLE-
SEX AND NORTHUMBERLAND, OF THE
CITY AND LIBERTY OF WESTMINSTER,
AND OF THE TOWN AND COUNTY OF
THE TOWN OF NEWCASTLE UPON TYNE;
VICE ADMIRAL OF ALL AMERICA, AND
OF THE COUNTY OF NORTHUMBER-
LAND; ONE OF THE LORDS OF HIS MA-
JESTY'S MOST HONORABLE PRIVY COUN-
CIL; KNIGHT OF THE MOST NOBLE
ORDER OF THE GARTER; AND FELLOW
OF THE ROYAL SOCIETY.

MY LORD,

IT is with equal deference and pleasure that I submit the following performance to your Grace's pe-
rusal;

DEDICATION.

rufal; being perfuaded you will not think it altogether unworthy of your notice from the important, but uncommon fubject it treats upon. Neither do I apprehend you will think my inducement to this work an unbecoming one, when I tell your Grace my intention was to refcue the originally untainted manners, and religious worfhip of a very ancient people from grofs mifreprefentation.

I thought it moft unjuft that the wifdom and tenets of BRAMAH and the ancient BRAMINS fhould be longer difgraced by the ftrange innovations and practices of their modern brethren; for from thefe unworthy fucceffors alone have been diffeminated the general accounts which we are hitherto made acquainted with of the theology of· thefe people.

Hence

DEDICATION.

Hence it is that although the wifdom of the Eaftern fages has been
proverbially famous, yet we find them
reprefented to us, in moft relations,
as a race, from the beginning, equally
credulous and ignorant. From fuch
imputations I have endeavoured to
vindicate them; not by labored apologies, but by a fimple difplay of
their primitive theology, which I
would willingly hope cannot but be
acceptable to the public, in fo inquifitive and learned an age as this.

Whatever fmall degree of appro-
bation my imperfect labors may obtain from the world, I reft affured it
will applaud my choice of a patron
on whofe judgement and candor I
can fecurely rely ; as being a perfonage whofe exalted titles are rendered

more

more refplendent by the amiable virtues and qualities that adorn them—
Virtues! which have endeared him
alike to prince and people.

I have the honor to fubfcribe
myfelf,

My Lord Duke,

Your Grace's moft obedient

and moft humble fervant,

Beenham Houfe, Berks,
Nov. 1ft, 1766.

J. Z. HOLWELL.

C H A P. IV.

The Religious Tenets of the Gentoos, followers of the Shaftah of Bramah.

INTRODUCTION.

WE have already premifed, that in the profecution of this our fourth general head, we fhould touch only on the original *principal* tenets of thefe ancient people the *Gentoos*; for were we to penetrate into, and difcufs the whole of their modern ceremonials, and complicated modes of worfhip; our labor would be without end : thefe are as diffufe, as the ancient fundamental tenets of *Bramah* are fhort, pure, fimple and uniform ; in this predicament the *Gentoos* are not fingular, as the original text of every theological fyftem, has, we prefume, from a fimilar caufe, unhappily undergone the fame fate ; though at firft promulged as a divine inftitution.

Part II.　　　　B　　　　We

We fhall not fay much regarding the antiquity of thefe people; nor fhall we amufe
ourfelves with the reveries of chronologers
and hiftorians; who have labored to fix with
precifion (though not two of them agree in
opinion) the various migrations after the
flood : it fhall fuffice for our purpofe, that
by their own fhewing, *Indoftan* was as
early peopled, as moft other parts of the
known world.

The firft invaders of this empire, found
the inhabitants a potent, opulent, civilized,
wife, and learned people; united under one
head, and one uniform profeffion of divine
worfhip ; by the fundamental principles of
which, they were precluded communication,
and focial converfe, with the reft of mankind;
and thefe invafions firft made them a warlike
people alfo.

Alexander the Great, invaded them in
later times, and found them in the fame
ftate; and though it fhould feem, from
Arrian's and *Quintus Curtius*'s hiftory of that
Prince's expeditions, that the different principalities he conquered, were independant
kingdoms, and governed by independant
Kings and Princes; yet the *Gentoo* records of
Bindoobund and *Banaras* fhew, that at that
period,

period, and much later, all the principalities of
this empire, were in fubjection to, and owned
allegiance to one head, ftiled the *Mhaahah
Rajah* of *Indoftan*; a Prince of the *Succadit*
family, faid to be lineally defcended from
their great Prince and Legiflator *Bramah*;
and that it was not until after the extinction
of this facred family (as the *Gentoos* call it)
that the *Rajahs* affumed an independency.

But it did not fufficiently footh the vanity
of *Alexander*, nor that of his hiftorians, to
record his conquefts of a few petty Rajahs
and Governors of provinces; and though
we do not conteft the fact of that invafion,
yet we think ourfelves juftified in concluding
the greateft part of its hiftory is fabulous;
yet, that it claims greater credit and belief,
than thofe of *Bacchus* and *Sefoftris:* the
Greek and *Latin* conftruction and termina-
tion of the names, and places, of the Princes
and kingdoms of *Indoftan*, faid by *Alexander's*
hiftorians to be conquered by him; bear not
the leaft analogy or idiom of the *Gentoo*
language, either ancient or modern; as any
one the leaft converfant in it can teftify;
and although the ground work of their hiftory was founded on fact, yet the fuperftructure carries ftrongly the femblance of invention and romance: And he who is ac-

quainted

quainted with this empire, and can give full credit to thofe legends, may upon as juft a foundation believe *Alexander* to have been the fon of *Jupiter Ammon*; or, with *Q. Curtius*, that the *Ganges* opened into the *Red fea*.

The annals of the *Gentoos*, give teftimony of *Alexander*'s invafion; where he is recorded under the epithets, of *Mhaabah Dukkoyt, é Kooneah*, a moft mightey robber and murderer; but they make not any mention of a *Porus*, nor of any name that has the fmalleft allufion or likenefs to it; and yet the action between *Alexander* and this imaginary King *Porus*, has been pompoufly exhibited by the hiftorians of the former, and has happily afforded fubject matter for reprefentations, that do the higheft honour to the art and genius of man.

The liberty we have taken with thefe fo long celebrated hiftorians, may feem to our readers to be foreign to our fubject, but in the end we hope it will appear otherwife; when they find that thefe authors have (either from their own fertile inventions, or from mif-information, or rather from want of a competent knowledge in the language of the nation) mif-reprefented, or to fpeak more

more favorably, mif-conceived their religious tenets as much as they have the genius and ftate of their government.

The fpace of time employed in *Alexander*'s expedition in this empire, did not afford a poffibility of acquiring any adequate knowledge of a language in itfelf fo highly difficult to attain in the fmalleft degree of perfection even from many years refidence and intimate converfe with the natives ; can it be poffibly believed then, that any of *Alexander*'s followers could in this fhort fpace acquire fuch perfection in the *Gentoo* language as could enable them juftly to tranfmit down the religious fyftem of a nation, with whom they can fcarcely be faid to have had any communication?

Touching the antiquity of the fcriptures, we are treating of, we have much more to fay, in fupport of our conjecture and belief, that the *Shaftah* of *Bramah*, is as ancient, at leaft, as any written body of divinity that was ever produced to the world. But it is previoufly neceffary, that we explain the word *Bramah*, which has been varioufly wrote, and indifcriminately applied by many authors, and particularly by *Baldeus*, who confounds *Birmah* and *Bramah* as being the fame per-

fon,

fon, though nothing in nature can be more different. This could proceed only, from the fpecific meaning and origin of thofe words not being clearly underftood; and this we conceive has led many other writers into the fame error: our prefent difquifition therefore calls, not only for the explanation of thefe words, but alfo of the other two fuppofed primary created beings *Biftnoo* and *Sieb*. For unlefs thefe three perfons *Birmah*, *Biftnoo*, and *Sieb*, are diftinctly comprehended, and held in remembrance, a confiderable portion of the allegorical part of the *Shaftah* of *Bramah*, will appear utterly unintelligible.

Different authors ftile him, *Bruma*, *Bramma*, *Burma*, *Brumma*, *Birmah*, *Bramah*; and although they write him thus varioufly, they are unanimous in thinking him the fame perfon, and give him the fame attributes. They are all, it is true, derivatives from the fame root, *Brum* or *Bram*, (for thefe are fynonimous in the *Shaftah*) but none of all the above appellatives are to be found in the *Shaftah*, but *Birmah* and *Bramah*. They are all compounded of *brum* or *bram*, *a fpirit*, or *effence*, and *mah*, *mighty*; *brum*, in an abfolute and fimple fenfe, fignifies *the fpirit or effence of God*, and is but upon one

occafion

occafion mentioned as a perfon, and that is when *brum* is reprefented with the habiliments and four arms of *Birmah*, floating on a leaf, upon the face of a troubled chaos, immediately preceding the act of the creation of the univerfe.—*Birmah* is underftood in an abfolute perfonal fenfe, and in a figurative one ; in the former as the firft of the three primary created angelic beings—in this fenfe the word fignifies literally the *mighty fecond.* For though *Birmah* is the firft of the three prime beings, he is ftiled *fecond* in power to God only, and fometimes in the *Shaftah* has the name of *Birmahah, the moft mighty fecond.*——In the figurative fenfe the word *Birmah* means creation, created, and fometimes creator, and reprefents what the *Bramins* call, the firft great attribute of God, *his power of creation.*

Bramah is the title folely appropriated to the Promulger of the *Shaftah*, and implies the fpirituality and divinity of his miffion and doctrines ; hence it is, that his fucceffors affumed the name of *Bramins*, fuppofing themfelves to inherit the fame divine fpirit.

As the word *Birmah*, is ufed in a perfonal, and figurative fenfe, fo is *Biftnoo* and *Sieb*; perfonally, as being the fecond and

B 4 third

third of the firſt created angelic beings, who
had pre-eminence in heaven; the word
Biſtnoo, literally ſignifies a *cheriſher*, a *preſerver*, a *comforter*; and *Sieb*, a *deſtroyer*,
an *avenger*, a *mutilator*, a *puniſher*; and
theſe three perſons, when figuratively applied in the *Shaſtah* (as they frequently are)
repreſent what the *Bramins* call the three
firſt and great attributes of God, his power
to create, his power *to preſerve*, and his
power *to change* or *deſtroy*. And we ſhall
ſee that in the diſtribution of the almighty's
commands to theſe primary perſons, taſks
are aſſigned to each, of a very different
nature; to *Birmah*, works of power, government and glory; to *Biſtnoo*, works of ten-
derneſs and benevolence; and to *Sieb*, works
of terror, ſeverity and deſtruction. This
laſt mentioned perſon is the object of great
diſmay and terror to the *Gentoos*, but modern expounders of *Bramah*'s *Shaſtah* have
ſoftened the rigor of his character by giving
him .names and attributes of a very different nature from that of *Sieb*. They call
him *Moiſoor* (a contraction of *Mahahſoor*,
the moſt mighty deſtroyer of evil) and under
this ſoothing title he is, worſhipped, not as
Sieb the deſtroyer, but as *the deſtroyer of
evil*. The other epithet they have given to
him is *Moidéb*, (a contraction of *Mahahdeb-
tah*,

tab, the moſt mighty angel) in this ſenſe
he is worſhipped as *the averter of evil,*
and under this character he has the moſt
altars erected to him.

This neceſſary interpretation and explanation premiſed, we proceed to the *Shaſtah*
itſelf; and ſhall faithfully give a detail of the
origin of this book; and the ſeveral innovations and changes it has ſuffered : a detail
—which although known by all the learned
amongſt the *Bramins,* is yet confeſſed but
by a few, and thoſe only, whoſe purity of
principle and manners, and zeal for the primitive doctrines of *Bramah's Shaſtah,* ſets
them above diſguiſing the truth; from many
of theſe, we have had the following recital.

" That, when part of the angelic bands
" rebelled, and were driven from the face
" of God, and expelled from the heavenly
" regions ; God doomed them in his wrath,
" to eternal puniſhment and baniſhment ;
" but, that by the interceſſion of the faith-
" ful remaining bands, he was at length
" inclined to mercy, and to ſoften the rigor
" of their ſentence, by inſtituting *a courſe*
" *only,* of puniſhment, purgation, and pu-
" rification ; through which, by due ſub-
" miſſion, they might work out a reſtoration
" to

" to the feats they had loft by their difobe-
" dience.

" That God in full affembly of the faith-
" ful bands fpecified *their courfe* of punifh-
" ment, purgation and purification ; regif-
" tered, and declared his decree, immutable,
" and irrevocable; and commanded *Birmah*,
" to defcend to the banifhed delinquents
" and fignify unto them the mercy and
" determination of their creator.

" That *Birmah* fulfilled God's command,
" defcended to the delinquent angels, and
" made known unto them the mercy and
" immutable fentence, that God their creator
" had pronounced and regiftered againft
" them.

" That the great and unexpected mercy
" of God, at firft made a deep impreffion
" upon all the delinquents, except on the
" leaders of their rebellion; thefe in procefs
" of time, regained their influence, and
" *confirmed* moft of the delinquents in their
" difobedience, and thereby the merciful
" intentions of the creator, became in a
" great meafure fruftrated.

" That about the beginning of the pre-
" fent age (i. e. 4866 years ago) the three
2   " primary

" primary created beings and the reft of the
" faithful angelic hoft, feeling the deepeft
" anguifh for the exalted wickednefs of their
" delinquent brethren, concluded it could
" only proceed, from their having by time,
" forgot the terms of their falvation; which
" had been only verbally delivered to them
" by *Birmah:* they therefore petitioned the
" Almighty, that he would be pleafed to
" fuffer his fentence, and the conditions of
" their reftoration, to be digefted into *a body*
" *of written laws* for their guidance; and
" that fome of the angelic beings, might
" have permiffion to defcend to the delin-
" quents, to promulge and preach this writ-
" ten body of laws unto them, that they
" might thereby be left without excufe, or
" the plea of ignorance, for their conti-
" nuance in difobedience.

" That God affented, to the petitions of
" the angelic bands; when they, one and
" all, offered to undertake this miffion, but
" God felected from amongft them thofe
" whom he deemed moft proper for this
" work of falvation; who were appointed
" to defcend *to the different regions* of the
" habitable univerfe. That a being from
" the firft rank of angels was deftined for
" the eaftern part of this globe, whom
. " God

" God dignified with the name of *Bramah*,
" in allufion to the divinity of the doctrine
" and miffion he had in charge.

" That *Birmah* by the command of God
" dictated to *Bramah* and the other deputed
" angels, the terms and conditions, which
" had been primarily delivered to the de-
" linquents, by the mouth of *Birmah*;
" that *Bramah* received, and entered the laws
" of God in *Debtah Nagur*, (literally, the
" language of angels) and that when *Bra-*
" *mah* defcended at the beginning of the
" prefent age, and affumed the human form
" and government of *Indoftan*, he tranflated
" them into the *Sanfcrit*, a language then
" univerfally known throughout *Indoftan*;
" and called the body of laws *the Chartah*
" *Bhade * Shaftah of Bramah* (literally, the
" *four fcriptures of divine words of the*
" *mighty fpirit)* which he promulged, and
" preached to the delinquents, as the only
" terms of their falvation and reftoration.

" That for the fpace of a thoufand years,
" the doctrines of the *Chartah Bhade*, were
" preached and propagated, without varia-
" tion or innovation; and many of the
" delinquents benefited from them and were

* A written book.

" faved :

(13)

" faved : but that about the clofe of this
" period, fome *Gofeyns* * and *Battezaaz* †
" *Bramins,* combining together, wrote a
" paraphrafe on the *Chartah Bhade,* which
" they called the *Chartah* ‡ *Bhade of Bra-*
" *mah* §, or the *fix fcriptures of the mighty*
" *fpirit* ; in this work the original text of
" *Bramah's Chartah Bhade* was ftill pre-
" ferved.—About this period alfo it was,
" that the *Gofeyns* and *Battezaaz Bramins,*
" began to appropriate to themfelves the ufe
" of the *Sanfcrit character,* and inftituted in
" the place of it the common *Indoftan* cha-
" racter in ufe at this day: it was now alfo
" that *they* firft began to veil in myfteries,
" the fimple doctrines of *Bramah.*

" That about five hundred years later,
" that is, fifteen hundred years from the firft
" promulgation of *Bramah's Shaftah*; the
" *Gofeyns,* and *Battezaaz Bramins,* pub-
" lifhed a fecond expofition, or commentary
" on the *Chartah Bhade* ; which fwelled
" the *Gentoo* fcriptures to eighteen books;
" thefe the commentators entitled the *Augh-*
" *torrah Bhade Shaftah,* or the *eighteen books*

* *Gentoo* Bifhops.
† Expounders of the *Shaftah.*   ‡ Six.
§ From the promulging this *Bhade,* the Polytheifm
of the *Gentoos* took its rife.

" *of*

" *of divine words*; it was drawn up in a
" compound character, of the common *In-*
" *doftan*, and *Sanfcrit*;—the original text of
" the *Chartah Bhade*, was in a manner funk
" and alluded to only ; the hiftories of their
" Rajahs and country, were introduced under
" figures and fymbols, and made a part of
" their religious worfhip, and a multitude
" of ceremonials, and exteriour modes of
" worfhip, were inftituted; which the com-
" mentators faid were implied in *Bramah's*
" *Chartah Bhade*, although not exprefly
" directed therein, by him; and the whole
" enveloped in impenetrable obfcurity by
" allegory and fable, beyond the compre-
" henfion even of the common tribe of
" *Bramins* themfelves ; the laity being thus
" precluded from the knowledge of their
" original fcriptures had a new fyftem of
" faith broached unto them, which their
" anceftors were utterly ftrangers to. ·

" That this innovation of the *Aughtorrah*
" *Bhade* produced a fchifm amongft the
" *Gentoos*, who until this period had fol-
" lowed one profeffion of faith throughout
" the vaft empire of *Indoftan*; for the *Bra-*
" *mins* of *Cormandell* and *Mallabar* finding
" their brethren upon the courfe of the *Ganges*
" had taken this hold ftep to inflave the laity,
" fet

" fet up for themfelves, and formed a fcripture
" of their own, founded as they faid upon
" the *Chartah Bhade* of *Bramah*; this they
" called *the Viedam* * *of Brummah*, or *divine*
" *words of the mighty fpirit*;—thefe com-
" mentators, by the example of their bre-
" thren, interfperfed in their new religious
" fyftem, the hiftories of their governors,
" and country, under various fymbols and
" allegories, but departed from that chaftity
" of manners, which was ftill preferved in
" the *Aughtorrah Bhade Shaftah*.

" Thus the original, plain, pure, and
" fimple tenets of the *Chartah Bhade* of
" *Bramah* (fifteen hundred years after its
" firft promulgation) became by degrees
" utterly loft; except, to three or four *Go-*
" *feyn* families, who at this day are only
" capable of reading, and expounding it,
" from the *Sanfcrit* character; to thefe may
" be added a few others of the tribe
" of *Battezaaz Bramins*, who can read
" and expound from the *Chartah Bhade*,
" which ftill preferved the text of the ori-
" ginal, as before remarked.

* *Viedam* in the *Mallabar* language fignifies the
fame as *Shaftah* in the *Sanfcrit*, viz. *divine words*——
and fometimes, *the words of God.*

" How

" How much foever the primitive reli-
" gion of the *Gentoos* fuffered by thefe inno-
" vations; their government underwent no
" change for many centuries after, all ac-
" knowledging allegiance to one univerfal
" Rajah of the *Succadit* family, lineally
" defcended from their Prince and Lawgiver
" *Bramah.*——— The Princes of this line
" oppofed the innovations made in their
" primitive faith, with a fruitlefs oppofition,
" which endangered the exiftence of their
" own government; fo that at length they
" were reduced to the neceffity of fubfcrib-
" ing, firft to the *Chartah Bhade*, and fub-
" fequently to the *Aughtorrah Bhade*; al-
" though their wifdom forefaw, and fore-
" told, the fatal confequences thefe inno-
" vations would have on the ftate and the
" nation: but the *Gofeyns* and *Bramins*,
" having tafted the fweets of prieftly power
" by the firft of thefe *Bhades*, determined
" to enlarge, and eftablifh it, by the pro-
" mulgation of the *laft*; for in this the
" exterior modes of worfhip were fo multi-
" plied, and fuch a numerous train of new
" divinities created, which the people never
" before had heard or dreamed of, and both
" the one and the other were fo enveloped
" by the *Gofeyns* and *Bramins* in darknefs,
" penetrable to themfelves only, that thofe

2   " profeffors

" profeffors of divinity, became of new and
" great importance, for the daily obliga-
" tions of religious duties, which were by
" thefe new inftitutes impofed on every
" *Gentoo*, from the higheft to the loweft
" rank of the people, were of fo intricate, and
" alarming a nature, as to require a *Bramin*
" to be at hand, to explain and officiate,
" in the performance of them : they had
" however the addrefs to captivate the minds
" of the vulgar, by introducing fhow and
" parade into all their principal religious
" feafts, as well as' fafts; and by a new.
" fingle political inftitution, to wit, *the pre-*
" *fervation of their caft or tribe*, the whole
" nation was reduced to facerdotal flavery.

" From the period that the *Aughtorrah*
" *Bhade* was publifhed as the rule of the
" *Gentoo* faith and worfhip, fuperftition, the
" fure fupport of prieftcraft, took faft pof-
" feffion of the people ; and their confcien-
" ces, actions, and conduct, in fpirituals
" and temporals, were lodged in the breafts
" of their *houfehold Bramins*, and at their
" difpofal; for every head of a family was
" obliged to have one of thofe ghoftly fa-
" thers at his elbow, and in fact the people
" became in general mere machines, ac-
" tuated and moved, as either the good

Part II.   C   " or

" or evil intentions of their houfehold tyrant
" dictated.

" The *Aughtorrah Bhade Shaftah*, has been
" invariably followed by the *Gentoos* inha-
" biting from the mouth of the *Ganges* to
" the *Indus*, for the laft three thoufand three
" hundred and fixty-fix years. This pre-
" cifely fixes the commencement of the *Gen-*
" *too mythology*, which, until the publication
" of that *Bhade*, had no exiftence amongft
" them: every *Gentoo* of rank or wealth,
" has a copy of this fcripture in his poffef-
" fion; under the care and infpection of
" his domeftic *Bramin*; who every day
" reads and expounds a portion of it to the
" family.

" Sixteen hundred and feventy nine years,
" from the promulgation of the *Aughtorrah*
" *Bhade Shaftah*, the facred line of *Bramah*
" became extinct, in the perfon of *Succa-*
" *dit*, the laft *Mahahmahah Rajah*; (moft
" mighty King) he reigned over all *Indof-*
" *tan*, fixty years; his deceafe caufed a ge-
" neral lamentation amongft the people; and
" from his death, a new *Gentoo Epocha*
" took place, called the *Æra of Succadit*;
" and the prefent year (A. D. 1766) is the
" year

1

" year of *Succadit,* fixteen hundred eighty
" feven.

" The death of *Succadit,* became not
" only remarkable for a new *Epocha* of
" time, but alfo for another fignal event in
" the *Gentoo* annals; namely, a total revo-
" lution of their government: the royal and
" facred line being extinct, the Vice-roys of
" this extenfive empire (who had been for
" fome years ftrengthening themfelves in
" their refpective governments, and prepa-
" ring for this expected event) on the demife
" of *Succadit,* fet up a claim of indepen-
" dency, to the lands over which they had
" ruled under the emperor: they all affumed
" the title of *Rajah,* a diftinction which,
" before this memorable period, had been
" only given to four or five of the firft
" officers of the ftate; who alfo generally
" filled the chief governments of the empire.
" ———Confufion followed———Thofe com-
" manders who found themfelves invefted
" with greater force and power, attacked,
" conquered, and joined to their govern-
" ments, the territories of thofe who lay
" contiguous to them; whilft others who
" lay more diftant preferved their indepen-
" dency: and thus the empire was divided
" into as many kingdoms, as there had

C 2   " been

" been Vice-royfhips and Governments.—
" Between thefe Rajahs, there fubfifted a
" continual warfare.—From an empire thus
" divided againft itfelf, what could be ex-
" pected, but that which, in a few centuries,
" confequently and naturally followed.

" For the fimple and intelligible tenets
" and religious duties, enjoined by the *Char-*
" *tah Bhade,* being thus abforbed and loft,
" in the attention and adherence, paid to
" the extravagant, abfurd, and unintelligible
" non-effentials of worfhip, inftituted by
" the *Aughtorrah Bhade*; laid the founda-
" tion of the miferies, with which, in fuc-
" ceeding times, *Indoftan* was vifited; and
" the merciful intention of God, for the
" redemption of the delinquent angels, (def-
" tined to inhabit this part of the earthly
" globe) was rendered fruitlefs.—The holy
" Tribe of *Bramins,* who were chofen and
" appointed by *Bramah* himfelf, to preach
" *the word of God,* and labor the falvation
" of the delinquents ; in procefs of time loft
" fight of their *divine original,* and in it's
" place fubftituted new and ftrange doctrines;
" that had no tendency, but to the eftablifh-
" ing their own power: the people heark-
" ened unto them, and their minds were
" fubdued and enflaved ; their ancient mili-
" tary

" tary genius, and fpirit of liberty was de-
" bilitated; difcord and diffention arofe
" amongft the rulers of the land, and the
" ftate grew ripe for falling at the firft con-
" vulfion; and in the end fuffered an utter
" fubverfion, under the yoke of *Mahom-*
" *medan* tyranny; as a juft punifhment in-
" flicted on them by God, for their neglect
" of his laws, commands and promifes,
" promulged to them, by his great and fa-
" vored angel *Bramah*, in the *Chartah*
" *Bhade Shaftah*."

The foregoing detail, contains the genuine conceptions and belief, which the
Bramins themfelves entertain of the antiquity of their fcriptures, and of the two remarkable innovations they have undergone;
particulars which we have had repeatedly
confirmed to us, in various conferences with
many of the moft learned and ingenuous,
amongft the laity of the *Koyt* *, and other
Cafts, who are often better verfed in the
doctrines of their *Shaftah* than the common
run of the *Bramins* themfelves.

We hope it will not be difpleafing to our
readers, if from the foregoing recital, we
reduce into a narrow compafs, and into one

* The tribe of Writers.

C 3   view,

view, the ftedfaft faith of the *Gentoos*,
Touching the antiquity of their fcriptures;
(the point now only under our confideration) it appears therefore that they date the
birth of the tenets and doctrines of the
Shaftah, from the expulfion of the angelic
beings from the heavenly regions; that
thofe tenets were reduced into a written
body of laws, four thoufand eight hundred
and fixty-fix years ago, and then by God's
permiffion were promulged and preached to
the inhabitants of *Indoftan*. That thefe original fcriptures underwent a remarkable
change or innovation a thoufand years after
the miffion of their Prophet and Law-giver
Bramah in the publication of the *Chartah
Bhade Shaftah*; and that three thoufand three
hundred and fixty-fix years paft, thefe original fcriptures fuffered a fecond and laft
change or innovation, in the publication of
the *Aughtorrah Bhade Shaftah*; which occafioned the firft and only fchifm amongft
the *Gentoos*, that fubfifts to this day, namely
between the followers of the *Aughtorrah
Bhade Shaftah*, and the followers of the
Viedam.

Without repofing an implicit confidence
in the relations the *Bramins* give of the
antiquity of their fcriptures; we will, with
our

our readers indulgence, humbly offer a few conjectures that have ſwayed us into a belief and concluſion, that the original tenets of *Bramah* are moſt ancient; that they are truly original, and not copied from any ſyſtem of theology, that has ever been promulged to, or obtruded upon the belief of mankind: what weight our conjectures may have with the curious, or how far it may rather appear in the proſecution of our work, that other theological ſyſtems have been framed from this, we readily ſubmit to thoſe, whoſe genius, learning and capacity in reſearches of this kind, are much ſuperior to our own.

It has been without reſerve aſſerted, that the *Gentoos* received their doctrines and worſhip, from the *Perſees* or *Egyptians*; but without (as we conceive) any degree of probability, or grounds, for the foundation of this opinion: reaſon and facts, ſeeming to us, to be on the ſide of the very contrary opinion.

That there was a very early communication between the empires of *Perſia*, *Egypt* and *Indoſtan*, is beyond controverſy; the former lay contiguous to *Indoſtan*; and although *Egypt* lay more remote from it, there ftill was an eafy paffage open between them, by the navigation from the *Red-fea*, to the *Indus*: therefore it will appear no ftrained conclufion, if we fay; it is moft likely there had been frequent intercourfe between the learned *Magi* of both thofe nations, and the *Bramins*, long before the laft mentioned fages were vifited by *Zoroafter* and *Pythagoras*.

It is neceffary to remark that the *Bramins* did not, indeed could not, feek this inter-courfe, for the principles of their religion forbad their travelling, or mixing with other nations; but fo famed were they in the earlieft known times for the purity of their manners, and the fublimity of their wifdom and doctrines, that their converfe was fought after, and folicited univerfally by the phi-lofophers, and fearchers after wifdom and truth. For this character of them, we have the concurring teftimony of all antiquity.

At what period of time, *Indoftan* was vifited by *Zoroafter* and *Pythagoras*, is not clearly determined by the learned; we will fuppofe it, with the generality of writers, to have been about the time of *Romulus*.— That thefe fages travelled not to *inftruct*, but, to be *inftructed*; is a fact that may be determined with more precifion; as well as, as, that they were not in *Indoſtan* together.— As they both made a long reſidence with the *Bramins* North Weſt of the *Ganges* (for the name of *Zardhurſt*, and *Pythagore* retain a place in the *Gentoo* annals " as travellers in " ſearch of wiſdom") it is reaſonable to conclude they might in ſome degree be inſtructed in the *Sanſcrit character*, and conſequently, in the doctrines and worſhip inſtituted by the *Chartah* and *Aughtorrah Bhades.*

It is worthy notice that the *Metempſychoſis*, as well as the three grand principles taught in the greater *Eleuſinian* myſteries ; namely, the *unity of the godhead, his general providence over all creation*, and *a future ſtate of rewards and puniſhments* ; were fundamental doctrines of *Bramah's Chartah Bhade Shaſtah*, and were preached by the *Bramins*, from time immemorial to this day, throughout *Indoſtan:* not as myſteries, but as religious tenets, publicly known and received, by every *Gentoo* of the meaneſt capacity ; this is a truth, which, we conceive, was unknown to the learned inveſtigator of the *Eleuſinian* myſteries ; or it is probable he would, with more caution, have aſſerted, that the Eaſtern nations received their doctrines from the *Egyptians*.

Although

Although the Polytheifm of the *Gentoos*
had its origin from the firft promulgation of
the *Chartah Bhade Shaftah*, and their Mythology from the publication of the *Aughtorrah
Bhade*; yet the abovementioned theological
dogma's remained inviolable and unchanged;
and as thefe, with the firm perfuafion of the
præ-exiftent ftate of the fpirit, or foul, have
ever been, and ftill are, the very bafis of all
the *Gentoo* worfhip; it appears to us moft
probable, (from the early communication
before remarked, and the reafons before
given) that the *Egyptians* borrowed thefe
tenets from the *Bramins*.

That *Pythagoras* took the doctrine of
the *Metempfychofis*, from the *Bramins*, is
not difputed: yet future times erroneoufly
ftiled it *Pythagorean*; an egregious miftake,
which could proceed only from ignorance
of its original.

Whatever may have been the period,
that *Indoftan* was vifited by the two travelling fages abovementioned; it is acknowledged that *Pythagoras* undertook that jour-
ney, fome years later than *Zoroafter:*———
when *Pythagoras* left *India*, he went into
Perfia, where he converfed with the Magi of
that country, and was inftructed in their
myfteries;

myfteries; and is faid (with probability of truth) to have held many conferences with *Zoroafter*, on the doctrines of the *Bramins*. They had both been initiated in all the myf-teries, and learning, of the *Egyptians*; and *Pythagoras*, in his fecond vifit to *Egypt*, be-fore his return to *Greece*, probably repaid the debt of wifdom he had received from the Magi, by giving them new, and ftronger lights into the theology, cofmogony and mythology of the *Bramins*, from their *Chartah*, and *Aughtorrah Bhades*.

The moral inftitutes, of *Zoroafter*, and *Pythagoras*; inculcated and taught by the one to the *Perfians*, and by the other, to the *Greeks*; truely bore the ftamp of divine! but their fyftem of theology, furely that of madnefs !—They had fo long and intenfely thought, and reafoned on the *divine nature*, and the *caufe of evil*; that the portion of divine nature they poffeffed, feemed utterly impaired, and bewildered, as foon as they began to form their crude principles into a *fyftem*;—they appear to have preferved the bafis and out-lines of *Bramah's Shaftah*, on which (probably in conjunction with the *Perfian* and *Egyptian* Magi) they raifed an aerial fuperftructure, wild and incompre-henfible! and labored to propagate an unin-telligible

telligible jargon of divinity, which neither themfelves, nor any mortal fince their time, could explain, or reduce to the level of human underftanding.

How far, on a comparifon between the modes of worfhip, inftituted by the *Chartah* and *Aughtorrah Bhades*, and thofe of the antient *Egyptians*, *Greeks* and *Romans*, it may appear that thofe of the *Bramins* are originals, and thofe of the latter copies only, we fubmit to the enquiry of the learned into thofe intricate ftudies, when in the courfe of our work we exhibit to the reader fome fpecimens of the *Gentoo* Mythology, and an account of their fafts and feftivals.

By the fundamental doctrines and laws of the *Gentoos*, they cannot admit of profelytes or converts, to their faith or worfhip; nor receive them into the pale of their communion, without the lofs of their Caft, or Tribe; a difgrace which every *Gentoo* would rather fuffer death than incur: and although this religious prohibition, in its confequences, reduced the people to a flavifh dependence on their *Bramins*; yet it proved the cement of their union as a nation; which to this day remains unmixed with any other race of people.—Thefe are circumftances which,

which, to the beſt of our knowledge, remembrance, and reading, peculiarly diſtinguiſh the *Gentoos*, from all the nations of
the known world, and plead ſtrongly in
favor of the great antiquity of this people,
as well as the originality of their ſcriptures.

Another conſideration, to the ſame purpoſe, claims our notice; namely the perpe-
tuity of the *Gentoo* doﬅrines, which through
a ſucceſſion of ſo many ages, have ﬅill remained unchanged, in their fundamental
tenets;—for although the *Chartah* and *Aughtorrah Bhades*, enlarged the exteriors of their
worſhip, yet theſe derive their authority
and eſſence, in the boſom of every *Gentoo*,
from the *Chartah Bhade* of *Bramah:* and it
is no uncommon thing, for a *Gentoo*, upon
any point of conſcience, or any important
emergency in his affairs or conduﬅ, to re-
jeﬅ the deciſion of the *Chartah* and *Aughtorrah Bhades*, and to procure, no matter
at what expence, the deciſion of the *Chartah Bhade*, expounded from the *Sanſcrit*.

Enough has been ſaid, to ſhew that the
genuine tenets of *Bramah*, are to be found
only in the *Chartah Bhade*; and as all who
have wrote on this ſubjeﬅ, have received
their information from crude, inconſiﬅent

3   reports,

reports, chiefly taken from the *Aughtorrah Bhade*, and the *Viedam*; it is no wonder that the religion of the *Gentoos*, has been traduced, by fome, as utterly unintelligible; and by others, as monftrous, abfurd, and difgraceful to humanity :——our defign is to refcue thefe ancient people, from thofe imputations; in order to which we fhall proceed, without further introduction or preface, to inveftigate their original fcriptures, as contained in the *Chartah Bhade*; at the clofe of each fection we fhall fubjoin, fuch remarks, and explanations, as may appear to us necefary and pertinent to our fubject.

For the greater perfpicuity, we will prefent to our readers the fundamental doctrines of the *Bramins*, under five diftinct fections; as they are ranged in the firft book of this *Shaftah:* viz.

I. Of God and his Attributes.
II. The creation of Angelic Beings.
III. The Lapfe of part of thofe Beings.
IV. Their Punifhment.
V. The mitigation of that Punifhment, and their final Sentence.

SECT. I.

" *Of God and his Attributes.*

"" God is ONE *.—Creator of all that
" *is.*———God is like a perfect fphere,
" without beginning or end.—God
" rules and governs all creation by a
" general providence refulting from
" firft determined and fixed principles.
" ———Thou fhalt not make enquiry
" into the effence and nature of the
" exiftence of the ETERNAL ONE, nor,
" by what laws he governs.—An en-
" quiry into either, is vain and crimi-
" nal.—It is enough, that day by day,
" and night by night, thou feeft in his
" works; his *wifdom, power,* and his
" *mercy.*———Benefit thereby."

* *Ekhummefha,* literally, *the one that ever was;*
which we tranflate, *the eternal one.*

REMARKS.

THE foregoing fimple and fublime defcription of the Supreme Being, conftitutes the firft chapter, or fection of the *Shaftah.*———The *Bramins* of the *Aughtorrah
Bhade* teach, that there originally exifted a
chapter

chapter of the *Shaftah*, which explained and
folely treated of the divine nature and effence; but that it was foon irrecoverably
loft, and never tranfmitted to pofterity by
Bramah, who *tore it out* of his *Chartah
Bhade.*

Baldeus, who refided thirty years on the
Ifland of *Ceylon*, and has given a laborious
tranflation of the *Viedam*; recites a fimilar
anecdote from thofe fcriptures, and fays,
" that the loft part treated of God, and the
" origin of the univerfe, or vifible worlds,
" the lofs of which is highly lamented by
" the *Bramins*."—In which this author feems
to have plunged into a double error; firft,
in alleging the part loft, treated of the origin
of the univerfe; whereas both the *Viedam*,
and *Shaftah*, are elaborate on the fubject;
and fix not only the period of its creation,
but alfo its precife age, and term of duration,
(as we fhall fhew hereafter); confequently
and fecondly, they could not properly be faid
to lament a lofs they never fuftained.——
But in truth, the whole of this matter is allegorical, a circumftance, which *Baldeus*, it
feems, never adverted to.

In various difcourfes, we have had, with
fome learned *Bramins*, on the above cited
paffage

paſſage of the *Aughtorrah Bhade*, they were
all unanimous in their ſenſe and interpretation of it : namely, that to man was given for
the exerciſe of his reaſon, and virtue, the contemplation of the viſible wonders of the creation ; but, that the ETERNAL ONE had precluded all enquiry into his origin, nature, and
eſſence, and the laws by which he governs;
as ſubjects inexplicable to, and beyond the
limited powers of created beings; therefore
it is emphatically ſaid, that *Bramah tore out*
that part, implying the prohibition of ſuch
enquiries, as uſeleſs and preſumptuous.

Had one tythe of the time and trouble,
which the juſt mentioned eccleſiaſtic beſtowed in rendering a literal tranſlation of the
Viedam, been employed in attempting an
explanation of its myſteries; his labors might
have proved worthy the attention of the
learned; whereas, by contenting himſelf with
a bare verſion, without aiming at the interpretation of the allegorical parts of thoſe
ſcriptures, his toils, which muſt have been
great and intenſe, have only produced a mon-
ſter, that ſhocks reaſon and probability.—
They are miſ-repreſentations like theſe, which
we have lamented in the preliminary diſcourſe, to the firſt part of this our work,
as injurious to human nature; various and

Part II.　　　　D　　　　enormous

enormous are the miftakes, which this author has fallen into from the above caufe,
through the whole of his voluminous work,
which might be proved in a multitude of
inftances; but one fhall fuffice as a fpecimen
of the whole, which nothing but the miftaken zeal of a chriftian divine can excufe.

" The *Viedam* (according to *Baldeus*) gives
" the fame place and power to *Birmah* or
" *Bramah* (for he erroneoufly makes thefe
" names fynonimous) as the *Shaftah* does;
" and as the *Mallabars* acknowledge *Bramah*
" to be the fon of God, and fupreme go-
" vernor of angels; nay even afcribe to him
" a human form: *fo it is evident, that thefe*
" *attributes, muft have their origin from*
" *what they have heard, though perhaps con-*
" *fufedly, of Jefus Chrift the fon of God.*"

S E C T. II.

" *The Creation of Angelic Beings.*

" The ETERNAL ONE, abforbed in the
" contemplation of his own exiftence; in
" the fullnefs of time, refolved to *par-*
" *ticipate* his glory and effence with
" beings capable of feeling, and fharing
" his beatitude, and of adminiftering
" to his glory.--Thefe beings then were
" not.—The ETERNAL ONE willed.—
" And they were. —He formed them
" in part of his own effence ; capable
" of perfection, but with the powers
" of imperfection ; both depending on
" their voluntary election.--The ETER-
" NAL ONE firft created *Birmah, Biftnoo,*
" and *Sieb* ; then *Moifafoor*, and all the
" *Debtah-Logue* *.———The *eternal one*
" gave pre-eminence to *Birmah, Bift-*
" *noo* and *Sieb.*———He appointed *Bir-*
" *mah*, Prince of the *Debtah-Logue,*
" and put the *Debtah* under fubjection
" to him; he alfo conftituted him his
" vicegerent in heaven, and *Biftnoo* and
" *Sieb*, were eftablifhed his co-adjutors.

* *Debtah*, angels; *Logue*, a people, multitude, or congregation; *Debtah-Logue*, the angelic hoft.

" —The

" —The ETERNAL ONE divided the
" *Debtah* into different bands, and
" ranks, and placed a leader or chief
" over each.—Thefe worfhipped round
" the throne of the *eternal one* accord-
" ing to their degree, and harmony
" was in heaven.—*Moifafoor*, chief of
" the firft angelic band, led the ce-
" leftial fong of praife and adoration
" to the Creator, and . the fong of
" obedience to *Birmah* his firft created.
" —And the Eternal One rejoiced in
" his new creation."

R E M A R K S.

MANKIND in general of every denomination, and religious profeffion,
have fubfcribed to the opinion of the exiftence of *angelic beings*; and have each
formed their crude, peculiar, and imaginary
conceptions of their origin and deftination.
—Crude and imaginary indeed ! muft be the
beft human conftruction, on fo marvellous
a fubject.—The fimple, rational, and fublime caufe, affigned by *Bramah*, for this act
of creation; is moft worthy a great and benign *being*, and conveys a ftriking and
interefting impreffion, not only of his
power, but of his *benevolence*.

Bramah, in the opening of this fection,
feems to place the *eternal one*, in the fituation
of

of an abfolute, good, and powerful *monarch*, without *fubjects*; which in fact is being no monarch at all: for however happy, or bleffed fuch a being may be, in the contemplation of his own fole exiftence and almighty power; yet he cannot (fay the *Bramins*) be completely fo, without partakers in his glory and beatitude; who fhould alfo, be confcious of the *tenure* of their own exiftence, as well as of the power, and benevolent intentions of their *creator*, and worfhip him, accordingly.

But a blind and neceffary obedience and worfhip, from any new creation of rational beings, (which muft have followed had they been created perfect) would have fallen fhort of their Creator's purpofe; therefore *Bramah* fays, *the eternal one*, formed them " capable " of *perfection*, but with the powers of im- " perfection ;" without fubjecting them to *either*, that their adoration and obedience fhould be the refult of their own *free-will*; the worfhip alone worthy his acceptance.

From the doctrine contained in this fection it appears, that the powers of perfection and imperfection, (or in other words the powers of *good and evil*) were coeval in the formation of the firft created beings:——The

Bramins

Bramins in their paraphrafe on this chapter, reconcile the fuppofed incompatibility of the exiftence of moral evil, confiftently with the juftice, power, and goodnefs of the *fupreme being*, by alleging, " that as the *Debtah* were invefted with the abfolute powers of *perfection*, their lapfe from that ftate, cannot impeach either the power, juftice, or goodnefs of the ETERNAL ONE; whofe motives for their creation were benevolent; and the duty enjoined them light and eafy.—To chaunt forth for ever, the praifes of their *creator* —To blefs him for their *creation*, and to acknowledge, and be obedient to *Birmah*, and his two coadjutors *Biftnoo* and *Sieb*."

Human penal laws, which have their exiftence in every well regulated government of the world; always pre-fuppofe that the individuals fubjected to thofe laws, are invefted with full powers and capacity of paying obedience to them; otherwife their impofition becomes an act of tyranny; but the premifes granted, then the breach and violation of them is criminal, and juftly punifhable, without an imputation of injuftice in the inftitutor.———Shall man then appear fcrupuloufly cautious in his inftitutes and laws, not to offend againft reafon and juftice, and

yet

yet dare to doubt of, or arraign the juftice of his Creator?

Whence the origin, and exiftence of *moral evil?* Is a queftion that has puzzled, and exercifed the imagination, and under-ftanding of the learned and fpeculative in all ages.——We confefs we have hitherto met with no folution of this interefting enquiry, fo fatisfactory, conclufive, and rational, as flows from the doctrine before us.——Au-thors have been driven to very ftrange con-clufions on this fubject, nay fome have thought it neceffary to form an apology in defence of their Creator, for the admiffion of moral evil into the world; and affert, " That God was neceffitated to admit moral evil in created beings, from the nature of the materials he had to work with; that God would have made all things perfect, but that there was in matter an evil bias, repugnant to his benevolence, which drew another way; whence arofe all manner of evils:" and that, therefore, " To endue created beings with perfection; that is to produce good exclufive of evil, is one of thofe im-poffibilities, which even infinite power cannot accomplifh." And confequently that from this *apologetical caufe only,* " The wickednefs and miferies of God's creatures

D 4   can

can be fairly reconciled, with his infinite power and goodnefs.

Interefting as this fubject is, and muft be, to every thinking being, our beft conceptions of it, muft fall far fhort of certainty ; it is however furely incumbent on us to adopt fuch fentiments (more efpecially when we refolve to broach them to the world) as will appear moft worthy infinite power and in-finite goodnefs.——How far this confidera-tion has been regarded in the reveries cited in the preceding paragraph, we fubmit to our readers ; in our own conceptions we cannot help faying thofe authors appear to us to have left the argument in a much worfe ftate than they found it ; and in place of a rational apology for their Creator, feem the rather tacitly to impeach his power, in the firft and greateft of his attributes ; his power of creation :—For God is not only the creator of angels and men; but creator of *matter* alfo ; and could have made *that* perfect, had he fo willed.——Whether God *could* endue created beings with perfection, or produce good exclufive of evil, we conceive is not the queftion; (although a doubt of it is highly prefumptuous, if not impious) but the quære is, whether God could create a race of beings, endued with the powers of

abfolute

abſolute free agency;—on the certainty of which poſition, the poſſibility of *ſin* in created beings abſolutely, and neceſſarily depends.

How much more rational and ſublime the text of *Bramah*, which ſuppoſes the Deity's voluntary creation, or permiſſion of evil; for the exaltation of a race of beings, whoſe *goodneſs* as free agents could not have ex- iſted without being endued with the con- traſted, or oppoſite powers of doing *evil*.

S E C T. III.

" *The Lapſe of Part of the Angelic Bands.*

" From the creation of the *Debtah*
" *Logue*, joy and harmony encompaſſed
" the throne of the eternal *one*, for
" the ſpace of *Hazaar par Hazaar*
" *Munnuntur* *; and would have con-
" tinued to the end of time, had not envy
" and jealouſy took poſſeſſion of *Moi-*
" *ſaſoor*, and other leaders of the angelic
" bands; amongſt whom was *Rhaabon*,
" the next in dignity to *Moiſaſoor*;—
" they, unmindful of the bleſſing of
" their creation, and the duties enjoined
" them, reject the powers of *perfection*,
" which the eternal ONE had gracioully
" beſtowed upon them, exerted their
" powers of *imperfection*, and did evil
" in the ſight of the eternal ONE.--They
" withheld their obedience from him,
" and denied ſubmiſſion to his *vice-*

---

* A phraſe often made uſe of in the *Shaſtah* to expreſs infinite extenſion or duration of time; the word
Munnu·tur in it's abſolute and literal ſenſe will be ſubſequently explained; the word *Hazaar*, literally ſignifies a thouſand; *Hazaar par Hazaar*, thouſands
upon thouſands.

" *gerent,*

" *gerent,* and his coadjutors, *Biſtnoo,*
" and *Sieb,* and ſaid to themſelves—
" We will rule!—And fearleſs of the
" omnipotence, and anger of their Crea-
" tor, they ſpread their evil imagina-
" tions amongſt the angelic hoſt, de-
" ceived them, and drew a large portion
" of them from their allegiance.—And
" there was a ſeparation from the throne
" of the eternal oNE.--Sorrow ſeized the
" faithful angelic ſpirits, and anguiſh
" was now firſt known in heaven."

S E C T. IV.

" The Punishment of the Delinquent Debtah.

" The eternal ONE, whofe omnifcience,
" prefcience and influence, extended to
" all things, except the actions of
" beings, which he had *created free*;
" beheld with grief and anger, the de-
" fection of *Moifafoor, Rhaabon*, and
" the other angelic leaders and fpirits.—
" Merciful in his wrath, he fent *Bir-*
" *mah*, *Biftnoo* and *Sieb*, to admonifh
" them of their crime, and to perfuade
" them to return to their duty;——
" but they exulting in the imagination
" of their independence, continued in
" difobedience.—The eternal ONE then
" commanded *Sieb* *, to go armed with
" his omnipotence, to drive them from
" the *Mahah Surgo* †, and plunge
" them into the *Onderah* ‡, there

---

* Why *Sieb* was fent on this command has been
already explained in our introduction.

† Supreme heaven, literally *the great eminence*, from
Mahah, great; and *Surgo, high*; eminent in a local
fenfe, the firmament being commonly diftinguifhed,
by the *Gentoos*, by the name of *Surgo*.

‡ *Onder, dark*; *Onderah, intenfe darknefs*.

" doomed

" doomed to fuffer unceafing *forrows*, for
" *Hazaar par Hazaar Munnunturs* *."

* In this place the expreffion (which we have explained in a preceding note) means *everlafting*.

REMARKS.

THAT there was a defection or rebellion in heaven, the records of antiquity, facred and prophane, bear allufive teftimony of;—we will not aver, that this opinion took its rife from the doctrines of the *Bramins*, though it is moft probable it did ; be this as it may, we cannot help concluding, that the conceptions conveyed by the *Shaftah*, of this extraordinary event, are more confiftent with, and do greater honor to the dignity of an omnipotent Being, than thofe handed down to us in fables of the Sages, Poets and Philofophers of *Egypt*, *Greece* and *Rome*.——From thefe our *Milton* copied, with extravagance of genius and invention.—— They all, without exception, unworthily impeach God's omnipotence by the powers of contention given to the apoftate angels, to oppofe their Creator in arms and battle ; and although facred writ † feems to countenance this warfare in heaven, it can only allude to the act of expulfion of the delinquents, as any other interpretation would leffen omnipotence.

† Revelations, chap xii. ver. 7.

The

The *Shaftah* opens this fection by dehying the prefcience of God `touching the actions of free agents; the *Bramins* defend this dogma by alleging, his prefcience in this cafe, is utterly repugnant and contradictory to the very nature and effence of free agency, which on fuch terms could not have exifted.

SECT. V.

" *The Mitigation of the Punifhment of the*
" *delinquent Debtah, and their final fen-*
" *tence.*

" The rebellious *Debtah* groaned under
" the difpleafure of their Creator in
" the *Onderah,* for the fpace of *one*
" *Munnuntur;* during which period,
" *Birmah, Biftnoo* and *Sieb,* and the
" reft of the faithful *Debtah,* never
" ceafed imploring the eternal ONE, for
" their pardon and reftoration.——
" The eternal ONE, by their interceffion
" at length relented,—and although he
" could not forefee the effect of his
" mercy on the future conduct of the
" delinquents: yet unwilling to relin-
" quifh the hopes of their repentance,
" he declared his will:—That they
" fhould be releafed from *the Onderah,*
" and be placed in fuch a ftate of
" *tryal* and *probation,* that they fhall
" ftill have power, to work out their
" own falvation. The eternal ONE then
" promulged his gracious intentions,
" and delegating the power and govern-
" ment of the *MahahSurgo, to Birmah,*
" he

" he retired into *himself*, and became in-
" vifible to all the angelic hoft, for the
" fpace of five thoufand years.——At
" the end of this period he manifefted
" himfelf again, refumed the throne of
" light, and appeared in his glory.-And
" the faithful angelic bands, celebrated
" his return in fongs of gladnefs.

" When all was hufhed !—the eter-
" nal ONE faid, Let the *Dunneahoudah**
" of the fifteen *Boboons* † of purgation
" and purification appear, for the re-
" fidence of the rebellious *Debtah*.—
" And it inftantly appeared.

" And the eternal ONE faid, Let *Bifl-*
" *noo* ‡, armed with my power, defcend
" to the new creation of the *Dunneahou-*
" *dah*, and releafe the rebellious *Debtah*
" from the *Onderah*, and place them
" in the loweft of the fifteen *Boboons*.

" *Biftnoo* ftood before the throne and
" faid, Eternal ONE, I have done as
" thou haft commanded.——And all

* *Dooneah*, or *dunneah*, the *world*, *Dunneahoudah*,
the *worlds*, or *the univerfe*.
§ *Boboons*, *regions* or *planets*.
‡ Why *Biftnoo* was fent on this fervice we have already explained in our introduction.

" the

" the faithful angelic hoſt, ſtood with
" aſtoniſhment, and beheld the won-
" ders, and ſplendor of the new creation
" of the *Dunneahoudah.*

" And the Eternal ONE ſpake again
" unto *Biſtnoo* and ſaid.—I will form
" *bodies* for each of the delinquent
" *Debtah*, which ſhall for a ſpace be
" their priſon and habitation; in the
" confines of which, they ſhall be ſub-
" ject to natural evils, in proportion
" to the degree of their original guilt.—
" Do thou go, and command them to
" hold themſelves prepared to enter
" therein, and they ſhall obey thee.

" And *Biſtnoo* ſtood again before the
" throne, and bowed and ſaid, Eternal
" ONE, thy commands are fulfilled.—
" And the faithful angelic hoſt, ſtood
" again aſtoniſhed, at the wonders
" they heard, and ſung forth the praiſe
" and mercy of the Eternal ONE.

" When all was huſhed! the Eternal
" one ſaid again unto *Biſtnoo*, The bodies
" which I will prepare for the recep-
" tion of the rebellious *Debtah*, ſhall
" be ſubject to change, decay, death,

Part II.   E   " and

" and renewal, from the principles
" wherewith I fhall form them ; and
" through thofe mortal bodies, fhall the
" delinquent *Debtah* undergo alternate-
" ly *eighty feven* changes, or *tranfmigra-*
" *tions* ; fubject more or lefs, to the
" confequences of natural and *moral*
" *evil*, in a juft proportion to the de-
" gree of their original guilt, and as
" their actions through thofe fucceffive
" forms, fhall correfpond with the li-
" mited powers which I fhall annex
" to each ;—and this fhall be their
" ftate of *punifhment* and *purgation.*

" And it fhall be,—That when the
" rebellious *Debtah* fhall have accom-
" plifhed and paffed through the eighty
" feven tranfmigrations——they fhall
" from my abundant favor, animate a
" new form, and thou *Biftnoo* fhalt call
" it GHOIJ ‡.

" And it fhall be,—That when the
" mortal body of the *Ghoij* fhall by a
" *natural* decay, become inanimate, the
" delinquent *Debtah* fhall, from my
" more abundant favor, animate the

---

‡ *Ghoij*, the cow ; *Ghoijal*, cows ; *Ghoijalbarry*, a cow-houfe.

" form

" form of M H U R D†,—and in this form
" I will enlarge their intellectual powers,
" even as when I firſt created them free;
" and in this form ſhall be their chief
" ſtate of their *trial* and *probation.*

" The *Ghoij* ſhall be, by the delin-
" quent *Debtah,* deemed ſacred and
" holy, for it ſhall yield them a new
" and more delectable food, and eaſe
" them of part of the labor, to which
" I have doomed them.—And they
" ſhall not eat of the *Ghoij,* nor of the
" fleſh of any of the mortal bodies,
" which I ſhall prepare for their habita-
" tion, whether it creepeth on *Murto,* or
" ſwimmeth in *Jhoale†,* or flyeth in
" *Ouſtmaan ‡,* for their food ſhall be
" the milk of the *Ghoij,* and the fruits
" of *Murto.*

" The mortal forms wherewith I
" ſhall encompaſs the delinquent *Deb-*
" *tah* are the work of my hand, they
" ſhall not be deſtroyed, but left to
" their natural decay; therefore which-
" foever of the *Debtah,* ſhall by de-

---

* *Mhurd,* the common name of *man,* from *Murto,*
matter, or earth.

† *Jhoale,* water, fluid.   ‡ The *air.*

E 2   " ſigned

" figned violence bring about the dif-
" folution of the mortal forms, ani-
" mated by their delinquent brethren,
" —Thou *Sieb*, fhalt plunge the of-
" fending fpirit into the *Onderah*, for
" a fpace, and he fhall be doomed to
" pafs again the eighty-nine tranfmi-
" grations, whatfoever ftage he may
" be arrived to, at the time of fuch
" his offence.—But whofoever of the
" delinquent *Debtah*, fhall dare to *free*
" *himfelf* by violence, from the mortal
" form wherewith I fhall inclofe him,
" —Thou *Sieb* fhalt plunge him into
" the *Onderah* for ever.——He fhall
" not again have the benefit of the
" fifteen *Boboons* of purgation, proba-
" tion, and purification.

" And I will diftinguifh by tribes and
" kinds, the mortal bodies which I have
" deftined for the punifhment of the
" delinquent *Debtah*, and to thefe bodies
" I will give different forms, qualities
" and faculties, and they fhall *unite* and
" propagate each other in their tribe
" and kind, according to a natural
" impulfe which I will implant in
" them; and from this natural union,
" there fhall proceed a fucceffion of
" forms;

(53)

" forms; each in his kind and tribe.
" that the progreffive tranfmigrations of
" the delinquent fpirits, may not ceafe.

" But whofoever of the delinquent
" *Debtah* fhall *unite* with any form out
" of his own tribe and kind; thou
" *Sieb* fhalt plunge the offending fpirit
" into the *Onderah*, for a fpace, and
" he fhall be doomed to pafs through
" the eighty-nine tranfmigrations, at
" whatfoever ftage he may be arrived,
" at the time he committed fuch of-
" fence.

" And if any of the delinquent
" *Debtah* fhall (contrary to the natural
" impulfe which I fhall implant in the
" forms which they fhall animate) dare
" to *unite* in fuch unnatural wife, as
" may fruftrate the increafe of his
" tribe and kind; thou *Sieb* fhalt plunge
" them into the *Onderah* for ever.—
" And they fhall not again be entitled
" to the benefit of the fifteen *Boboons*
" of purgation, probation and purifi-
" cation.

" The delinquent and unhappy *Deb-*
" *tah*, fhall yet have it in their power,

E 3   " to

" to leſſen and ſoften their pains and
" puniſhment, by the ſweet intercourſe
" of ſocial compacts ; and if they love
" and cheriſh one another, and do mu-
" tual good offices, and aſſiſt and en-
" courage each other in the work of
" repentance for their crime of diſ-
" obedience ; I will ſtrengthen their
" good intentions, and they ſhall find
" favor.——But if they perſecute one
" another, I will comfort the perſecuted,
" and the perſecutors ſhall never enter
" the ninth *Boboon*, even the *firſt Bo-*
" *boon* of purification.

" And it ſhall be,—That if the *Deb-*
" *tab* benefit themſelves of my favor
" in their eighty-ninth tranſmigration
" of *Mhurd*, by repentance and good
" works, thou *Biſtnoo* ſhalt receive
" them into thy boſom and convey them
" to the ſecond *Boboon* of puniſhment
" and purgation, and in this wiſe ſhalt
" thou do, until they have paſſed pro-
" greſſively the eight *Boboons* of puniſh-
" ment, purgation, and probation, when
" their puniſhment ſhall ceaſe, and thou
" ſhalt convey them to the ninth ; even
" the firſt *Boboon* of purification.

" But

" But it fhall be,—That if the re-
" bellious *Debtah*, do not benefit of
" my favor in the eighty-ninth tranf-
" migration of *Mhurd*, according to
" the powers, wherewith I will inveft
" them;—Thou *Sieb*, fhalt return them
" for a fpace into the *Onderah*, and
" from thence after a time which I
" fhall appoint, *Biftnoo* fhall replace
" them in the loweft *Boboon* of punifh-
" ment and purgation for a fecond
" trial; and in this wife fhall they
" fuffer, until by their repentance and
" perfeverance in good works, during
" their eighty-ninth mortal tranfmigra-
" tion of *Mhurd*, they fhall attain the
" ninth *Boboon*, even the firft of the
" feven *Boboons* of purification.—For it
" is decreed that the rebellious *Debtah*
" fhall not enter the *Mahah Surgo*,
" nor behold my face, until they have
" paffed the eight *Boboons* of punifh-
" ment, and the feven *Boboons* of pu-
" rification.

" When the angelic faithful hoft,
" heard all that the Eternal ONE had
" fpoken, and decreed, concerning the
" rebellious *Debtah*; they fung forth
" his praife, his power, and juftice.

" When

" When all was hufhed! the Eternal
" ONE faid to the angelic hoft, I will
" extend my grace to the rebellious
" *Debtah*, for a certain fpace, which I
" will divide into four *Jogues* *.—In the
" firft of the four *Jogues*, I will, that
" the term of their probation in the
" eighty-ninth tranfmigration of *Mhurd*,
" fhall extend to 100,000 years—in
" the fecond of the four *Jogues*, their
" term of their probation in *Mhurd*,
" fhall be abridged to 10,000 years
" —in the third of the four *Jogues*, it
" fhall be yet abridged to 1000 years
" —and in the fourth *Jogue* to 100
" years only.—And the angelic hoft,
" celebrated in fhouts of joy, the
" mercy and forbearance of God.

" When all was hufhed! the Eternal
" ONE faid, It fhall be,—That when
" the fpace of time, which I have
" decreed for the duration of the *Dun-*
" *n'aboudah*, and the fpace which my
" mercy has allotted for the probation
" of the fallen *Debtah*, fhall be ac-
" complifhed, by the revolutions of the
" four *Jogues*,—in that day, fhould
" there be any of them who remaining

* *Jogues*, ages, precife periods of time.

" reprobate,

" reprobate, have not paſſed the eighth
" *Boboon* of puniſhment and probation,
" and have not entered the ninth *Bo-*
" *boon*, even the firſt *Boboon* of purifi-
" cation;—thou *Sieb* ſhalt, armed with
" my power, caſt them into the *Onde-*
" *rab* for ever.—And thou ſhalt then
" deſtroy the eight *Boboons* of puniſh-
" ment, purgation and probation, and
" they ſhall be no more.—And thou
" *Biſtnoo* ſhalt yet for a ſpace preſerve
" the ſeven *Boboons* of *purification*,
" until the *Debtah*, who have benefited
" of my grace and mercy, have by thee
" been purified from their ſin:——
" and in the day when that ſhall be
" accompliſhed, and they are reſtored
" to their ſtate, and admitted to my
" preſence,—thou *Sieb* ſhalt then de-
" ſtroy the ſeven *Boboons* of purification,
" and they ſhall be no more.

" And the angelic faithful hoſt trem-
" bled at the power, and words of
" the Eternal ONE.

" The Eternal ONE, ſpoke again and
" ſaid.—I have not withheld my mercy
" from *Moiſaſoor*, *Rhaboon*, and the
" reſt of the leaders of the rebellious
" *Debtah*;

" *Debtah* ;——but as they thirſted for
" power, I will enlarge their powers *of*
" *evil* ;——they ſhall have liberty to
" pervade, and enter into the *eight*
" *Boboons* of purgation and probation,
" and the delinquent *Debtah*, ſhall be
" expoſed and open to the ſame temp-
" tations, that firſt inſtigated their re-
" volt : but the exertion of thoſe en-
" larged powers, which I will give to
" the rebellious leaders, ſhall be *to them*,
" the ſource of aggravated guilt, and
" puniſhment; and the reſiſtance made
" to their temptations, by the perverted
" *Debtah*, ſhall be *to me* the *great*
" *proof*, of the ſincerity of their ſorrow
" and repentance.

" The Eternal oɴe ceaſed.—And
" the faithful hoſt ſhouted forth ſongs
" of praiſe and adoration, mixed with
" grief, and lamentation for the fate
" of their lapſed brethren.——They
" communed amongſt themſelves, and
" with one voice by the mouth of
" *Biſtnoo*, beſought the Eternal oɴe, that
" they might have permiſſion to de-
" ſcend occaſionally to the *eight Bo-*
" *boons* of puniſhment, and purgation,
" to aſſume the form of *Mhurd*, and

" by

" by their prefence, council and ex-
" ample, guard the unhappy and per-
" verted *Debtah*, againft the further
" temptations of *Moifafoor*, and the
" rebellious leaders.—The Eternal ONE
" affented, and the faithful heavenly
" bands, fhouted their fongs of glad-
" nefs and thankfgiving.

" When all was hufhed ! the Eternal
" ONE fpake again, and faid,—Do thou
" *Birmah*, arrayed in my glory, and
" armed with my power, defcend to
" the loweft *Boboon* of punifhment and
" purgation, and make known to the
" rebellious *Debtah*, the words that I
" have uttered, and the decrees which
" I have pronounced againft them, and
" fee they enter into the bodies, which
" I have prepared for them.

" And *Birmah* ftood before the
" throne, and faid, Eternal ONE, I have
" done as thou haft commanded.——
" The delinquent *Debtah* rejoice in
" thy mercy, confefs the juftice of thy
" decrees, avow their forrow and re-
" pentance, and have entered into the
" mortal bodies which thou haft pre-
" pared for them."

R E M A R K S,

T H E foregoing is almoſt a literal tranſlation from the *Chartah Bhade of Bramah*, as we deſpaired of reaching the ſublime ſtile and diction of the original ;—it
will not we hope be diſpleaſing to our reader, if we aſſiſt his memory and recollection by a recapitulation of the ground work
of theſe doctrines, preſented to him in one
connected view ; the more eſpecially, as we
ſhall alſo be thereby the better enabled to
form our neceſſary explanatory remarks.

We have ſeen that the original divine in-
ſtitutes of *Bramah* are ſimple and ſublime,
comprehending the whole compaſs of all
that is ; God, Angels, the viſible and inviſible worlds, man and beaſts; and is com-
prized under the following articles of the
Gentoo creed. To wit—

" That there is one God, eternal, omni-
fic, omnipotent, and omniſcient, in all things
excepting a *preſcience* of the future actions
of *free agents*.—*That* God from an impulſe of
divine love and goodneſs, firſt created T H R E E
angelic perſons to whom he gave precedence,
though not in equal degree——*That* he
afterwards

afterwards from the fame impulfe created
an angelic hoft, whom he placed in fubjection to *Birmah* his firft created, and to
Biftnoo and *Sieb*, as coadjutors to *Birmah*.—
That God created them all free, and intended
they fhould all be partakers of his glory and
beatitude, on the eafy conditions of their
acknowledging him their Creator, and paying
obedience to him, and to the three primary
created perfonages, whom he had put over
them.—*That*, in procefs of time, a large portion of the angelic hoft, at the inftigation
of *Moifafoor* and others of their chief leaders, rebelled and denied the fupremacy of
their Creator, and refufed obedience to his
commands. *That* in confequence the rebels
were excluded heaven, and the fight of their
Creator, and doomed to languifh for ever in
forrow and *darknefs*. *That*, after a time,
by the interceffion of the three primary,
and the reft of the faithful angelic beings,
God relented, and placed the delinquents in
a more fufferable ftate of punifhment and
probation, with powers to gain their loft
happy fituation.—*That* for that purpofe a
new creation of the vifible and invifible
worlds inftantaneoufly took place, deftined
for the delinquents.—*That* the new creation
confifted of fifteen regions, feven below,
and feven above this terraqueous globe, and
that

that this globe and the feven regions below
it are ftages of punifhment and purgation,
and the feven above ftages of purification,
and confequently that this globe is the eighth,
laft and chief ftage of punifhment, purgation
and trial.—*That* mortal bodies were prepared
by God, for the rebel angels, *in which* they
were for a fpace to be imprifoned, and fubject to natural and moral evils, more or lefs
painful in proportion to their original guilt,
and *through which* they were doomed to
tranfmigrate under eighty-nine different
forms, the laft into that of *man*, when the
powers of the animating rebel fpirits, are
fuppofed to be enlarged equal to the ftate
of their firft creation.—*That* under this form
God refts his chief expectations of their
repentance and reftoration, and if they fail,
and continue reprobate under this form, they
are returned to the loweft region, and fentenced to go through the fame courfe of punifhment, until they reach the ninth region,
or firft ftage of purification, where although
they ceafe from punifhment, and gain ré-
miffion and forgivenefs of their guilt of
rebellion; yet, they are not permitted to
enter heaven, nor behold their Creator, before they have paffed the feven regions of
purification.——*That* the rebel-leaders had
power given them by God, to enter the
eight

eight regions of punifhment and probation, and that the faithful angelic fpirits, had per- miffion occafionally to defcend to thofe re- gions, to guard the delinquents againft the future attempts of their leaders.—*And that*, confequently, the fouls, or fpirits which ani- mate every mortal form, are delinquent angels in a ftate of punifhmept, for a lapfe from innocence, in a *pre-exiftent* ftate."

We will prefume to fay, that the *difference* between the doctrines hitherto imputed, to thefe ancient people, when compared with the original tenets of the *Chartah Bhade*, will now appear fo obvious to the learned and curious reader, that a further difcuffion of this point, is we conceive needlefs, and would in truth be a tacit reflection upon his underftanding.———Yet we are far from con- demning the authors, who have treated on this fubject; they took their information from the beft lights they had;—it is only to be regretted, that in place of drinking at the fountain head, they have fwallowed the muddy ftreams which flowed from the *Char- tah* and *Aughtorrah Bhades*.—The author on his departure from *Bengal* in the year 1750, imagined himfelf well informed in the *Gen- too* religion, his knowledge had been ac- quired by converfations with the *Bramins* of

of thofe *Bhades* who were near, as little acquainted with the *Chartah Bhade* of *Bramah*, as he was himfelf; and he had then
thoughts of obtruding his crude notions on
the public, had not a different neceffary application of his time luckily prevented him.

When we perufe fome portions of *Milton*'s
account of the rebellion and expulfion of the
angels, we are almoft led to imagine, on
comparifon, that *Bramah* and he were both
inftructed by the fame fpirit; had not the
foaring, ungovernable, inventive genius of
the latter, inftigated him to illuftrate his
poem with fcenes too grofs and ludicrous,
as well as manifeftly repugnant to, and in-
confiftent with, fentiments we ought to entertain of an omnipotent Being (as before
remarked) in which we rather fear he was
infpired by one of thefe malignant fpirits
(alluded to in the *Shaftah* and elfewhere)
who have from their original defection, been
the declared enemies of God and Man.———
For however we are aftonifhed and admire the
fublimity of *Milton*'s genius, we can hardly
fometimes avoid concluding his conceits
truely diabolical.—But this by the by.—

Our readers are now poffeffed for the firft
time of a faithful account of the *Metempfychofis*

fychofis of the *Bramins*—commonly called
the tranfmigration of fouls, a term hitherto
we believe little underftood, that this doctrine was originally peculiar to the *Gentoos*,
will not admit of doubt, although in after
times it was embraced by the *Egyptian* Magi,
and by fome fects amongft the *Chinefe* and
Tartars.——*Pythagoras*, who favored this
doctrine, and was a convert to it, labored
to introduce it amongft his country-men the
Greeks, but failed in the attempt. He fucceeded better with them in the theogony, cofmogony and mythology of the *Bramins*
Aughtorrah Bhade Shaftah, although thefe
conftituted no part of the original theology
of *Bramah*.

As we have referved a part exprefly for a
differtation on the doctrine of the *Metempfychofis*, we will avoid further mention of it
here; but as the *Bramins* of the *Chartah* and
Aughtorrah Bhades, inculcate and teach many
corollary branches of doctrine which fpring
from this root, it is neceffary that we recite
a few of the moft eftablifhed ones.

" When the delinquent *Debtah*, by the
mediation of *Birmah*, *Biftnoo* and *Moifoor*,
and the faithful angelic hoft, were releafed
from the *Onderah*; all, except *Moifafoor*,

Part II.   F   *Rhaabon*,

Rhaabon, and the reft of the rebel leaders, were fo ftruck with the goodnefs and mercy of the Eternal ONE, that they perfevered in a pious refignation and true penitence, during the firft of the *four Jogues*, and multitudes afcended, and paffed through the fifteen *Boboons*, and regained their forfeited eftate. —This period of time is called in the *Shaftah* the *Suttee Jogue*, when the term of the fpirits probation in *Mhurd*, was extended to one hundred thoufand years.

" In the *fecond* of the *four Jogues*, *Moifafoor* and the rebel leaders fo effectually exerted their influence over the delinquent *Debtah*, that they foon began to forget their crime and difregard their punifhment in the *Onderah*; they rejected the councils and examples of the guardian *Debtah*, and ftood a *fecond time* in defiance of their Creator; and *Moifafoor* drew over *one third* of the remaining unpurified fpirits.——This period is diftinguifhed in the *Shaftah*, by the name of the *Tirtah Jogue*, in which the Eternal ONE retrenched the term of the fpirits probation in *Mhurd*, to ten thoufand years. In this *Jogue* however, many perfevered in goodnefs, afcended through the fifteen *Boboons*, and regained the *Mahah Surgo*.

3   " In

" In the third of the four *Jogues*, *Moifafoor's* influence increafed, and he drew over half of the remaining unpurified fpirits, in each of the eight *Boboons* of punifhment and probation. This period is called in the *Shaftah*, the *Duapaar*, or *Dwapaar Jogue*, in which the term of probation in *Mhurd*, was reduced to one thoufand years; yet in this *Jogue* there were many who afcended and regained the *Mahah Surgo*.

" In the fourth *Jogue*, *Moifafoor* acquired as full poffeffion of the hearts of the remaining delinquent *Debtah* as when they firft rofe in rebellion with him, with very few exceptions; this period in the *Shaftah* is called the *Kolee Jogue*, in which the term of probation in *Mhurd* is limited to one hundred years only.—Yet even this *Jogue* affords fome inftances of the delinquent fpirits furmounting the eight lower *Boboons*, by penitence and good works; notwithftanding the unwearied diligence of *Moifafoor*, *Rhaabon*, and the reft of the rebellious leaders, and delinquent *Debtah*, who had a fecond time fallen under his influence."

The *four Jogues* or ages having been fo frequently mentioned in the laft paragraphs, we cannot do better than explain their mean-

ing

ing here, as fuch explanation would prove too long for a note, it may be remembered, they are called the *Suttee Jogue*, the *Tirtah Jogue*, the *Duapaar Jogue*, and the *Kolee Jogue*; we will fpeak to each in their order.

The *Suttee Jogue*, or the firſt age, literally the age of truth, figuratively the age of goodnefs;—in this age *Endeer* is fabled to be born, according to the *Aughtorrah Bhade*; and appointed King of the Univerfe—the word *Endeer* literally fignifies good, and is in that *Shaſlah* oppofed to *Moiſaſoor* or *evil*, and the various battles faid to be fought between this rebel angel and *Endeer*, and their defcendants in every *Jogue*, allegorically exhibit the conflicts and progrefs of *good* and *evil* in the univerfe; *Endeer*'s being appointed univerfal Monarch in the *Suttee Jogue*, alludes to the ſtate of the delinquent *Debtah* in this age, upon their emerging from the *Onderah*, when the imprefſion of God's mercy acted fo powerfully on their hearts, as to preſerve them in penitence and purity, during this age, notwithſtanding the utmoſt efforts of *Moiſaſoor* (or *evil*) and his adherents, to engage them in a fecond defection.—From the word *Suttee* (truth) the word *Sanfah* in *Bengals*, and *Sutch*, in the Moors are derived,—any one acquainted

in

in the leaft degree with thofe tongues, knows
that the phrafe *Sanfah Kotah*, in the one,
and *Sutch Bhaat*, in the other, is commonly
ufed to affert the verity of any thing advanced, and fimply fignifies, *words of truth*.

The *Tirtah Jogue*, or fecond age.—By
the term prefixed to this age, the order of
the *Jogues* fhould feem inverted, as the word
in its fimple conftruction fignifies *third*.—
The words *teen, tarah, tife, trefe,* and *tetrefe,*
which exprefs the numbers three, thirteen,
twenty-three, thirty and thirty-three, are all
derivatives from the *Sanfcrit, Tirtah,* or
Tirtea, as it is fometimes wrote, and means
the third, but oftener the *third part*, as in
the prefent inftance, where the term *Tirtah
Jogue* given to the fecond age, is allufive to
the fecond defection of one third of the remaining unpurified delinquent fpirits, from
that penitence and purity which governed
them in the *Suttee Jogue.*—In this age *Rhaam*
is fabled to be born for the protection of the
delinquent *Debtah*, againft the fnares and
attempt of *Moifafoor* and his adherents.—
The word *Rhaam* in the *Sanfcrit*, literally
fignifies protector, but in many parts of the
Aughtorrah Bhade this perfonage is mentioned in a more extended fenfe, as the protector of kingdoms, ftates and property.—

F 3 *Rhaam!*

Rhaam! Rhaam! is ufed as a pious faluta-tion, between two *Gentoos* when they meet in the morning, thereby recommending each other's perfon and property to the protection of this Demi-god.

The *Duapaar Jogue*, or third age.—This term prefixed to the third age, alludes to the fecond defection from penitence and goodnefs of *one half* of the remaining unpu-rified *Debtah—dua*, or *dwa* fimply fignifies, two, or the fecond, but here by the addition of *paar*, it means the half; thus *duapaar deen*, expreffes half the day, and *duapaar rhaat*, half the night,—that is if the phrafe iffues from the mouth of a polite *Gentoo*—but the vulgar would fay *adah deen* and *adah rhaat*, *adah* being the common *Bengal* word for half.—In the beginning of this *Jogue* the *Aughtorrah Bhade* fixes the birth of *Kif-fen Taghoor*.—The word *kiffen* in the *San-fcrit* fignifies a fcourge, and this *being* is in that *Bhade* frequently diftinguifhed as the fcourge of tyrants and tyranny.—*Tagoor* li-terally means *revered*, *refpected*, and is a common appellation given to *Bramins*.

The *Kolee Jogue*, or the fourth and pre-fent age.—*Kolee* in the *Sanfcrit* fignifies cor-ruption, pollution, impurity, confequently

Kolee

Kolee Jogue means the age of pollution.—
In this age (fay the *Bramins*) children fhall
bear falfe witnefs againft their parents, and
before the expiration of it—the ftature of
the *Mhurd* by the wickednefs of the rebellious *Debtah* that animates it, fhall be fo reduced, that he will not be able to pluck a
Bygon (berengelah *) without the help of a
hooked ftick.—We have often, whilft at the
head of the judicial court of *Cutcherry* at
Calcutta, heard the moft atrocious murders
and crimes confeffed, and an extenuation of
them attempted, by pleading, *it was the
Kolee Jogue.*—How far the poetical conceits
of *Ovid,* and others, touching the golden,
&c. ages, have been framed from *Bramah*'s
four Jogues, we leave to the inveftigation of
the curious.

It is an eftablifhed doctrine of the *Aughtorrah Bhade,* that the three primary created
perfonages, as well as the reft of the heavenly angelic faithful fpirits, have from time
to time according to the permiffion given
them by God, defcended to the eight *Boboons* of punifhment, and have voluntarily
fubjected themfelves to the feelings of natural and moral evil, for the fake of their
brethren, the delinquent *Debtah.* And to

* The *Egg Plant.*

F 4   this

this end, have undergone the eighty-nine tranfmigrations *; and that it is thofe benevolent fpirits, who have at different times appeared on this earthly region, under the mortal forms and names of *Endeer*, *Bramah*, *Jaggernaut*, *Kiffen Tagoor*, *Rhaam*, *Luccon*, *Kalkee*, (or *Kallee*) *Surfuttee*, *Gunnis*, *Kartic*, *&c.*—that have oppofed and fought againft *Moifafoor*, *Rhaabon*, and their iniquitous adherents——and have proved themfelves under the various characters of Kings, Generals, Philofophers, Lawgivers and Prophets, fhining examples to the delinquent *Debtah*, of ftupendous courage, fortitude, purity and piety.—That their vifitations were frequent during the *Tirtah*, and *Duapaar Jogues*, but rare fince the commencement of the *Kolee Jogue*, becaufe in this age the delinquent *Debtah* in general are deemed utterly reprobate, and hardened in their wickednefs beyond the power of counfel or example; fo that they are in a manner left, and given úp to their *own powers*, and abandoned to the full influence of *Moifafoor.*——But that there are ftill in every

* Hence the *Gentoos* dread of killing even by accident any thing that has life, as thereby they may not only difpoffefs the fpirits of their allied *Debtah*, but alfo, thofe of the celeftial *Debtah*, who are working for their redemption,

period

period of time fome few inftances of the delinquents exertion of their *own powers* for
their falvation, and that when this is manifeft to God, he permits the celeftial *Debtah*
invifibly to aid, confirm, and fupport them.

Although the *Shaftah* of *Bramah* denies
the prefcience of God refpecting the actions
of free-agents, yet the *Bramins* maintain
that his knowledge extends to the thoughts of
every created being, and that the moment a
thought is conceived by the foul or fpirit, it
is fympathetically conveyed to God.—It is
upon this principle that the adorations, prayers, petitions and thankfgivings, which the
Gentoos prefer to the Deity himfelf, are offered
in folemn filence; but it is not fo with regard
to the invocations and worfhip, inftituted by
the *Aughtorrah Bhade* to be paid to the fubordinate celeftial beings, for thefe are ad-
dreffed in loud prayer, joined to the clang
of various mufical inftruments.

We have already flightly touched on the
religious veneration paid to the *Ghoij* in a
particular diftrict of *Bengall*, although it is
beyond doubt, that their devotion to this
animal was univerfal throughout *Indoftan* in
former times.—The original fource of this
regard, was of a two-fold nature, as a reli-
2   gious

gious and political inftitution: firft, in a religious fenfe; as holding in the rotation of the
Metempfychofis, the rank immediately preceding the human form ; this conception is
the true caufe of that devout, and fometimes
enthufiaftic veneration paid to this animated
form, for the *Bramins* inculcate that when
the *Ghuj* fuffers death by accident or violence, or through the neglect of the owner,
it is a token of God's wrath againft the
wickednefs of the fpirit of *the proprietor*,
who from thence is warned that at the diffolution of his human form, he will not be
deemed worthy of entering the firft *Boboon* of
purification, but be again condemned to return
to the loweft region of punifhment : hence
it is, that not only mourning and lamentation enfue on the violent death of either cow
or calf—but the proprietor is frequently enjoined, and often voluntarily undertakes, a
three years pilgrimage in expiation of his
crime, forfaking his family, friends and relations, he fubfifts during his pilgrimage on
charity and alms.—It is worthy remark,
that the penitent thus circumftanced, ever
meets with the deepeft commiferation, as his
ftate is deemed truely pitiable ; two inftances
have fallen within our own knowledge where
the penitents have devoted themfelves to the
fervice of God, and a pilgrimage during the
term of their life.

Secondly,

Secondly, the *Ghoij* is venerated by the *Gentoos* in a political fenfe, as being the moft ufeful and neceffary of the whole animal creation, to a people forbid feeding on flefh, or on any thing that had breathed the breath of life; for it not only yielded to them delectable food, but was otherways effentially ferviceable in the cultivation of their lands; on which depended their vegetable fubfiftence.

The *Gentoos* hold that the females of all animated forms are, more or lefs, favored of God, but more eminently in the form of *Moiyah* in the eighty-ninth tranfmigration; the word fignifies *excellent*, and is applied to the female of *Mhurd*; *Rhaan* is the common name for woman, though it ufually means a married *Moiyah*, and the *Gentoo* Princeffes have no higher title than *Rhaance*. The female or *Moiyah* of *Mhurd*, is fuppofed to be animated by the moft benign and leaft culpable of the apoftate angels, and that from this form, in every period of the *four Jogues*, an infinitely greater number of the delinquent fpirits, have entered the firft region of purification, than from the form of *Mhurd*.

The fudden death of infants, the *Bramins* fay, marks the fpirits favored of God, and
that

that it is immediately received into the bofom of *Biftnoo*, (the preferver) and conveyed to the firft region of purification.—The fudden death of adults, on the contrary, they pronounce a mark of God's wrath againft the animating fpirit, as it's term of probation in *Mburd*, is cut fhort.——The great age of man, when it is accompanied with the enjoyments of his faculties and underftanding, is pronounced by the *Bramins* to be the greateft blefling God can beftow upon this mortal ftate, as thereby the term of the fpirits probation is prolonged; adding that the limited fpace of one hundred years, decreed by God in the prefent *Kolee Jogue*, is full fhort for the works of repentance and goodnefs, and that when the life and underftanding is preferved beyond that limited term, it ought to be deemed a fignal mark of God's fpecial grace and favor.

Longevity, in (what we call) the brute creation, is by the *Bramins* efteemed a mark of the great delinquency of the fpirits which animate thofe tribes, becaufe they are fo long debarred and with-held from their great and chief ftate of probation in *Mburd*.—The *Gentoos* eftimate the greater or leffer delinquency of the apoftate fpirits, by the clafs of mortal forms they are doomed to inhabit;

thus,

thus, all voracious and unclean animals are
fuppofed to be animated by the moft malignant fpirits ;—if a hog or dog touch a *Gentoo*, he is defiled, not from the animal form,
but from the perfwafion, that the *Debtah*
animating that form, is a malignant fpirit.
—Every voracious animal, that inhabits the
earth, air and waters, and men whofe lives
and actions are publickly and atrocioufly
wicked, come under that clafs of fpirits:—
On the contrary, thofe fpirits that animate
the forms which fubfift on vegetables, and
do not prey upon each other, are pronounced
favored of God.

The *general warfare* which is obferved in
the animal world, whereby the deftruction
of one fpecies is the neceffary fupport and
fubfiftence of others, the *Bramins* affert is
the lot of punifhment decreed by God for
the moft guilty of the apoftate angels, who
are thereby made *his* inftruments of punifhment to *each other*, every of thefe tribes
being a deftined prey to one another.—The
natural enmity which fome claffes of animals bear to others, whereby they live in a
continued ftate of war and contention, when-
ever they meet, although they do not fubfift on each other, proceeds they fay from
the fame caufe; the delinquent *Debtah* being
deftined

deftined as a punifhment, in thofe forms to exercife that propenfity to hatred, envy, and animofity, on one another, which they had fo impotently dared to exert againft their Creator.

The rotation of animal forms deftined for the habitation of the delinquent *Debtah*, are not, fay the *Bramins*, precifely the fame, on repetition of the eighty-nine tranfmigrations; but are arbitrary and refts with the will of God; but it is their belief that the leaft guilty of the *Debtah*, tranfmigrate only through thofe forms which by their nature are deftined to fubfift on the vegetable creation; and that the three changes immediately preceding the fpirits animating the *Ghoij* (that is the eighty-fifth, eighty-fixth, and eighty-feventh) are into the moft innocent of the fpecies of *birds*, the *goat* and the *fheep*, the animals moft favored of God, next to the *Ghoij* and *Mhurd*.—From hence the rigid *Bramins* execrate with bitternefs, the cruelty of thofe nations, who wickedly and wantonly felect and flaughter the beft beloved created forms of God, namely the birds, the goat, the fheep, and the cow, to fatisfy their unnatural luft of appetite, in defiance not only to his exprefs command and prohibition, but in oppofition to the

natural

natural and obvious conſtruction of the
mouth and digeſtive faculties of *Mhurd,* which
marks him, deſtined with other forms moſt
favored of God, to feed and ſubſiſt on the fruits
and produce of the earth, with the additional
bleſſing of the milk of the *Ghoïj,* and of
other animals.—For this degeneracy, they
account no otherwiſe, than piouſly lamenting
the pitiable ſtate of *Mhurd,* ſince the commencement of the *Kolee Jogue,* adding, that
by juſt conſequence the tranſgreſſion carries
its puniſhment along with it, for by this aſ-
ſemblage of unnatural and forbidden food,
variety of diſeaſes are entailed, which cut
ſhort the term of probation in *Mhurd,* by
which the delinquent ſpirit robs himſelf of
more than half of that ſpace of indulgence
and trial which his Creator has graciouſly
beſtowed upon him, and which he by a freſh
inſtance of his diſobedience, ungratefully
rejects.

Ovid in his fifteenth book of *Metamorpho-*
ſes introduces *Pythagoras* diſſuading mankind
from killing and feeding on his fellow creatures. Our readers will excuſe us, if we tranſ-
cribe ſuch parts of his pathetic arguments,
as are ſtrictly in point with the ſubject of the
preceding paragraph.

" He

" He firſt the taſte of fleſh, from tables drove,
And argued well, if arguments could move.
O mortals ! from your fellows blood abſtain,
Nor taint your bodies, with a food prophane ;
While corn and pulſe by nature are beſtow'd,
And planted orchards bend their willing load ;
While labor'd gardens wholeſome herbs produce,
And teeming vines afford their gen'rous juice ;
Nor tardier fruits of cruder kind are loſt,
But tam'd by fire or mellow'd by the froſt ;
While kine to pails, diſtended udders bring,
And bees their honey, redolent of ſpring ;
While earth, not only can your needs ſupply, .
But laviſh of her ſtores, provides for luxury ;
A guiltleſs feaſt, adminiſters with eaſe,
And without blood, is prodigal to pleaſe ;
Wild beaſts their maws, with their ſlain brethren fill,
And yet not all,—for ſome refuſe to kill ;
Sheep, goats, and oxen, and the nobler ſteed,
On browſe and corn, and flow'ry meadows feed ;
Bears, tigers, wolves, the angry lions brood,
Whom heaven endu'd with principles of blood,
He wiſely ſunder'd, from the reſt to yell,
In foreſt, and in lonely caves to dwell ;
Where ſtronger beaſts oppreſs the weak by night,
And all in prey, and purple feaſts delight.

" O impious uſe ! to Nature's laws oppoſed,
Where bowels are in others bowels cloſed ;
Where fatten'd, by their fellows' fat they thrive,
Maintain'd by murder, and by death they live ;

'Tis

'Tis then for nought, that mother Earth provides
The ſtores of all ſhe ſhows, and all ſhe hides;
If men with fleſhy morſels muſt be fed,
And chaw with bloody teeth the breathing bread;
What elſe is this, but to devour our gueſts,
And barb'rouſly renew Cyclopean feaſts.
We by deſtroying life, our life ſuſtain,
And gorge th' ungodly maw, with meats obſcene.

    " Not ſo the golden age, who fed on fruit,
Nor durſt with bloody meals their mouths pollute;
Then birds, in airy ſpace, might ſafely move,
And tim'rous hares on heaths ſecurely rove,
Nor needed fiſh the guileful hooks to fear,
For all was peaceful, and that peace ſincere.
Whoever was the wretch, and curs'd be he,
That envy'd firſt, our food's ſimplicity;
The eſſay of bloody feaſts, on brutes began,
And after forged the ſword to murder man;
Had he the ſharpened ſteel, alone employed
On beaſts of prey, which other beaſts deſtroyed,
Or man invaded, with their fangs and paws,
This had been juſtified by Nature's laws,
And ſelf defence :—but who did feaſts begin
Of fleſh, he ſtretch'd neceſſity, to ſin.
To kill man-killers, man has lawful power,
But not the extended licence to devour.

    " Ill habits gather, by unſeen degrees,
As brooks make rivers, rivers run to ſeas;
The ſow, with her broad ſnout, for rooting up,
Th' entruſted ſeed, was judg'd to ſpoil the crop;
And intercept the ſweating farmer's hope.

Part II.   G   The

The covetous churl, of unforgiving kind,
The offender to the bloody prieft refign'd ;
Her hunger was no plea, for that fhe dy'd ;
The goat came next in order to be tried.
The goat had crop'd the tendrils of the vine,
In vengeance the laity, and clergy join,
Where one had loft his profit, one his wine.
Here was, at leaft, fome fhadow of offence ;
The fheep was facrificed, on no pretence,
But meek, and unrefifting innocence.
A patient, ufeful creature, born to bear,
The warm and woolly fleece, that cloth'd her murderer ;
And daily to give down the milk fhe bred,
A tribute for the grafs on which fhe fed :
Living both food and raiment fhe fupplies,
And is of leaft advantage when fhe dies.

" How did the toiling ox, his death deferve,
A downright fimple drudge, and born to ferve ?
O tyrant ! with what juftice canft thou hope,
The promife of the year a plenteous crop,
When thou deftroy'ft thy lab'ring fteer, who till'd
And plough'd with pain, thy elfe ungrateful field ;
From his yet reeking neck, to draw the yoke,
That neck with which the furly clods he broke ;
And to the hatchet, yield thy hufbandman,
Who finifhed autumn, and the fpring began.

" Nor this alone ! but heaven itfelf to bribe,
We to the gods, our impious acts afcribe ;
Firft recompence with death, their creatures toil,
Then call the bleft above to fhare the fpoil.

3   The

The faireſt victim, muſt the pow'rs appeaſe
(So fatal 'tis ſometimes too much to pleaſe)
A purple fillet his broad brow adorns,
With flow'ry garlands crown'd and gilded horns :
He hears the murd'rous prayer the prieſt prefers,
But underſtands not ! 'tis his doom he hears :
Beholds the meal, betwixt his temples caſt,
(The fruit and product of his labors paſt,)
And in the water, views perhaps the knife,
Uplifted to deprive him of his life ;
Then broken up alive, his entrails ſees
Torn out for prieſts t'inſpect the gods decrees.

" From whence, O mortal man ! this guſt of blood
Have you deriv'd ? and interdicted food ?
Be taught by me, this dire delight to ſhun,
Warn'd by my precepts, by my practice, won ;
And when you eat the well-deſerving beaſt,
Think, on the lab'rer of your field, you feaſt.

" Then let not piety be put to flight,
To pleaſe the taſte of glutton appetite ;
But ſuffer inmate ſouls ſecure to dwell,
Leſt from their ſeats your parents you expell ;
With rabid hunger feed upon your kind,
Or from a beaſt diſlodge a brother's mind."

That *Pythagoras* carried ſuch ſentiments
from the *Bramins*, and labored to obtrude
them upon his countrymen, is beyond controverſy ; the pathetic perſwaſives he urged
to them in that age to abſtain from the

G 2   feeding

feeding on their brethren of the creatiori, proved however as ineffectual then, as we conceive it would be in the prefent, the more's the pity—for it is to be feared we fhall to the end of the chapter—Rife, kill, and eat.

Regarding the defcription (which *Ovid* puts in the mouth of *Pythagoras*) of the ancient religious facrifices, we muft in juftice to the *Bramins* fay he could not borrow it from them; in this particular the original religious tenets of the *Gentoos* differ from all the ancients, for they were ftrangers to thofe bloody facrifices and offerings; neither of the *Gentoo Bhades* having the leaft allufion to that mode of worfhipping the deity; and the *Bramins* fay, nothing but *Moifafoor* himfelf could have invented fo infatuated and cruel an inftitution, which is manifeftly fo repugnant to the true fpirit of devotion, and abhorrent to the Eternal ONE.

That every animal form is endued, with cogitation, memory and reflection, is one of the moft eftablifhed tenets of the *Bramins*; indeed it muft confequentially be fo, on the fuppofed *Metempfychofis* of the apoftate fpirits, through thefe mortal forms.—Every ftate of the delinquent fpirits abode in the eight *Boboons*, they fay, is a ftate of humilia-

humiliation, punifhment and purgation, that of *Mhurd* not excepted; and that the purpofe of the Eternal ONE would be defeated by himfelf, had he not endued them with rationality and a confcioufnefs of their fituation.——In the form of *Mhurd* alone, is the fpirit's ftate of probation, becaufe in this form only, he again becomes an abfolute and *free agent*; and in this alone lies the difference between *Mhurd,* and the reft of the animal created forms, for in thefe, the fpirit's intellectual faculties are circumfcribed, more or lefs, by the varied conftruction of the forms, and limited within certain bounds, which they cannot exceed,—that confcioufnefs of thofe confined powers, and envy at the fuperior ftate of *Mhurd,* conftitutes their chief punifhment; that this unceafing envy, and *refentment* of the ufurped tyranny which *Mhurd* affumed over the animal creation (from the beginning of the *Kolee Jogue)* are the caufes which made them in general fhun his fociety, and live in a ftate of enmity with him, according to the force of the natural powers, which the Eternal ONE has endued them with; that where fome of the fpecies appear an exception to this general bent, it proceeds from the weaknefs of their natural powers; or the fuperior craft and fubtility of *Mhurd,* who firft deceitfully

allured

allured them to flavery and deftruction.——
That neither *envy* or enmity in the animal
created forms, nor ufurped tyranny on the
part of *Mhurd*, had exiftence in the breafts
of either, before the beginning of the *Kolee
Jogue*, when a univerfal degeneracy of almoft all the remaining unpurified *Debtah*
prevailed through all their mortal forms—
which until that period had lived in amity
and harmony, as confcious of being involved
under the fame fentence and difpleafure of
their Creator; and laftly—That the ufurped
tyranny of *Mhurd* over the reft of the delinquent angels was difpleafing to the Eternal
ONE, and will be a charge exhibited againft
the fpirit by *Biftnoo* at the diffolution of
Mhurd, for that in place of cherifhing the
unhappy delinquents during their ftate of
humiliation and punifhment, they do, by the
force of their tyrannic ufurpation, labor
to make their ftate more miferable, than the
Eternal ONE intended it fhould be, in violation of his exprefs injunction, *that they fhould
love one another.*

The *Bramins* hold, that every diftinct
fpecies of animal creation have a compre-
henfive mode of communicating their ideas,
peculiar to themfelves; and that the *Metempfychofis*

fychofis of the delinquent fpirits extends through every organifed body, even to the fmalleft infect and reptile;—they highly venerate the bee, and fome fpecies of the ant, and conceive the fpirits animating thofe forms are favored of God, and that its intellectual faculties, are more enlarged under them, than in moft others.

Although we have already fhewn that the bloody facrifices of the ancients was no part of the *Gentoo* tenets, yet there fubfifts amongft them at this day, a *voluntary facrifice*, of too fingular a nature, to pafs by us unnoticed; the rather as it has been frequently mentioned by various authors, without we conceive that knowledge and perfpicuity which the matter calls for ; the facrifice we allude to, is the *Gentoo wives burning with the bodies of their deceafed hufbands*. We have taken no fmall pains to inveftigate this feeming cruel cuftom, and hope we fhall be able to throw fame fatisfactory lights on this very extraordinary fubject, which has hitherto been hid in obfcurity ; in order to which we will firft remove one or two obftructions that lie in our way, and hinder our nearer and more perfect view of it.

G 4   The

The caufe commonly affigned for the origin of this facrifice (peculiar to the wives of this nation) is, that *it was a law confti-tuted to put a period to a wicked practice that the Gentoos wives had of poifoning their huf-bands* ;—for this affertion we cannot trace the fmalleft femblance of truth, and indeed the known fact, that the facrifice muft be *voluntary*, of it's felf refutes that common miftake.—It has alfo been a received opinion, that *if the wife refufes to burn, fhe lofes her caft* (or tribe) *and is ftamped with difgrace and infamy* ; an opinion equally void of foundation in fact as the other.—The real ftate of this cafe is thus circumftanced.—The firft wife (for the *Gentoo* laws allow bigamy, although they frequently do not benefit themfelves of the indulgence, if they have iffue by the firft) has it in her choice to burn, but *is not permitted* to declare her re-folution before twenty-four hours after the deceafe of her hufband ;—if fhe refufes, the right devolves to the fecond,—if either, after the expiration of twenty-four hours, publicly declare, before the *Bramins* and *witneffes*, their refolution to *burn*, they cannot then retract. If they both refufe at the expira-tion of that term, the worft confequence that attends their refufal, is lying under the imputation of being wanting to their own

2 honor,

honor, purification, and the prosperity of their family, for from their infancy, they are in-ftructed by the houfehold *Bramin* to look upon this cataftrophe, as moft glorious to themfelves, and beneficial to their children : the truth is, that the children of the wife who burns, become thereby illuftrious, and are fought after in marriage by the moft opulent and honourable of their *caft*, and fometimes received into a caft fuperiour to their own.

That the *Bramins* take unwearied pains to encourage, promote, and confirm in the minds of the *Gentoo* wives, *this fpirit of burning*, is certain (their motives for it, the penetration of our readers may by and by probably difcover) and although they feldom lofe their labor, yet inftances happen, where fear, or love of life, fets at nought all their preaching; for it fometimes falls out that the firft wife refufes, and the fecond burns ; at others, they both refufe; and as but one can burn, it fo happens, that when the fecond wife has iffue by the deceafed, and the firft none, there commonly enfues a violent contention between them, which of the two fhall make the facrifice; but this difpute is generally determined by the *Bra-mins*, in favor of the firft, unlefs fhe is pre-vailed

vailed on by perfwafion, or other motives to
wave her right, in favor of the fecond.——
Having elucidated thefe matters, we will
proceed to give our readers the beft account
we have been able to obtain of the origin
of this remarkable cuftom.

At the demife of the mortal part of the
Gentoos' great Law-giver and Prophet BRA-
MAH, his wives, inconfolable for his lofs,
refolved not to furvive him, and offered
themfelves voluntary victims on his funeral
pile.——The wives of the chief *Rajahs*, the
firft officers of the ftate, being unwilling to
have it thought that they were deficient in
fidelity and affection, followed the heroic
example fet them by the wives of *Bramah*;
——the *Bramins* (a tribe then newly conftituted by their great legiflator) pronounced
and declared, *that the delinquent fpirits of
thofe heroines, immediately ceafed from their
tranfmigrations, and had entered the firft
Boboon of purification*—it followed, that *their*
wives claimed a right of making the fame
facrifice of their mortal forms *to God*, and
the manes of their deceafed hufbands ;——
The wives of every *Gentoo* caught the enthufiaftic (now pious) flame.——Thus the
heroic acts of a few women brought about
a general cuftom, the *Bramins* had given it

the

the ftamp of religion, they foifted it into the *Chartah* and *Aughtorrah Bhades,* and infti- tuted the forms and ceremonials that were to accompany the facrifice, ftrained fome ob- fcure paffages of *Bramah's Chartah Bhade,* to countenance their *declared fenfe* of the action, and eftablifhed it as a religious tenet throughout *Indoftan,* fubject to the reftric- tions before recited, which leaves it a volun- tary act of glory, piety and fortitude.——— Whether the *Bramins* were fincere in their declared fenfe, and confecration of this act, or had a view to the fecuring the fidelity of their own wives, or were actuated by any other motives, we will not determine.———

When people have lived together to an advanced age, in mutual acts of confidence, friendfhip and affection; the facrifice a *Gen- too* widow makes of her perfon (under fuch an affecting circumftance as the lofs of friend and hufband) feems lefs an object of wonder; ———but when we fee women in the bloom of youth, and beauty, in the calm poffeffion of their reafon and underftanding, with af- tonifhing fortitude, fet at nought, the tender confiderations of parents, children, friends, and the horror and torments of the death they court, we cannot refift viewing fuch

an

an act, and such a victim, with tears of commiferation, awe and reverence.

We have been prefent at many of thefe facrifices: in fome of the victims, we have obferved a pitiable dread, tremor, and re-luctance, that ftrongly fpoke repentance for their *declared refolution*; but it was now too late to retract, or retreat; *Biftnoo* was *waiting for the fpirit*.—If the felf doomed victim difcovers want of courage and fortitude, fhe is with gentle force obliged to afcend the pile, where fhe is held down with long poles, held by men on each fide of the pile, until the flames reach her; her fcreams and cries, in the mean time, being drowned amidft the deafening noife of loud mufick, and the acclamations of the multitude.——Others we have feen go through this fiery trial, with moft amazing fteady, calm, re-folution, and joyous fortitude.——It will not we hope be unacceptable, if we prefent our readers with an inftance of the latter, which happened fome years paft at the *Eaft India* company's factory at *Coffimbuzaar*, in the time of Sir *Francis Ruffel's* chieffhip; the author, and feveral other gentlemen of the factory were prefent, fome of whom are now living:—from a narrative, which the author then tranfmitted to *England*, he is

now

now enabled to give the particulars of this moft remarkable proof of female fortitude, and conftancy.

" At five of the clock in the morning of the 4th of *February*, 1742-3, died *Rhaam ChundPundit* of the *Mahabrattor* tribe, aged twenty-eight years; his widow (for he had but one wife) aged between feventeen and eighteen, as foon as he expired, difdaining to wait the term allowed her for reflection, immediately declared to the *Bramins* and witneffes prefent her refolution to burn ; as the family was of no fmall confideration, all the merchants of *Coffimbuzaar*, and her relations, left no arguments uneffayed to diffuade her from it—Lady *Ruffel*, with the tendereft humanity, fent her feveral meffages to the fame purpofe; —the infant ftate of her children (two girls and a boy, the eldeft not four years of age) and the terrors and pain of the death fhe fought, were painted to her in the ftrongeft and moft lively colouring—fhe was deaf to all,—fhe gratefully thanked Lady *Ruffel*, and fent her word *fhe had now nothing to live for*, but *recommended her children to her protection*.—When the torments of burning were urged in terrorem to her, fhe with a refolved and calm countenance, put her finger into the fire, and held it there a confiderable time,

time, fhe then with one hand put fire in
the palm of the other, fprinkled incenfe on
it, and fumigated the *Bramins*. The confideration of her children left deftitute of a
parent was again urged to her.—She replied,
he that made them, would take care of them.—
She was at laft given to underftand, fhe
fhould not be permitted to burn *; this for
a fhort fpace feemed to give her deep afflic-
tion, but foon recollecting herfelf, fhe told
them, *death was in her power, and that if fhe
was not allowed to burn, according to the
principles of her caft, fhe would ftarve herfelf.*—
Her friends, finding her thus peremptory and
refolved, were obliged at laft to affent.

" The body of the deccafed was carried
down to the water fide, early the following
morning, the widow followed about ten
o'clock, accompanied by three very principal
Bramins, her children, parents, and relations,
and a numerous concourfe of people. The
order of leave for her burning did not arrive
from *Hoffeyn Khan, Fouzdaar* of *Morfhada-
bad*, until after one, and it was then brought
by one of the *Soubah*'s own officers, who

---

* The *Gentoos* are not permitted to burn, without
an order from the *Mahommedan* government, and this
permiffion is commonly made a perquifite of ——

had

had orders to fee that fhe burnt voluntarily. —— The time they waited for the order was employed in praying with the *Bramins*, and wafhing in the *Ganges*; as foon as it arrived, fhe retired and ftayed for the fpace of half an hour in the midft of her female relations, amongft whom was her mother; fhe then divefted herfelf of her bracelets, and other ornaments, and tyed them in a cloth, which hung like an apron before her, and was conducted by her female relations to one corner of the pile; on the pile was an arched arbor formed of dry fticks, boughs and leaves, open only at one end to admit her entrance; in this the body of the deceafed was depofited, his head at the end oppofite to the opening.—At the corner of the pile to which fhe had been conducted, the *Bramin* had made a fmall fire, round which fhe and the three *Bramins* fat for fome minutes, one of them gave into her hand a leaf of the bale tree (the wood commonly confecrated to form part of the funeral pile) with fundry things on it, which fhe threw into the fire; one of the others gave her a fecond leaf, which fhe held over the flame, whilft he dropped *three times* fome ghee on it, which melted, and fell into the fire (thefe two operations, were preparatory fymbols of her approaching diffolution

by

by fire) and whilft they were performing this, the third *Bramin* read to her fome portions of the *Aughtorrah Bhade*, and afked her fome queftions, to which fhe anfwered with a fteady, and ferene countenance; but the noife was fo great, we could not under-ftand what fhe faid, although we were with-in a yard of her.—Thefe over, fhe was led with great folemnity *three times* round the pile, the *Bramins* reading before her; when fhe came the third time to the fmall fire, fhe ftopped, took her rings off her toes and fingers, and put them to her other orna-ments; here fhe took a folemn majeftic leave of her children, parents, and relations; after which, one of the *Bramins* dip'd a large wick of cotton in fome ghee, and gave it ready lighted into her hand, and led her to the open fide of the arbor; there, all the *Bramins* fell at her feet;——after fhe had bleffed them, they retired weeping;—by two fteps, fhe afcended the pile and entered the arbor; on her entrance, fhe made a profound reverence at the feet of the de-ceafed, and advanced and feated herfelf by his head; fhe looked, in filent meditation on his face, for the fpace of a minute, then fet fire to the arbor, in *three places*; obferv-ing that fhe had fet fire to leeward, and that the flames blew from her, inftantly feeing

her

her error she rose, and set fire to windward, and resumed her station; ensign *Daniel* with his cane, separated the grass and leaves on the windward side, by which means we had a distinct view of her as she sat. With what dignity, and undaunted a countenance she set fire to the pile the last time, and assumed her seat, can only be conceived, for words cannot convey a just idea of her.—The pile being of combustible matters, the supporters of the roof were presently consumed, and it tumbled upon her."

We see our fair country-women shudder at an action, which we fear they will look upon, as a proof of the highest infatuation in their sex.—Although it is not our intention here to defend the tenets of the *Bramins*, yet we may be allowed to offer some justification on behalf of the *Gentoo* women in the action before us—Let us view it (as we should every other action) without prejudice, and without keeping always in sight *our own* tenets and customs, and prepossessions that too generally result therefrom, to the injury of others ;—if we view these women in a just light, we shall think more candidly of them, and confess they act upon heroic, as well as rational and pious principles : In order to this we must consider them as a race of females

Part II.   H   trained

trained from their infancy, in the full conviction of their *celeſtial rank*; and that this world, and the corporeal form that incloſes them, is deſtined by God, the one as their place of puniſhment, the other as their priſon.——— That their ideas are conſequently raiſed to a ſoothing degree of dignity befitting angelic beings.——They are nurſed and inſtructed in the firm faith—that this voluntary ſacrifice, is the moſt glorious period of their lives, and that thereby the celeſtial ſpirit is releaſed from its tranſmigrations, and evils of a miſerable exiſtence, and flies to join the ſpirit of their departed huſband, in a ſtate of purification : add to this, the ſubordinate conſideration of raiſing the luſtre of their children, and of contributing by this action to *their* temporal proſperity;—all theſe it muſt be owned are prevalent motives, for chearfully embracing death, and ſetting at nought every common attachment which the weakneſs of humanity urges, for a longer exiſtence in a world of evil.—Although theſe principles are in general ſo diametrically contrary to the prevailing ſpirit and genius of our fair country-women, who (from a happy train of education) in captivating amuſements and diſſipation, find charms ſufficient in this world, to engage their wiſhes for a perpetual

reſidence

refidence in it; yet we will depend on their natural goodnefs of heart, generofity and candor, that they will in future look on thefe their *Gentoo* fifters of the creation, in a more favorable, and confiftent light, than probably they have hitherto done; and not deem *that action* an infatuation, which re-fults from principle. Let them alfo recollect that their own hiftory affords illuftrious ex-amples in both fexes of voluntary facrifices by fire, becaufe they would not fubfcribe even to a different mode of profeffing the fame faith. Befides—a contempt of death, is not peculiar to the women of *India*, it is the characteriftic of the nation; every *Gentoo* meets that moment of diffolution, with a fteady, noble, and philofophic refignation, flowing from the eftablifhed principles of their faith.

Before we clofe this fubject, we will men-tion one or two more particulars relative to it.—It has been already remarked in a mar-ginal note, that the *Gentoo* women are not allowed to burn, without an order of leave from the *Mahommedan* government; it is proper alfo to inform our readers this pri-vilege is never withheld from them.—There have been inftances known, when the victim has, *by Europeans,* been forcibly refcued

H 2   from

from the pile; it is currently faid and believed (how true we will not aver) that the
wife of Mr. *Job Charnock* was by him
fnatched from this facrifice; be this as it
may, the outrage is confidered by the *Gen-*
toos, an atrocious, and wicked violation of
their facred rites and privileges.

Having now brought our fourth general
head to a conclufion, and faithfully, to the
beft of our knowledge (with the materials we
are poffeffed of) exhibited the original tenets
of the ancient *Bramins*, according to the
firft book of *Bramah's Chartah Bhade*;
and having in our remarks given fuch eluci-
dations as we thought our fubject called
for, we fubmit our imperfect work (for
imperfect we muft ftill call it) with all due
deference to the public; hoping that fome
more capable head and hand, will be ftimulated by our endeavours, to produce a
more full, and fatisfactory relation, of the
reft of his doctrines.—A large field is yet
left open, for the excercife of induftry and
talents. *Bramah's* firft fection of his fecond
book on the creation of this globe, will be
the fubject of our next general head.——
His third book, directing the plain and
fimple modes of worfhip to be paid to God,
and the three primary created beings, and
his

his fourth *fublime book*, (which the *Gentoos*
commonly call **Bramah Ka, Infoff Bhade**,
or, **Bramah**'s book of juftice) wherein is
exprefly recited and enjoined, the duties and
offices which the delinquent *Debtah* fhall
obferve and pay to each other; thefe two
laft mentioned books, and part of the fecond,
we fay, muft lie in oblivion, until fome
one, bleffed with opportunity, leifure, application, and genius, brings them to light.

The End of the Fourth Chapter.

II 3   C H A P.

C H A P. V.

Of the Creation of the Worlds.

INTRODUCTION.

IN the fifth section of our laſt general head, *Bramah* recites, that the Eternal ONE, (after he had promulged his gracious intention, of mitigating the puniſhment of the fallen angels, at the interceſſion of the remaining faithful hoſt ;) " retired into himſelf, and became inviſible to them, for the ſpace of five thouſand years."—In his introduction to the act of creation of the worlds in his ſecond book, he takes again occaſion to repeat the above mentioned paſ-ſage, and explains it by an inference, that during THAT SPACE, the Eternal ONE was employed in meditation on his intended new creation ;—and although it appears, from the ſame ſection, that this ſtupendous work, was produced by an *inſtantaneous fiat* of the

Deity,

Deity, yet *Bramah*, to difplay the infinite and amazing wifdom of his Creator, enters into a fublime, and philofophic difquifition and defcription, of his modes (if we may be allowed the expreffion) and manner of creation, in the marvellous conftruction of the fifteen *Boboons*, that conftitute the *Dunneahoudah*, or univerfe ;—thefe defcriptions, he couches under allegories, then commonly and familiarly underftood, at which the reader will the lefs wonder, when he knows, that at this day it is the ufual mode of converfing, amongft well educated *Gentoos*.

In this exhibition of infinite wifdom, *Bramah* gives a fhort, fimple and elevated defcription, of each of the fifteen *Boboons*, their fituation, their rank, and peculiar deftination, with the appellations appropriated to the angelic inhabitants, in their progreffive ·paffage from one fphere to another. Our memory only fupplies us with the names of the fojourners of the ninth, fifth, fixth, and feventh, that is, the firft, and three laft of the feven regions of purification, to wit, the fpheres of the *Pereeth logue* *, the *Munnoo*

---

* *Logue*, literally people. *Pereeth logue*, purified people.

logue,

logue *, the *Debtah logue* †, and the *Bir-mah logue* ‡; in the laft mentioned fpherc, according to the *Bramins* computation, a complete day is equal to twenty-eight *Mun-nunturs* of vulgar time. (Vid. fixth or next general head.)

On the foundation of *Bramah*'s defcrip-tion of the fifteen *Boboons*, the compilers of the *Aughtorrah Bhade* have raifed an elabo-rate chimerical fuperftruðure, that confounds the underftanding.

As the *Bramins* conceptions and calcula-tion of the age and future duration of the univerfe, will be the fubjeð of our next general head, we fhall fay nothing more of it here, than to remind our readers, that they date it's exiftence from the rebellious angels being releafed from the *Onderah*.

We again lament the lofs of our materials, which confines us to the eighth feðion of

---

* *Munnoo logue, people* of *contemplation*, from *mun*, or *mon*, *thought*, *refleðion*, alludes to God's being worfhipped in this fphere in filent meditation.

† In this fphere the angels are firft fuppofed to re-gain properly their title of *Debtah*.

‡ In this fphere the delinquents are fuppofed to be cleanfed from the pollution of their fin, regenerated, and fit to enter again the *Mahah Surgo*, and to be re-admitted to the prefence of their Creator.

Bramah's

Bramah's fecond book that treats only of
the creation of this terreftrial planet, to which
we will now proceed, premifing that it is
diftinguifhed by the title of *the eighth Boboon of Murto*, which literally fignifies *the
region of earth.*

SECT. VIII.

" *Birmahah* * or *Creation.*

" And it was————that when the
" Eternal ONE, refolved to form the
" new creation of the *Dunneahou-*
" *dah*, he gave the rule of *Mahah*
" *Surgo* to his firft created *Birmah*,
" and became invifible to the whole
" angelic hoft.

" When the Eternal ONE, firft began
" his intended new creation of the
" *Dunneahoudah*, he was oppofed by two
" mighty *Ofloors* †, which *proceeded*
" from the *wax* of *Brum*'s ear ; and
" their names were *Modco* ‡ and *Kytoo* §.

" And the Eternal ONE, contended
" and *fought* with *Modoo* and *Kytoo*,
" five thoufand years, and he fmote

---

* This title is prefixed to every fection of *Bramah's*
fecond book, *Birmah* in the figurative fenfe (before
explained) fignifying *creation.*

† The common appellation given to *giants*, but is
varioufly ufed in the *Shaftah*, to exprefs *excrefcence*, *ex-*
cretion, and *fecretion.*

‡ *Difcord, enmity.*   § *Confufion, tumult.*

" them

" them on his *thigh* *, and they were
" *loſt* and aſſimilated with *Murto*:

" And it was,—that when *Modoo*
" and *Kytco* were ſubdued, the Eternal
" ONE emerged from his ſtate of in-
" viſibility, and glory encompaſſed him
" on every ſide!

" And the Eternal ONE ſpoke, and
" ſaid, Thou *Birmah* † ſhalt *create* and
" form all things that ſhall be made
" in the new creation of the fifteen
" *Boboons* of puniſhment, and puriſi-
" cation, according to the powers of the
" ſpirit, wherewith thou ſhalt be in-
" ſpired.——And thou, *Biſtnoo* ‡, ſhalt
" ſuperintend, cheriſh, and *preſerve* all
" the things and forms which ſhall be
" created.—And thou, *Sieb* §, ſhalt
" *change*, or *deſtroy*, all creation, ac-
" cording to the powers, wherewith I
" will inveſt thee."

* Reduced them to ſubjection, or obedience : *touching the thigh*, amongſt the ancient *Gentoos*, was a token
of *ſubjection*.
† *Power of creation*. Vid. introduction to the fourth
chapter.
‡ *Preſerver*. Vid. introduction to the fourth chapter.
§ *Mutilator*, *deſtroyer*. Vid. introduction, &c.

" And

" And when *Birmah*, *Biftnoo*, and
" *Sieb*, had heard the words of the
" Eternal ONE, they all bowed obe-
" dience *.

" The Eternal ONE fpoke again,
" and faid to *Birmah*, Do thou begin
" the creation and formation of *the*
" *eighth Boboon*, of punifhment and *pro-*
" *bation*, even the *Boboon* of *Murto*,
" according to the powers of the fpirit
" wherewith I have endued thee, and
" do thou, *Biftnoo*, proceed to execute
" thy part.

" And when *Brum* † heard the
" command, which the mouth of the
" Eternal ONE had uttered; he ftraight-
" ways formed a *leaf of beetle*, and he
" floated on the *beetle leaf* over the fur-
" face of the *Jhoale*; and the children ‡
" of *Modoo* and *Kytoo*, fled before

* The foregoing exordium of the general act of
creation of the *Dunneahoudah*, preceeds every one of
the fifteen fections of *Bramah's* fecond book.
† *Birmah* and *Brum*, are, in the act of creation, fynonimous terms.
‡ Suppofed remains of difcordant matter. The
Bramins fuppofed the firft principles of things prior to
the creation of the univerfe, to have been in a fluid
ftate.

" him,

" him, and vanished from his pre-
" fence.

" And when the agitation of the
" *Jhoale* had fubfided, by the powers
" of the fpirit of *Brum*, *Biftnoo* ftraight-
" ways transformed himfelf into a
" *mighty boar* *, and defcending into
" the abyfs of *Jhoale*, he brought up
" *the Murto* on his tufks.—Then fpon-
" taneoufly iffued from him, a *mighty*
" *tortoife* †, and a *mighty fnake* ‡.

" And *Biftnoo* put the fnake erect
" upon the *back* of the tortoife, and
" placed *Murto* upon the *head* of the
" fnake.

" And all things were created and
" formed by *Birmah* in the eighth
" *Boboon* of punifhment and *probation*,
" even the eighth of *Murto*, according
" to the powers of the fpirit, where-
" with the Eternal ONE had endued
" him.

* The *Gentoos* fymbol of *ftrength*, becaufe, in pro-
portion to his fize, he is the ftrongeft of all animals.
† The *Gentoos* fymbol of *ftability*.
‡ The *Gentoos* fymbol of *wifdom*.

" And

" And *Biſtnoo* took upon him the
" ſuperintendance and charge of all
" that was created, and formed, by
" *Birmah* in the eighth *Boboon* of
" *Murto* ; and he cheriſhed and pre-
" *ſerved* them, as the words of the
" Eternal ONE had directed, and com-
" manded."

R E M A R K S.

IN the ſame ſublime allegorical manner,
has *Bramah* deſcribed the creation of *Surjee* *, and *Chunder* †, and the other twelve
Boboons of the *Dunneahoudah*, without pre-
tending, or aiming to dive into, and explain,
the principles of matter, or the nature of
thoſe eſſential laws of motion by which the
Deity guides and governs his creation ; the
wiſdom of *Bramah* has elſewhere marked
ſuch fruitleſs enquiries, with the *ſtamp* of
preſumption and folly ; and that the knowledge of *theſe*, and the mode of the exiſtence
of God, is concealed even from the three
primary created beings themſelves.

From the foregoing ſpecimen of the
creation of the eighth region, as well as

---

* The *Sun*.   † The *Moon*.

from

from *Bramah*'s hiftorical difcuffion of the
other fourteen, it is moft obvious, that the
perfonages which he introduces as actors in
the work of that creation were intended by
him to be taken only in a figurative fenfe,
as expreffive of the three fupreme attributes
of the Deity, his power *to create*, his power
to preferve, and his power *to change* or
deftroy, as before hinted *.—For if they were
to be underftood in any other fenfe, it would
exprefly contradict his own text, where he
reprefents the creation of the *Dunneahoudah*
as proceeding from the *inftantaneous* fiat
of the Eternal ONE ; and a further proof
of *Bramah*'s plain intention, refults from
his prefixing the fame exordium to each of
his fections of creation.

But as the real fenfe and meaning of the
allegory (then clearly underftood by all) was,
in procefs of time, loft to the generality of
the *Gentoos*, the compilers of the *Chartah*
and *Aughtorrah Bhades*, took the advantage
(which ignorance and time gave them) and
not only realifed *Bramah*'s three myftical
beings, but created alfo a multitude of fubordinate actors, and made Demi-gods and Divinities of them all, inftituting particular
days, fafts, and feftivals; and other exterior

* Vid. Introduction to the fourth chapter.

worfhip,

worſhip, to each:—Thus *Surjee* and *Chunder*, *Modoo* and *Kytoo*, and a race of their children and deſcendants, became Demi-gods and heroes; and ſcorning to confine themſelves to the eighth *Boboon*, they ranſacked the fourteen, and framed divinities of the prin‑ cipal perſonages which their wild imagina‑ tion ſuppoſed reſident in each of them, and allotted to them peculiar divine worſhip, which ſubſiſts to this day.

It will not, we hope, be thought an im‑ probable conjecture, if we ſay, that the allegorical parts of *Bramah*'s *Chartah Bhade*, (which truely bears a divine ſemblance) being thus perverted or groſly miſtaken by the very tribe, which he had inſtituted guardians over it, and being ſubſequently communicated to the *Egyptian* Magi, and by them circulated through the ſtates of *Greece*, afforded them, as well as *Rome* and the whole *Weſtern* world, thoſe inexhauſtible ſupplies of *mythological ſyſtems*, which held their exiſtence and au‑ thority even long after the light of chriſtia‑ nity had ſhone upon them.——But to re‑ ſume our more immediate ſubject.

The act of creation of the *Boboon of Murto* is repreſented in the annexed plate No. 1. which (with others we ſhall have occaſion

to

to prefent to the reader) was drawn by the inftructions, and under the eye of a judicious *Bramin* of the *Battezaar* tribe, the tribe, as before noticed, ufually employed in expounding the *Shaftahs*.

Brum * is reprefented lying and floating on a leaf of *beetle*, over the troubled furface of the abyfs of *Jhoale*; the three primary beings appear before it, in the pofture of adoration, *Birmah* on the right, *Biftnoo* in the middle, and *Sieb* on the left.——On the right, above the abyfs, is figured a huge *boar*, bearing on his tufks a lump of earth. —On the left, above the abyfs, is reprefented a *tortoife*, on which a fnake refts his tail, bearing *Murto* (or the *earth*) on his head.— *Brum* and *Birmah* are habited alike; and are each figured with four heads and four arms.—The *three* primary beings, are fuppofed in the pofture of adoration, to be receiving the commands of the Eternal ONE, touching his projected new creation; and the other figures exprefs the *three* gradations of the work, namely the beginning, the progrefs, and completion †.

---

* *Spirit* or *effence* of the Eternal ONE: vide Introduction to the fourth chapter.

† Vide Plate No. 1.

Notwithſtanding the ſagacious reader, by a bare reference to the marginal notes which we have affixed to the text of *Bramah*, will readily conceive the ſpirit of the allegory contained in it; yet as ſome paſſages of it require a further explanation than could be huddled into a note, we will add the whole interpretation of it under one connected view.

The Eternal ONE having determined on the creation of the univerſe, like a ſupreme wiſe architect, he *retired* for a ſpace to project his ſtupendous plan, and prepare his materials.—He was *oppoſed* in the operation by the *diſcord, confuſion* and *tumult* of the elements that compoſe the *abyſs of Jhoale*; —he ſeparated, ſubdued, brought them under *ſubjection*, and prepared them to receive his intended impreſſions.—He exerts his *three* great attributes, to *create, preſerve*, or *deſtroy*, which are figuratively repreſented by the *three* primary created beings—His *ſpirit* floats upon the ſurface of the abyſs of *Jhoale*, or fluid matter,—Creation takes place.—*Birmah* (or Creation) is repreſented with four heads and four arms, to denote the *power* of God in the act of creation. *Biſtnoo the preſerver* is transformed into a mighty *boar*, emblematically ſignifying *the ſtrength* of God in the act of creation.—
The

The tortoife myftically denotes the *ftability* and *permanency* of the foundation of *the earth*, and the fnake the *wifdom* by which it is *fupported*. Thefe latter operations are given to *Biftnoo*, becaufe the *earth* was the grand principle or parent, from whence he was to draw the means for the *prefervation* of the future animal creation, deftined for the prifons of the rebellious *Debtah*; a work which we may gather from *Bramah*'s text, was referved for the hand of *God himfelf*, as *they* were to be endued with *rational powers*.—It may be afked why *Brum*, is reprefented floating, particularly on a *beetle leaf?* To this we can only reply, that the plant is deemed facred amongft the *Gentoos*, it's culture is made under the aufpices of the *Shaftah*, and inftruction of the *Bramins*; *unclean perfons* are prohibited entering into a *beetle garden*, as the approach of any impurity is pronounced fatal to the plant, in the infancy of its growth.

To conclude this general head—How far *Homer, Virgil, Lucretius, Ovid, Lucian*, &c. have in their conceptions of the creation, (by means of the *Egyptians)* built on, and availed themfelves of the fimple *cofmogony* of *Bramah*, we leave the learned and curious to trace.—Although in fact, it is obvious,

· I 2   that

that this ancient fage, aimed at no other folution of that ftupendous and incomprehenfible act, than to inculcate, that the univerfe was produced by *the effence* and voluntary *power, ftrength* and *wifdom* of GOD. That it is *preferved* and fuftained by original conftituent *powers* impreffed on it by the Deity, and that it is liable *to change* and diffolution, at his divine pleafure and will.

The End of the Fifth Chapter.

C H A P. VI.

The Gentoo manner of computing Time, and their conception of the age of the univerſe, and the period of its diſſolution.

[From Bramah's Chartah Bhade, in the ſupplement to his Birmahah.]

SIXTY *mimicks*, or winks of the eye, make one *pull*.

Sixty *pulls*, make one *gurree*.

Sixty *gurrees*, make one complete day, or one day and one night.

Three hundred and ſixty-five compl̄ete days and fifteen *gurrees* make one ſolar year.

The *Gentoos* divide the complete day into eight parts, to which they give the term *paar*; commencing their day at ſix in the morning;—thus *ek paar dheen* * equals our nine in the morning; *duapaar dheen*, our noon; *teenpaar dheen*, our three afternoon; *Chaarpaar dheen*, our ſix in the evening:— the diviſions of the night are diſtinguiſhed by the word *rhaat* (night) in place of

* Literally, *one part* of *day.*

I 3

dheen,

dheen, as *ek paar rhaat,* equals our nine at
night; and fo on.

It is the province of the *Bramins* in this
country to keep the account of time, and
there is no *Gentoo* of diftinction but retains,
in his houfe and on his journeys one of
thefe time keepers, whofe intire bufinefs it is
to regulate time, and ftrike the *gurrees* as
they pafs, on the *Ghong,* an extended fheet
of copper, which yields the found of a
folemn bell.

Bramah meafures fpace or duration of time,
from the creation of the *Dunneahoudah,* or
univerfe, by the revolutions of the *four*
Jogues.

	Years.
The firft age, or *Suttee Jogue,* contains thirty-two lac years of vulgar time, or	3,200,000
The fecond age, or *Tirta Jo-gue,* fixteen lac, or	1,600,000
The third age, or *Dwapaar Jogue,* eight lac, or	800,000
The fourth age, or *Kolee Jo-gue,* four lac, or	400,000
	6,000,000

Ekutter

Ekutter (feventy one) revolutions of the four *Jogues* make one *Munnuntur* of vulgar time, or years 426,000,000.

(The word *Munnuntur*, is in this place ftriátly applied by *Bramah* to *fpace of time*, but it is by him frequently ufed with a re-trofpeét fignification to the aét of *creation*, and is fometimes given as an additional name to *Birmah*, as *Birmah Munnuah*, alluding to the creation being the refult of thought and meditation ;—the word, as we before re-marked in a marginal note, fprings from *Mon*, or *Mun*, thought, refleétion ; *Munnoo Logue*, the people of thought, or contem-plation.—The compilers of the *Aughtorrah Bhade* derive the word *Munnuntur* from *Munnuah* or *Munnooah*, whom (by perverting the fenfe of *Bramah*) they make to be the fabulous perfonal offspring of *Birmah*, and report mighty feats of his prowefs in war, againft *Moifafoor*, and his adhcrents.)

When *Bramah* defcended to promulge the written law and commands of the Eter-nal ONE to the *Gentoos*, he at the fame time (namely, the beginning of the prefent *Kolee Jogue* *) declared, " *from the regifters*

* Vide Introduétion to the fourth chapter.

I 4 *of*

of Surgo, that the *Dunneahoudah,* was then entering into the eighth revolution of the four *Jogues,* in the *fecond Munnuntur* ;" confcquently, according to *Bramah*'s account, (and if our calculation be right) the precife age of *this,* and the other fourteen planets of the univerfe, amounted to, at that period, four hundred and fixty eight millions of years. And if we fubftract the 4866 years, which have elapfed fince the defcent of *Bramah,* we fhall find the remainder of the *Kolee Jogue* will be 359,134 years; at the expiration of which, *Bramah* pronounced and prophecied, that the patience and forbearance of the Eternal ONE would be withdrawn from the delinquent *Debtah,* and deftruction *by fire* fall upon the eight regions of punifhment, purgation and probation †.

In the fupplement to his BIRMAHAH, *Bramah* likewife taught, that the *Boboon* of *Murto,* had undergone *three* remarkable changes, and would undergo *three* more, before its final diffolution in common with the other feven *Boboons* ; but he fpecifies not of what nature *thofe changes* were, or would be ;—he alfo declares, " *that after a long* " *fpace, a fecond new creation will take place* ; " *but of what kind, or on what principles it*

† Vide towards the clofe of the fifth fection.

2   " *would*

" would be conftrucected, was only known to the
" ETERNAL ONE."

The caufe of the fuperftitious veneration
paid by the *Gentoos* to the numericals ONE
and THREE has, we conceive, been obvious
to the difcerning reader as he travelled thro'
thefe fheets.—It is remarkable, that a *Gentoo* never gives or receives an obligation for
an even fum; if he borrows or lends a
hundred, a thoufand, or ten thoufand ru-
pees, the obligation runs for a hundred and
one, a thoufand and *one*, ten thoufand and
one, &c. The *Mahommedans*, in conformity
only, have generally adopted this cuftom;
hence it was, that the revenues ftipulated
to be paid annually by *Soujah Khan* into
the royal treafury, were *one* khorore, *one* lac,
one thoufand, *one* hundred, and *one* rupee.

The End of the Sixth Chapter.

CHAP. VII.

Of the Gentoo Fasts, and Festivals, &c.

[From the Chatah and Aughtorrah Bhade Shaftahs.]

INTRODUCTION.

AS the *Gentoo* year begins the firſt of *April*, we will trace their holy days as they fall in turn from that day, premiſing that the word *Oupoſs* ſignifies a faſt, *Pur-rup* a feaſt, and *Poojah* worſhip, but when accompanied with an offering, it is then called *Birto Poojah.*—*Poojah* is alſo ſometimes uſed to ſignify the altar on which they offer.

The *Gentoo* holy days are guided by the courſe and age of the moon, and generally take their denomination from that, or from the religious duties that are enjoined on thoſe particular days, and ſometimes from both.

Their

Their offerings confift of fruits, fome particular facred plants and flowers, powdered
fugar, falt, meal, and different kinds of grain.

Firft Holy Day. *Oupofs.*

OKHUIJ TERTEA, falls on the *third*
day of the new moon in *April*, and is dedicated to the giving *alms* and benefactions
to the *Bramins*, as the word *Okhuij* imports.
—This day is alfo ordained for making the April.
Gentoo pickle called *Koffundee*, made only on
this day, by the wives of the *Bramins*; it
is compofed of green mango's, tamarind,
muftard feed, and frefh muftard feed oil;
it is deemed a holy pickle, and the only one
the *Gentoos* ufe with their food.

Second. *Oupofs.*

POORNEMEE †, falls on the full moon
in *April*, and is ftrictly ordained for wafhing and purifying in the river *Ganges*, and
for diftributing charity.

Third. *Oupofs Poojah—Purrup.*

ORUN ‡ SUSTEE, falls on the fixth day
of the new moon in *May*, and is dedicated May.
to the goddefs *Suftee*, the goddefs of gene-

† *Poorah*, full.
‡ *Orun*, the *morning ftar*, often ufed to exprefs the
dawn of day.

ration,

ration, who is worſhipped when the *morning ſtar* appears, or at dawn of day, for the propagation of children, and to remove barrennefs.—On this day prefents are ufually made by the parents to their fons in law, and the day ends with a *purrup* or feaſt.

Fourth. *Purrup*, at night *Poojah*.

DUSSARRAH, as the word imports, falls on the tenth day of the new moon in *May*; it is dedicated to the God *Gunga*, the God of the *Ganges*, who is fabled to have arrived on earth on this day of the moon, and in this month—it is alfo dedicated to the Goddefs *Moonſhee Tagooran* *, Goddefs of fnakes, and fabulous daughter of *Sieb*.

Fifth. *Oupofs-Poojah*.

POORNEMEE falls on the full moon in *May*, and is dedicated to *Jaggernaut*, (fynonimous with *Biſtnoo*.) This day is otherwife called from the duty enjoined on it, the *Sinan* †, *Jattra* ‡, or *general waſhing* in the *Ganges*—and it is almoſt incredible to think the immenfe multitude of every age and fex that appears on both fides of the river,

* *Tagooran*, prieftefs, fometimes goddefs.
† *Sinan*, bathing.
‡ *Jattra*, literally fignifies *a dance of many*.

throughout

throughout it's whole courfe, at one and the fame time.

Sixth. *Oupofs-Purrup.*

RHUTT JATTRA, falls on the fecond day of the new moon in *June*; it is dedicated to *Jaggernaut* and *Biftnoo.*—On this day the *Rhutt*, or triumphal car of *Jaggernaut*, is carried forth about a mile, refts, and is returned on the ninth day of the moon.—— From the feventh day of the moon to the tenth, both inclufive, is the UMBOOBISSEE ; June. during which fpace, the earth is left to *her purgations*, and neither plough, fpade, or any other inftrument of tillage, permitted to moleft her.—The term UMBOOBISSEE, which needs no further explanation, is ap-plied to women under the fame circumftances.

Seventh. *Oupofs.*

SYON † EKKADUSSEE, as the laft word imports, falls on the *eleventh* day of the new moon in *June*, and is a folemn faft. *Jaggernaut* (or *Biftnoo*) is fabled to *fleep* for four months ;—which only fignifies that the rainy feafon about this time fetting in for four months, the care of *Biftnoo* (the pre-

† *Syon,* fleep, repofe.

ferver)

ſerver) is ſuſpended, as immaterial, the rains
ſecuring their crops of grain.

Eighth. *Oupoſs.*

POORNEMEE, as the word imports, falls
on the *full moon* in *June*, and is dedicated
to waſhing in the *Ganges*, and charity to the
Bramins.

Ninth. *Oupoſs.*

DUADUSSEE, as the word ſignifies, falls
on the *twelfth* day of the new moon in
July, and is devoted to waſhing in the
Ganges, and giving alms.

Tenth. *Oupoſs-Purrup.*

EKKADUSSEE, TERADUSSEE, CHOWTA-
DUSSEE and POORNEMEE, the eleventh,
thirteenth, fourteenth, of the new moon in
July, to the *Poornemee* or full incluſive,
are dedicated to the *Joolna Jattra* of *Kiſſen Tagoor*; but theſe are not directed by the
Shaſtah, and are only obſerved by the *Gentoos* of the *Kettery* tribe.

Eleventh. *Oupoſs.*

JURMO†OOSTOOMEE falls on the eighth
day after the full, or twenty-third day of

† *Jurmo*, nativity.

3

the

the moon in *July*, and is dedicated to the birth of *Kiſſen Tagoor*, who is fabled to have then deſcended for the deſtruction of *Kunkſoo Rajah*, a famous *Oſſoor* and tyrant. It is obſerved as a ſolemn faſt,

Twelfth. *Purrup.*

Lukee † *Poojah* falls on the firſt *Thurſ-day* in the month of *Auguſt*; ſhe is the *Gentoo* Goddeſs of all kinds of grain, and is Auguſt. fabled to be the wife of *Biſtnoo*, the *preſerver*; ſhe is worſhipped at this time on the coming in the *Paddy*, the name given to rice in the huſk.—The day concludes with a feaſt.

Thirteenth. *Purrup.*

UNNUNTO BIRTO, falls on the fourteenth day of the moon in *Auguſt*, and is dedicated to *Biſtnoo* with the epithet of *Unnunto*, or the *unknown*; an offering of grain is made to him, and the day concludes with a feaſt,

Fourteenth. *Oupoſs.*

ARUNDAH POOJAH falls on the thirtieth day of *Auguſt*, and is dedicated to *Moonſhee Tagooran* (the feminine of *Tagoor)* Goddeſs of ſnakes.——The precife interpretation of *Arundah* we have loſt, and will not impoſe

† *Lukee,* plenty, affluence.

on

on our readers.—Although this day is a faſt, it ends in a feaſt of the *new rice*, boiled early, and *eaten cold*; to which eſſential circumſtance we think the word *Arundah*, given to this *Poojah*, alludes; but we are not poſitive.

Fifteenth. *Purrup*.

DRUGAH POOJAH falls on the ſeventh day of the new moon in *September*, and continues the eighth and ninth. The eighth is obſerved as a faſt by thoſe who have no children.—*This* is the grand general feaſt of the *Gentoos*, uſually viſited by all

Septem-
ber.

Europeans, (by invitation) who are treated by the proprietor of the feaſt with the fruits and flowers in ſeaſon, and are entertained every evening whilſt the feaſt laſts, with bands of ſingers and dancers.—This Goddeſs is the firſt in rank and dignity, and the moſt active of all the fabulous deities of the *Aughtorrah Bhade*, and is ſtiled the wife of *Sieb*, the *deſtroyer*, the third of the three primary created beings. She is as often ſtiled *Bowannee* †, as *Drugah* ‡ ; and frequently *Bowannee Drugah*: the cauſe of her deſcent is thus derived :—God having appointed *Endeer* § and his deſcendants uni-

† *Perſevering.*   ‡ *Virtue.*   § *Goodneſs.*

verſal

verfal *Rajahs* of the world, the appointment
was illy brooked by *Moifafoor* *; he there-
upon drew together his adherents, and waged
war againft *Endeer* and his defcendants, who
were at laft in the *Duapaar Jogue* obliged
to fly, and leave the government of the
world to *Moifafoor*; which proved the
⁻fource of ravages, murders, and confufion.
—*Endeer*, and his few adherents, were
confined to a fmall portion of the world,
from whence, in compaffion to mankind,
they with piety and humility petitioned the
three primary created beings to implore
the Eternal ONE to redrefs the grievances
refulting from the ufurped power of *Moifafoor*.—The three beings interceded, and obtained permiffion that *Bowannee Drugah*
fhould defcend on the earth, for the deftruction of *Moifafoor* and his adherents, which
the *Gentoos* are taught to believe fhe will
in the end effect, and finally reftore the
government of the world to *Endeer* and his
defcendants, according to the firft intention
of the Eternal ONE. Hence was the *Drugah Poojah* inftituted, during which the
Supreme Being is invoked, through her mediation, to haften that wifhed-for period.—
The allegory in the foregoing recital is fo
plain by a reference to the marginal notes,

* *Evil.*

Part II.　　　K　　　　　that

that we will not affront the underftanding
of our readers by offering an explanation,
although we fhall illuftrate it further when
we give a particular interpretation of the
plate N°. 2.

Sixteenth. *Purrup*.

DUSSUMEE, or the tenth day of the new
moon in *September*, when the image of
DRUGAH is caft into the *Ganges*, with the
univerfal acclamations of the people, and is
faid to be returned to her hufband *Sieb*. Purification by wafhing in the *Ganges* on this
day is ftrictly enjoined.

Seventeenth. *Oupofs*.

LUKEE POOJAH falls on the full moon
in *September*, on which fhe is worfhipped
all night, during which nothing is drank
but the water of the coco nut.

Eighteenth. *Oupofs*.

KALLEKA, *Kalkee* or *Kalle Poojah*, (for
they are fynonimous) falls on the laft day
of the moon in *September*. This goddefs is
worfhipped all the night of that day univerfally, but in a more particular manner at
Kallee Ghat, about three miles fouth of *Calcutta*; an ancient *Pagoda* dedicated to her
there, ftands clofe to a fmall brook, which
is

is by the *Bramins* deemed to be the original courfe of the *Ganges.*——The parts of the *Gentoo* Goddefs (like the parts of fome modern faints) are worfhipped in various parts of *Indoftan*; her *eyes* at *Kallee Ghat*, her head at *Banaras*, her hand at *Bindoobund*; but where the remains of her are diftributed has efcaped our memory *.—She takes her name from her ufual habiliment, which is *black*, and is frequently called the *black Goddefs*; *Kallee* is the common name for ink.—— She is fabled to have fprung, completely armed, from the *eye of Drugah*, at a time when fhe was hard preffed in battle by the tyrants of the earth †.—On this faft, worfhip and offerings are paid to the *manes* of deceafed *anceftors*. Befides the laft mentioned annual cuftom, every *Gentoo* keeps the anniverfary of their father's death, in fafting and worfhip to his *manes*, which is called *Baap ka Surraad*‡.—It is worthy remark (by the bye) that in all *Devonfhire*, the word *Kallee* expreffes black or fmut : why the fame combination of letters fhould convey the fame idea to people fo far removed from each other, we leave the curious to account for.

* Plate Nº. 3.
† The various heads which appear fcattered over the plate, fignify the many tyrants and monfters fhe flew in conjunction with *Drugah*.
‡ *Sacred to the father.*

K 2   Nine-

Nineteenth. *Purrup.*

RAAS ‡ JATTRA, falls on the full moon in *October,* and is continued to the feventeenth of the moon; it is dedicated to *Kiffen Tagoor Kettry.*—This feaft is univerfally obferved, but in a moft extraordinary manner celebrated at *Bindoobund,* in commemoration of a marvellous event which is fabled to have happened in the neighbourhood of that place.—A number of virgins met to celebrate, in mirth and fports, the defcent of *Kiffen* §: in the heighth of their joy, the God appeared amongft them, and propofed to them a *dance,* to which they objected, as *they* were many, and *he* but one; to obviate this objection, he divided himfelf into as many *Kiffens* as there were virgins, who immediately entered into a *circular* dance with them, as reprefented in the plate N° 4. In the centre circle he is reprefented ftanding in a difengaged attitude, attended by the nymphs *Nundee* and *Bringbee* (joys and fports) who are making him offerings of flowers and fruits.

October.

Twentieth. *Oupofs.*

KARTIK *Poojah* falls on the laft day of the moon in *October.*—This divinity is fabled to be the youngeft fon of *Moifoor* (or *Sieb)*

‡ A *circle.* § Plate N° 4.

and

and *Drugab*; he is worſhipped on this day by thoſe who have not been bleſſed with children, and man and woman are enjoined a ſtrict faſt.——The word *Kartik*, ſtrictly means *conſecration*, hence this divinity is ſaid to be the inviſible guardian, and ſuperintendant of the *Gentoo Pagodas*. The word alſo ſometimes ſignifies *holineſs*.. ' The month of *October* takes its name from him, becauſe in this month the *Pagodas* are generally conſecrated.

Twenty-firſt. *Purrup.*

NOVONO † is celebrated on the firſt *lucky Thurſday* in *November*, on the firſt coming in of the new grain of the ſecond crop; the *lucky Thurſday* is fixed in a conſultation of *Bramins*, and is a general feaſt. November.

Twenty-ſecond. *Oupoſs-Purrup.*

LUKEE POOJAH falls on the firſt *Thurſday* in the month of *December*, on getting in all the new.harveſt, when this favorite Goddeſs of the *Gentoos* receives a ſolemn thankſgiving for all the bleſſings of the year; the day is paſſed in faſting, worſhip, waſhing and purifying in the *Ganges*; at night they feaſt. December.

† *New rice.*

K 3 Twenty-

Twenty-third. *Purrup.*

LUKEE POOJAH SANKRANTEE * falls on the laſt day in *December*, when this Goddeſs is again worſhipped as on the laſt mentioned holy-day, excepting the faſt. On this day bread is diſtributed in alms, according to every one's ability.

Twenty-fourth. *Purrup.*

SEEREE PUNCHEMEE falls on the fifth day of the new moon in *January*, and is dedicated to *Surſuttee* †, the *Gentoo* Goddeſs of arts, and letters.—She is fabled to be the daughter of *Birmah* and *Birmaanee*. anuary. The *Koyt Caſt*, or tribe of writers, are prohibited the uſe of pen and ink on this feſtival, *which* are conſecrated to her for the day, and a ceſſation is put to buſineſs of every kind.—*Seeree* ſignifies *fortune, ſucceſs*, and is the *firſt* word of every epiſtolary correſpondence in the *Gentoo* language.

Twenty-fifth. *Birto.*

ORUN OODEE, ‡ SUPTIMEE, falls on the ſeventh day of the new moon in *January*, and is called *Soorjee Poojah*, or *worſhip to the*

* *Sunkrantee* ſignifies the laſt day in every month.
† *Invention, contrivance, ingenuity, genius.*
‡ *Riſing of the dawn.*

ſun ;

fun ; to whom offerings are made of peculiar flowers in the *Ganges*.

Twenty-fixth. *Oupofs.*

BHIM EKADUSSEE falls on the eleventh day of the new moon in *January*; the day is dedicated to *Kiffen*, and commemorates the abftinence of *Bhim*, a voracious *Eater*, who fafted on this day; he is called the brother of *Judifteen*. *Bhim* is the common name of reproach for a *Glutton*, but who this *Judifteen* is, or what the occult meaning and real fignification of this faft, has flipped our memory, and we will not fubftitute any interpretation that is not warranted by our materials, or from our certain and clear knowledge.

Twenty-feventh. *Oupofs.*

POORNEMEE, or the full moon in *January*, is dedicated to *Biftnoo*, the *cherifher.*—— Fafting, wafhing and alms.

Twenty-eighth. *Oupofs.*

SIEBRATEER, *Chowturduffee,* or the fourteenth after the full, falls on the twentyninth day of the moon in *January*, and is dedicated to *Sieb*, the deftroyer, who is worfhipped with fafting, offerings, and prayer *all the night*, as the additional *rateer* annexed to the title of this holy-day imports.

K 4 Twenty-

Twenty-ninth. *Oupofs.*

GOVINDUSSEE falls on the twelfth day
of the moon in *February*, and is dedicated
bruary. to *Eifnoo* the *comforter*, as the word *Govin*,
or *Govindu* fignifies, and is one of the many
appellatives given to the fecond of the *three*
primary created perfons, and he is worfhipped
on this day with fafting, prayer, &c.

Thirtieth. *Purrup.*

DOLE † JATTRA falls on the *Poornemee*
or full moon in *February*, and is facred to
Kiffen Tagoor. On this feaft day it is that
the *Gentoos* caft the powder of a certain red
flower, called *Faag*, on all they meet; but
whence this cuftom, or for what caufe this
feaft was firft inftituted, has efcaped us.

Thirty-firft. *Oupofs.*

BARRANEE JATTRA, or *Modoo Kiftna ‡
Tiraduffee* (the thirteenth after the full) falls
on the twenty-eighth day of the moon in
February: if this falls on a *Saturday*, it is
called *Barranee*, and if the ftar *Satoo Biffah*
is then on the meridian, it is called *Mahah
Barranee*; and again, if the ftar *Soobo Jogue*
is in conjunction with *Satoo Biffah*, it is

† *Dole*, a drum.
‡ *Kiffen, Kiftna*, are fynonimous with *Biftnoo*, but
allude to different attributes.

then

then called * *Mahab Mahab Barrance:*
——Thefe conjunctions are uncertain, but
when they happen, it is deemed a moſt
holy day, and is obſerved by univerſal
purification in the *Ganges*, and worſhip and
offerings to *Soorjee*, or the *fun*. It fell out
laſt on the twenty-eighth of *February*,
1759.—As we have loſt the precife meaning and etymology of the word *Barrance*,
and confefs ourſelves ignorant of the aſtro-
nomy of the *Bramins*, we will not attempt
an explanation of this faſt.

Thirty-two. *Oupofs-Purrup.*

LUKEE POOJAH falls on the firſt *Thurf-
day* in *March*, when this goddefs is wor- March,
ſhipped univerſally, and thanked for all the
productions of the earth, all being brought
forth by this time.

Thirty-fecond. *Purrup.*

DURGAH *Poojah*, and *Bhafuntee* † *Poojah*,
falls on the feventh day of the new moon
in *March*, and continues the eighth, ninth
and tenth—on the laſt, her image is caſt into
the *Ganges*. This feaſt is inſtituted for the

* *Moſt great.*
† *The end, final, conclufive,* alluding to this being
the laſt feaſt of the year, preceding the *Gentoo* Lent.

2   fame

fame purpofes as the other grand one, but not with that parade and univerfality.

Thirty-third. *Oupofs.*

SIEB, or *Sunnias* * *Poojah*, is from the firft to the thirtieth of *March*, with only a fhort fufpenfion during the term of the *Durgah Poojah* above-mentioned—The *Sunnias Poojah*, is the *Gentoo* Lent; their penances, mortifications, and *felf* corporal punifhments, have been fo often defcribed, we will not particularize any of them. The *Churruck* †, or day of *fwinging*, falls on the thirtieth. From this penance the three cafts, or tribes, of *Bramins, Bydees* ‡, and *Koyts*, are exempted by the *Aughtorrah Bhade*; and, in fact, none but the very loweft of the people go through any of the publick penances; but, every caft fafts and worfhips the twenty-ninth, the day preceding the *Churruck.*—This folemn faft is dedicated to *Sieh*, or *Moideb*, or *Moifoor*, the *Mutilator*, and *averter of evil*; through whom, at this feafon, the Eternal ONE is invoked, to defend them from the influence of *Moifafoor* and his adherents, and avert

---

* *Penitents.* † Literally fignifies a *Wheel*—— but the circle which the penitent defcribes in fwinging round has given it this appellation.

‡ *Bydees,* the tribe that profefs the practice of phyfick.

the

the final doom pronounced againft the delinquent *Debtah.*

There is a feftival inftituted to *Rhaam*, the *protector*, which is entitled the RHAAM JATTRA, but the precife time of it's celebration we have utterly forgot.—*Rhaam* is another of the multitude of names, or rather attributes, given to *Biftnoo*, the *preferver.*

How far the origin of the fafts, feftivals, terms, &c. of the *Egyptians, Greeks* and *Latins,* may be traced from the *Chatah* and *Aughtorrah Bhade Shaftahs,* we fubmit and recommend to the elucidation of our learned readers, who will be the better enabled to make fuch an enquiry from what follows.

Explanation of the Plate or Reprefentation of the Gentoos grand feaft of the Drugah.

Plate N° 2.

The reprefentation of the Drama in this grand *Gentoo* feaft will, we doubt not, appear genuine to many thoufands now in *England,* as it is a fight that few who have vifited *Bengall* have not indulged themfelves with; and we may take the liberty of faying, that but very few amongft the multitude who have

have feen it could form the fmalleft judgment of it's *intention* or fignification; to
thefe, therefore, we flatter ourfelves it will
afford fome pleafure, the having a fubject
explained to them, on which they have
often looked with pity and amazement!
becaufe they did not underftand it.—The
intention of this feaft we have already given
in it's proper place, to which the reader may
advert, under the title of *Drugah Poojah*
N° 15. and fhall now proceed to the explanation of the chief perfonages in the plate.

The center and principal figure is DRU-
GAH or Virtue; fhe is reprefented, with ten
arms, defcending on a dragon—myftically
fhewing the *power* and irrefiftable force of
virtue, when exerted with vigor.—She is
crowned, one of her hands is armed with a
fpear, and fhe is environed with a fnake—
with another hand fhe binds *Moifafoor* (or
Evil) with a *fnake*, and kills him by thruft-
ing her fpear through his *heart*, thereby
implying that Virtue's fafeft and fureft guard
againft vice or *evil* is *wifdom*, of which the
fnake, as before obferved, is the fymbol.—
The battles * faid to have been fought between *Endeer* †, and *Moifafoor* ‡, in which
the latter generally proved victorious, with-

* Vide *Drugah Poojah*, fifteenth.
† *Good.*   ‡ *Evil.*

out

out the affiftance of *Drugah Bowannee*, or *perfevering virtue*, implies that *moral evil* can only be fuccefsfully combated *therewith*. --The ravages, murders, and confufion, which are faid to be the confequences in the world of the flight of *Endeer* and victory of *Moifafoor* *, emblematically fignify the fatal and natural effects of vice or evil triumphant, which muft neceffarily be attended with deftructive fcenes of violence.—Hence, *Moifafoor* is fabled to have transformed himfelf, after his victory, into a *mad buffola*, the fymbol of ungovernable rage, whofe head is feen in the annexed plate lying at the feet of *Drugah*.—Although *Moifafoor* in the plate appears to be flain by *Drugah*, yet this act is only a prophetic reprefentation of the death and deftruction he will in the end fuffer by her hand, when *Endeer* fhall be reftored, and *Good* be predominant in the world again, and triumph over *Moifafoor* or Evil.—*Endeer* being appointed by God univerfal Rajah of the world, myftically points out his benevolent intentions, that it fhould be governed by goodnefs and piety, and the allegory is as obvious, where *Moifafoor* is faid *illy to brook the appointment* †.

On the right of *Drugah* are reprefented the figures of *Sieb*, her hufband, and of

* Vide *Drugah Poojah*.   † Vide *Drugah Poojah*.

Lukee,

Lukee, the goddefs of grain.—*Sieb* is fitting on a *white bull,* the fymbol of purity and dominion; he is environed with a fnake, holding in one hand a *Dumboor* †, and in the other a *Singee* ‡, mufical inftruments in ufe at all the *Gentoo* feftivals; allegorically pointing out that wifdom is the moft effectual *averter* of *evil,* and that mirth, joy and gladnefs, are the natural effects of it's being averted from us.

The goddefs *Lukee* is reprefented ftanding in an eafy attitude; fhe is crowned with ears of grain, and is encircled by a plant bearing fruit, which paffes through both her hands, the root of which is under her feet; fhe (as all the fuperiour *Gentoo* divinities are) is environed by a fnake.——The meaning conveyed by this figure is fo obvious it needs no explanation.

Underneath the figure of *Sieb* is reprefented the divinity named GHUNNIS §.— He has no peculiar day of worfhip inftituted in honour of him, for this manifeft reafon, becaufe all the addreffes, offerings and worfhip, which are made to the fupreme, and fuperior beings, are preferred through his mediation, and promoted by a prior offering

† A *fmall drum.*　　　‡ A *mufical horn.*
§ *Purity,* or *fincerity of heart.*

and

and worſhip paid to him; ſo that he may be properly ſtiled the *God of offerings*.—He is fabled to be the firſt born of *Moiſoor* (or *Sieb*) and *Drugah*; all worſhip and offerings being made through him, myſtically ſignifies that *purity* and *ſincerity of heart* muſt be the ſource from whence the Deity is invoked.—He is repreſented with four arms, ſiting on an altar, environed with a ſnake, and with the head of a *white elephant*, the ſymbols of *purity*, *riches* and *dominion* or *ſtrength*, which, the *Gentoos* ſay, includes every bleſſing, and cannot be juſtly and properly acquired but by pure and ſincere acts of devotion to God, and good works to man and his fellow creatures.—His four arms are only repreſentative of the power, force and efficacy of ſincerity in worſhip and prayer.

On the left of *Drugah* is repreſented the figure of *Surſuttee*, the *Gentoo* Goddeſs of arts, letters and eloquence, ſo fully deſcribed under the feaſt called *Seeree Punchumee* (twenty-fourth.) In the plate, ſhe appears environed with a ſnake, ſtanding in a careleſs, diſengaged poſture, holding in her hands a reed, of which the writing pens are uſually made.

On the left of *Surſuttee* is repreſented the idol of RHAAM, the protector of *empires*,

pires, flates, and property, already explained*.
—In the plate, he is figured crowned, encircled with a fnake, and riding upon a
monkey; in his left hand he holds a bow,
and is reprefented in the attitude of having
juft difcharged an arrow from it. To under-
ftand this reprefentation, a fhort hiftorical
recital becomes neceffary.—*Rhaaboon* †, the
fubverter of empires, ftates and *property,* is
ever contrafted with *Rhaam* in the courfe of
the *Aughtorrah Bhade Shaftah*—This prime
agent of *Moifafoor* is fabled to have run
away with SITHEE ‡, the wife of *Rhaam;*
and for the recovery of her, that book exhibits a long detail of furious battles fought
between *Rhaam* and *Rhaaboon* with various
fuccefs; myftically painting the contentions
that ever have fubfifted in the world touching *empires* and *property,* in general. Under
thefe the ancient hiftory of *Indoftan* and it's
Rajahs is obfcurely couched.—In one of
the moft bloody of thefe battles, *Rhaam*
being fore prefled, was obliged to call in as
an auxiliary, *Hoonmhon* Prince of the *mon-
keys,* by whofe affiftance he routed *Rhaaboon*
and recovered his wife—*Sithee;* implying
only, that *lawlefs force,* muft be fometimes

* Vide explanation of the *Tirtah Jogue,* or fecond
age, chap. 4.
† *Lawlefs violence.*   ‡ Literally, *property.*

                                combated

combated with craft, policy, and ftratagem, of which the *monkey* throughout *Indoftan* is the known emblem.—The laft mentioned battle is reprefented in the plate number 5. where *Rhaam* appears engaged with *Rhaaboon*, and the attitude of *Rhaam* (in the plate of the *Drugah*) as having difcharged the fatal arrows from the back of the monkey, alludes to *that* battle : in the plate No. 5. *Rhaam* is fupported by his brother *Lukkon*, or *fortitude*, each encircled with fnakes ; and *Rhaaboon* (as he generally is) is reprefented with ten arms, and as many heads of monfters, which intimate the *force* of lawlefs tyranny and power.—Although the emblematic fenfe of the *monkey* is fo obvious, yet the crafty *Bramins* have eftablifhed a belief that *Rhaam* transformed himfelf into, and is always prefent under *that form* ; the people fwallowed the delufion in a literal fenfe, and it is upon this principle, that numerous colleges of *Bramins* are fupported by the people for the maintainance of thofe animals, near the groves where they ufually refort ; one of them is at *Amboah* in the neighbourhood of *Culna*, on the *Ganges*.—In the time of the *Rhaam Jattra* the *Bramins* exhibit a kind of theatrical mafque, wherein the many flights, and efcapes of *Sithee*, and the various ftratagems of *Rhaaboon* to retain her, and of

Part II.   L   *Rhaam*

Rhaam to recover her, with the final battle, which gave him the repoffeffion of her, are all thrown into action, and the ·dialogue taken from the *Aughtorrah Bhade Shaftah.* We have been frequently prefent at this theatrical exhibition, and received much plea- fure and amufement ; one circumftance at the conclufion is worth mentioning—when *Rhaam* had recovered his wife *Sithee*, he refufes to cohabit with her, until fhe has given fome fignal proof, that fhe had fuffered no contamination, or ·violation, during her abode with *Rhaaboon*; on which (by an in- genious piece of machinery) fhe paffes thro' a fire, comes out unhurt, and then *Rhaam* with raptures, receives her to his arms.

Below the idol of *Rhaam* on the plate of the *Drugah*, is that of *Kartik* ; for the ex- planation of this faft, fee number twenty- four.—He is reprefented, armed at all points for war, and riding on a *peacock*, the *Gentoo* fymbol of *pride* and *oftentation*, intimating that thofe qualities and vices of the mind muft be fubdued, as being previoufly necef- fary to the approach and admiffion into their *Pagodas* ; he is armed as a guardian, capable of defending from violation the divinity with- in ; wherever there is a congregation of idols, in a *Tagoor Bharree* *, his idol is placed

* Literally *a houfe for divinities.*

2   at

at the door.—A *Gentoo* had within our memory an only fon dangeroufly ill of a fever;
he paid folemn worfhip, vows and offerings,
for his recovery, not only to the *goddefs of
fevers*, but to all the other Gods, and Goddeffes befides—His fon died—the father,
frantic with grief and defpair, fallied out
before day, broke open a *Tagoor Bharree*
in a buzaar fouth of the town of *Calcutta*,
where *Kartik* being off his guard and mingled
with the other divinities—he cut all their
heads off; his intention was to have proceeded round the town (as he confeffed on
examination) and to have decollated every
God in all the *Tagoor* bharries of the place;
but the fecond he came to, *Kartik* was
upon his guard at the door, and prefenting
his dart at him, brought him to his fenfes;
and providentially faved the reft of his brother divinities.

Below the figures of *Lukee* and *Surfuttee*,
ftand the reprefentation of two divine nymphs,
Nundee joy, and *Bringee* fports ; they are
both encircled by *fnakes*, implying, that
joy and fports at all their feftivals, fhould
be circumfcribed by prudence and *wifdom*.

On the right between *Sieb* and *Ghunnis*,
is reprefented a boat, in which *Nundee* and
Bringee are carrying *Drugah* to her huf-

L 2   band

band *Sieb*, after fhe had been caft into the *Ganges*; and in the copartment oppofite between the figures of *Rhaam* and *Kartik*, are reprefented two nymphs in a kind of threatening pofture, advifing him to take better care of *his wife* another time, and keep her at home.

In the centre of the arch is reprefented *Surfuttee* and four female attendants, one prefenting to her the palmira leaf, the original paper, another a piece of wax, the third an ink ftand, the fourth a pen, the ufe of which are all interdicted on her feftival, and made an offering to her.——The two end copartments *Kallee* and *Drugah*, each engaged with two giants tyrants of the earth.—The other divifion of the arch, allude to different paffages of the *Aughtorrah Bhade*, which have efcaped our memory.

End of the Explanation of plate N° 2.

As we referve the eighth chapter or general head, namely, " the differtation on the metempfychofis," for a third and *laft part* of this work, there remains nothing more to clofe this chapter, but to add a fhort recital of the genealogy of the *Gentoo* divinities, on which fubject, as our materials are few, we fhall not, we fear, afford any great fatisfaction to the curious, as we are confined to the

the progeny of *Birmah* and *Birmanee* only. The fabulous legend of the *Aughtorrah Bhade* fays,

That God created *three* females, or affociates, for the *three* primary created Beings. To *Birmah* he gave *Birmaanee*, to *Biftnoo Lukee*, and to *Sieb Bowannee Drugah*.

That to *Birmah* and *Birmangee* were born two fons, the eldeft named *Kuffiebmunnoo*, the youngeft *Dookee Rajah*; the eldeft was governed by a pious and laudable fpirit, the youngeft by a vicious and turbulent one.

Dookee Rajah had a daughter (but how he came by her the legend fayeth not) named *Dithee*, whom he married to his brother *Kuffiebmunnoo*, and fhe brought him a fon, whom he called ENDEER; he and his defcendants, after the example of their father *Kuffiebmunnoo*, were truly virtuous, and obfervant of the laws of God, communicated to them by *Birmah* and *Birmaanee*.

Dookee Rajah had a fecond daughter, whom he called *Odithee*, who was alfo married to *Kuffiebmunnoo*, and fhe likewife brought him a fon, who was named MOISASOOR; he and his defcendants, after the example of their grandfather *Dookee Rajah*, flighting

flighting the precepts of *Birmah* and *Bir-maanee*, became abandoned to every vice, and contemners of the laws of God.

All the benefit that accrues from the foregoing fhort - recital of the progeny of *Birmah* and *Birmaanee*, is, that thus we find in *Endeer*, and *Moifafoor*, the roots from whence the doctrine of two contending principles in nature, *Good* and *Evil*, fprung; that this was the ground-work of all the doctrines of the *Bramins*, after they had loft fight of the fimple and fublime theology of the *Chartah Bhade* of *Bramah*, is beyond all controverfy; as the whole tendency of the two *later Bhades*, exemplify the natural hiftory of thofe two contending principles in the *human mind*, and the concomitant effects, they will have on *it*, and on the government of the *world*, as they alternately happen to prefide.—Hence the unceafing ftruggles and conflicts for fuperiority between *Endeer* and *Moifafoor* and their adherents, which fay the *Bramins* fubfift to this day; fo well founded, was the conjecture of the learned and ingenious Mr. *Bayle*, touching the great antiquity of the origin of the *Ma-nechean* doctrine—nor is it at all improbable, that arch heretic *Manes* might have received fome notions of this doctrine from the tenets of the *Bramins*, which he per-verted

verted to the worſt and moſt dangerous
purpoſes and opinions :—on the contrary the
ſimplicity, with which the doctrine is profeſſed by the *Gentoos*, has in it's ſelf (but
otherwiſe in it's conſequences) no ſuch manifeſt tendency; although by their adherence
to it, they ſeem utterly to forget the conſideration of their original exiſtence and delinquency, and the merciful cauſe of their
eſtabliſhment, in the eight *Boboons* of puniſhment and probation, as well as the laws
and injunctions of their prophet *Bramah*,
who obviouſly reſts the reſtoration and ſalvation of the offending *Debtah*, upon *two*
ſimple and plain conditions, *a ſincere penitent*
impreſſion of their original delinquency; and an
atonement by good works, according to the powers
of exertion, which God annexed to their animal
forms.—But it is not at all to be wondered
at, that they ſhould thus loſe ſight of their
original ſin and defection, as well as the
means laid down for their ſalvation ; when
the very ſpirit of the faſts and feſtivals, and
whole conduct of the drama of the *Chatah*,
and *Aughtorrah Bhades*, are relative only to
the *averting* the evils of their preſent exiſtence, without the ſmalleſt retroſpect to
their firſt tranſgreſſion, or the means of
atoning for it.—This is the ſituation of the
bulk of the people of *Indoſtan*, as well as
of the modern *Bramins*; amongſt the latter,

if

if we except one in a thoufand, we give
them over meafure; the confequences from
thefe premifes are obvious—the *Gentoos* in
general, are as degenerate, crafty, fuperftitious, litigious and wicked a people, as any
race of beings in the known world, if not
eminently more fo, efpecially the common run
of the *Bramins*; and we can truly aver, that
during almoft five years, that we prefided in
the judicial cutcherry court of *Calcutta*, never
any murder, or other atrocious crime, came
before us, but it was proved in the end, a
Bramin was at the bottom of it : but then,
the *remnant* of *Bramins* (whom we have
before excepted) who feclude themfelves
from the communications of the bufy world,
in a philofophic, and religious retirement, and
ftrictly purfue the tenets and true fpirit of
the *Chartah Bhade of Bramah*, we may with
equal truth and juftice pronounce, *are the
pureft models of genuine piety that now exift,
or can be found on the face of the earth.*——
And now, my friends, and moft refpectable
readers, we will, with your permiffion,
adopt one cuftom of the *Gentoos*, and make
an offering, for fome time at leaft, of our
pen, ink, and paper, to the goddefs SUR-
SUTTEE.

The End of the Second Part.

Beenham Houfe, Berks,
the 1ft of Aug. 1766.

INTERESTING

HISTORICAL EVENTS,

Relative to the

PROVINCES of BENGAL,

AND THE

EMPIRE of INDOSTAN.

WITH

A Seafonable HINT and PERSUASIVE

To the Honorable

The COURT of DIRECTORS of the
EAST INDIA COMPANY.

AS ALSO

The MYTHOLOGY and COSMOGONY, FASTS
and FESTIVALS of the GENTOOS,
Followers of the SHASTAH.

AND

A DISSERTATION on the METEMPSYCHOSIS,
commonly, though erroneoufly, called the
PYTHAGOREAN Doctrine.

By J. Z. HOLWELL, Efq;

PART III.

LONDON:

Printed for T. BECKET and P. A. DE HONDT, near
Surry-Street, in the Strand.

MDCCLXXI.

TO THE MOST NOBLE

THE DUKE OF NORTHUMBERLAND,

NOT MORE CONSPICUOUS

FROM

THE SPLENDOR OF HIS TITLES,

THAN

DISTINGUISHED BY THE LUSTRE OF HIS MERITS,

BELOVED FOR HIS AMIABLE QUALITIES,

REVERED FOR HIS PUBLIC AND PRIVATE VIRTUES,

THE LOVER OF ARTS, THE FRIEND OF LEARNING,

THE PATRON OF SCIENCE,

THIS ESSAY

(INTENDED TO RESCUE FROM ERROR AND

OBLIVION THE ANCIENT RELIGION OF INDOSTAN)

IS DEDICATED,

BY (A LOVER OF TRUTH, AND AN ADMIRER OF

HIS GRACE's EXALTED CHARACTER)

J. Z. HOLWELL.

CHAP. VIII.

A Differtation on the Metempfychofis of the Bramins, *or Tranfmigrations of the fallen Angelic Spirits; with a Defence of the original Scriptures of* Bramah, *and an occafional comparifon between them and the Chriftian Doctrines.*

INTRODUCTION.

PART I.

WE have hitherto floated upon the materials which the wreck of *Calcutta* in the year 1765 afforded us, and now for the firft time, launch out into the ocean of hypothefis and fpeculation upon our own bottom. Difficult and hazardous as our courfe is, we will hope our voyage may not be unprofperous. We invoke no aid to lead us on our way, but that POWER ALONE, which can ALONE ENLIGHTEN; that POWER! which in every age (but more particularly in fome) has gracioufly been

B   pleafed,

pleafed to convey a divine revelation to the HEART OF MAN.

2. Various foils and climates, as they influence the conftitutions, fo they do in part the difpofitions of mankind; and this it is, that may have made it neceffary to difpenfe different modes of revealing the WILL OF GOD to the different parts of this (and poffibly every other) habitable globe; and as the minds of focieties, and even nations, are fubject, with all things elfe, to revolution and change; it may alfo have been neceffary to vary the mode of revelation *to the fame people*, at different periods of time, as the immoral ftate, or imperfections of mankind may have indicated. The hiftory of the world is pregnant with many inftances in fupport of thefe probable conclufions, befides that of the double revelation to the Hebrews, the Mofaic, and the Chriftian : the minds of men are impreffed by, and open to conviction, and the acceptance of TRUTH, under one peculiar form, which they will reject under another: How deeply then ought we to adore and reverence that fupreme Being, who thus condefcends to model his commands, and infpire his chofen writers, in conformity to the weaknefs, and failings of his creatures?

3. It

3. It is an allowed truth, that there never was yet any fyſtem of theology broached to mankind, whoſe firſt profeſſors and propagators did not announce *its deſcent from* God ; and God forbid, we ſhould doubt of, or impeach the divine origin, of any of them ; for ſuch eulogium they poſſibly all merited in their primitive purity, could they be traced up to that ſtate, notwithſtanding many learned pens have labored to prove, that ſuch a claim was generally a political impoſition only ; a fuggeſtion that we think has not much contributed to the advancement of either the piety, or morals of mankind, and therefore better had it been ſuppreſſed, and kept from their knowledge, as we hope to make appear preſently. ——Various as we may obſerve the religious fyſtems fcattered throughout the world, and ſingular as our following opinion, and our reaſoning thereon may appear to be ; we ſhall not heſitate to lay it down as a principle, That—howfoever mankind, either of *Europe, Aſia, Africa* or *America,* may differ in the exterior modes of worſhip paid to the Deity, according to their various genius ; yet, that there are ſome *fundamental points* of every fyſtem, wherein *all agree* and profeſs unanimous faith ; as may be gathered, either from their *expreſs doctrines,* or evidently implied, from their

modes,

modes, or ceremonials of worſhip, howfoever differing in manner and form, from
each other.

4. The *fundamental points* of religion
above alluded to, we chuſe to diſtinguiſh
by the title of PRIMITIVE TRUTHS, truths!
which forceably ſtruck, and impreſſed the
human heart at the period of man's creation, and although from an original unhappy taint, he in ſucceeding times, ſtrange-
ly deviated from them, yet he never has,
nor ever will be able, wholly to obliterate
and efface them, however he may ſometimes for a greater, or leſſer ſpace, utterly
loſe ſight of them.——We will enumerate
the principal of theſe *primitive truths* ——
1ſt, The being of a GOD, eternal, creator,
and conſervator of all things, animate and
inanimate ;——2dly, The exiſtence of three
prime created celeſtial beings, either confounded with the Deity, or excluſive of,
and ſubordinate to him ;——3dly, The creation of angelic beings ;——4thly, A defection, or rebellion of a portion of thoſe beings ;——5thly, Their expulſion from the
heavenly regions ;——6thly, The immortality of the human ſoul ;——7thly, A future ſtate of rewards and puniſhments of the
human ſoul ;——8thly, That man is here
in a ſtate of puniſhment and probation, for
a tranſ-

a tranfgreffion committed in a prior ftate of exiftence againft his Creator;——9thly, That there exifts a Being, who inftigated the revolt of the angelic fpirits, and ftill continues the enemy and deceiver of mankind;——10thly, The neceffity of a mediator, or mediators, between God and man, over and above repentance and good works, for the expiation of fin, and obtaining a reftoration to a ftate, from which he now ftands expelled;——11thly, That there is an intermediate ftate of punifhment and purification between death and the perfect reftoration of the human foul;——12thly, The exiftence of *a golden age*;——13thly, That there exifted a period when mankind was fuftained by, and fubfifted only on the fruits of the earth;——and *laftly*, The doctrine of the miniftration of angels, in human affairs. Thefe were the *primitive truths* revealed by a gracious God to man, in the early days of his creation, at a time when it may be reafonably prefumed he retained a lively fenfe of his foul's former tranfgreffion; as well as of the grace then offered to him. That thefe are the only *primitive truths* neceffary to man's falvation, and reftoration, appears from hence, that they have, from the earlieft records of time to this day, remained more or lefs *the ftock* upon which the blindnefs, or wickednefs

of

of man has engrafted very extravagant, unprofitable, as well as unintelligible doctrines, to delude their fellow-creatures, and seduce them from a strict adherence to, and reliance on, those *primitive truths only.*

5. This being the case, how much is it to be lamented, that our learned divines, some of whom are the greatest ornaments of our church and profeffion, have not taken the advantage of the concurring testimony of all mankind, touching these *fundamental principles,* to enforce their relative duties, in their preaching and writings? in place of which, moved by a vain oftentation, and shew of deep learning, the rubbish of antiquity is raked up, and sifted, to prove that nations, and individuals amongst the ancients, and some of the wisest and best of mankind, were infidels with respect to any sincere faith in religion at all; and that the fable of religion was invented by lawgivers, purely to keep the populace in awe: and we are told by these profound refearchers, that the great *Socrates* was the only one amongst the ancient philosophers, who believed what he taught, *the unity of the Godhead, the immortality of the foul, and a future ftate of rewards and punifhments:*——a ftrange mode this, of enlightening modern times! to record and

circulate

circulate fuch fentiments in the mother tongue of a Chriftian people, although on fuppofition only, that fuch principles ever exifted in any country or age whatfoever.

6. We are aware that the motives and plea urged in defence of the publication of the infidel opinions of the ancient philofo-phers are, the reputation of modern atheifts, deifts, and free-thinkers: vain pretence,, and no lefs vain the attempt, where the flighteft review of the bent and genius *of man* would have convinced them, that when once a writer, can fo far get the better of fhame and decorum, as to dare publifh opinions, not only contrary to, but fubverfive of all religious faith, that man is incorrigi-ble, and beyond the reach of conviction. To reafon with writers of that ftamp, carries as much propriety with it, as if our divines would go and difpiay their oratory upon the miferable inhabitants of Bedlam ; and their endeavors would be as falutary. The fame may be faid of fanatics in every religion ; as the one believes nothing at all, thefe be-lieve too much, and both have always thrived, and acquired ftrength from difpu-tation and perfecution.

7. Religious controverfy never yet did, nor ever will do good to the caufe of true

religion,

religion, for this plain and cogent reafon; conviction on either fide cannot follow, becaufe the nature of the fubject matter in difpute cannot, like a propofition in *Euclid,* admit of demonftration ;——befides another mifchievous confequence refults from the canvaffing and laying open the opinions of the ancient philofophers touching facred matters, for it puts weapons into the hands of the modern enemies of religion, which probably they would otherwife never have been in poffeffion of; and it muft be the height of glory to infidels and free-thinkers, to find themfelves claffed with the *Platos, Plutarchs, Ciceros, &c.* of antiquity.—— A fimilar mode of reputation poffeffed the primitive fathers of the church, which, added to an inflamed miftaken zeal and doctrines never dictated by their divine mafter, laid the foundation of thofe fchifms, and heretical evils, which have ever fince diftracted and divided the Chriftian ftates, fo that they may with more propriety be ftiled *the deftroyers,* than *the fathers* of it.

8. For how long a fpace man after his creation retained a lively fenfe of the fpecial grace offered to him by his Creator, or benefited himfelf by a ftrict adherence to, and obfervance of the divine *primitive truths,* then revealed to him, are circumftances not determinable;

determinable; but we may with reafon conclude, that a long feries of time paffed
away, before he poffibly could, from the
nature of things lofe fight of them. All
nations have by tradition a conception that
there once exifted *a golden or comparative
age* of innocence; and if there ever did
exift fuch a period (which we think highly
probable at leaft) it fhould appear to have
been the fpace juft above hinted at, between
man's creation, and the time when firft he
began to fet at nought the faving precepts
which had been gracioufly delivered to him.
Although mankind differ fo widely refpecting the epocha of the creation of the univerfe and man, yet they are generally
agreed, that they were coeval; the enlightened *Mofes* did not venture to fay when,
nor is it very material to us, fo we believe
that GOD made it for wife and neceffary
purpofes, fubfequently to be confidered in
a new point of view.

9. When we attentively perufe *Mofes*'s
detail of the *creation and fall of man*, we
find it clogged with too many incomprehenfible difficulties to gain our belief, that
that confummate legiflator ever intended it
fhould be underftood in a literal fenfe;
and as a part of the law of *Mofes* was
" typical to the *Jews* of the coming of
" their

" their Meffiah, and calculated to prepare
" them for it," (as has been proved by the
Author of the Divine Legation) fo we hope
to prove that his detail of *the fall of man*
was *typical only* of the angelic fall; to
which, we doubt not, but *Mofes* believed
(and had good grounds for that belief) that
man? had a much *nearer relation* than is
commonly imagined.

10. It is pretty manifeft, that the *golden
age* of innocence and truth was not a con-
fequent of *Mofes's fuppofed creation*; for,
excepting a very few individuals, mankind
by his own fhewing were far gone in
wickednefs, almoft as foon as created;
therefore, we muft look higher for it,
which we will do in good time, for we
cannot relinquifh the fact, that there was a
period of time, in which *fuch an age* really
exifted.

11. We find that mankind throve and
grew in vice until GOD, perceiving the
meafure of their wickednefs was full,
thought it neceffary to, bring about a ftupendous change on the face of this habitable globe, by which we are told the whole
race of animated beings, faving a remnant
of each, were deftroyed; and of thefe, that
the human fpecies fcarcely emerged drip-
ping

ping from the deluge, than they were again *drowned in fin*; and from the earlieft accounts which can be depended upon, free from fable, we learn that the fuppofed moft ancient inhabitants in the world, to wit, the *Chaldeans, Egyptians, Hebrews, Phœnicians*, &c. were all profoundly funk in rank idolatries, and every fpecies of wickednefs; and we find, that the fo much boafted and celebrated wifdom of *Egypt*, confifted only in their fuperior art and cunning in political legiflation; whereby they were better enabled to deceive and inflave the unhappy people, who fell under their government : thus we fee that all the benefit we gain by our deep and learned refearches into the antiquities of thofe nations, is,' to be afcertained that men were as bad in the moft early known times as they well could be ; a piece of knowledge for which we need not have travelled farther than our own fcriptures. If the *Egyptians* muft have the honor of being the moft wife of the ancients, they have undoubtedly the honor alfo of being the moft wicked and fuperftitious, not excepting the ancient pofleffors of the land of *Canaan*. This part of their character we will not conteft with the learned explorers of their tenets; but we think ourfelves well warranted to difpute, both the fuperiority

of

of their wifdom and antiquity *. Indeed
the conteft refpecting the wifdom of the
Egyptians, as well as the *Perfian* Magi, and
the whole tribe of the *Grecian* and *Roman*
philofophers, who copied from them (*Socrates* alone excepted) may be reduced into
a very narrow compafs ; for the whole total
of it, upon fumming up the evidence
produced by the advocates in its favor,
amounts to FOLLY ; and folly of fo egregious a nature, that nothing lefs than the
wit of a Lucian is equal to the expofing it
in a juft point of ridicule.—Of what utility
is that kind of wifdom (howfoever profound) either to the poffeffors, or to mankind, which leads to the eftablifhment of
laws, doctrines, and worfhip, moft unworthy the conceptions we ought to harbor
of the *Divine Nature,* and his attributes ?
—Such was the wifdom of the *Egyptians,*
&c. and yet thefe men acquired the vene-
rable titles of Sages and Philofophers, to the
utter violation of the true fpirit and meaning of the words; for every fpecies of
what is commonly called wifdom, that does
not lead us into juft ideas of GOD, and *of
ourfelves,* is folly.—It is faid—they were *the
firft* who cultivated the arts and fciences :
fuppofe it granted, were they the better men

* Vid. Introduction to Part ii. from page 23. to 29.

for

for it? It is proved they were not, but rather worfe, by thofe very pens who labored to demonftrate that prior claim.——
Indeed the hiftory of mankind affords us
this melancholy truth, that the moft enlightened ages, in the kind of fpurious and
ufelefs wifdom we have been fpeaking of,
have been *the moft wicked*, and we could
wifh the application did not reach the
prefent age.

12. That the *Egyptians* were an ancient
race we do not deny, and yet modern times
have brought us to the knowledge of an
empire of people, who, from the moft probable concurring circumftances, were a
potent and numerous nation in the earlieft
known times, although frcm caufes peculiar to themfelves, which we have before
recited in our fecond Part, *they were little
known to the world.* Our readers will not
be at a lofs to guefs, that we here mean the
people of *Indoftan*, a people that exifted *a
feparate and unmixed nation*, without any
intercommunity of manners or religious
worfhip, from the period of the *firft migrations* of the inhabitants of the earth ;——
(a period, which is hid, as well from our
knowledge, as our conceptions) and fo continue to this day, notwithftanding they
groan under *Mahomedan* tyranny : a ftrong
prefumption,

presumption, almost amounting to proof, of
this people being, *as a nation,* more ancient
than any other.—Such *a separation* was the
great aim of the inspired Legislator of the
Hebrews, although he was never able to
accomplish it : he was able to separate their
bodies, but their souls still languished for
the *flesh-pots* of *Egypt,* and their infamous
idolatries, until captivity had softened their
hearts, and made them look (when it was
too late) towards their One God, and King.
—The difference between the cases of the
Gentoos and the *Hebrews* was, that whereas the former for a deviation from their
primitive truths were enslaved at home, and
the latter were driven for deviating from
the law into captivity in a foreign land ;
as a greater punishment (we may rationally
suppose) for the greater crime. For,

13. Although the *Gentoos* had offended
by raising an idolatrous superstructure upon
the *primitive truths* of *Bramah,* (which they *
had held sacred and inviolate for the space
of a thousand years, as elsewhere shewn)
yet, his fundamentals, *viz.* the unity of the
Godhead, the Metempsychosis, and its concomitant essential doctrines, the angelic
origin, and immortality of the human soul,
and its present and future state of rewards
and punishments, *&c.* still kept their
ground;

ground; and remained, as they do to this day, the bafis of their faith and worfhip.

14. The angelic fall, and the doctrine of the Metempfychofis, the one the crime, the other the punifhment of thofe unhappy free-agents, being the *fine qua non* of the *Gentoo* fyftem, it is incumbent upon us to prove from reafon and the nature of things, that *the latter* was the original growth of *Indoftan*, and not borrowed by them from the *Egyptians*, as has been more than once infinuated by that learned cafuift and divine, the Author of the Divine Legation of *Mofes*, and inveftigator of the *Eleufinian* myfteries.—When his Lordfhip, with great ftrength of argument, labors to refute the fuppofition that the *Egyptians* borrowed any of their fuperftitions from the *Hebrews*, he urges with great propriety, " the utter " improbability of a potent, and powerful " nation, borrowing any part of their re- " ligious worfhip from a people, who was " then in a ftate of flavery to them, and " held by them in the higheft deteftation;" or words to this effect ;———now, furely it is *much more improbable to conceive*, that a *potent*, and *powerful nation* (for fuch *Indoftan* was found to be at the firft known intercourfe with them) fhould borrow *a fundamental*, on which the whole fyftem of their moft

moſt ancient worſhip hinged, from a few
ſtraggling *Egyptians.*—If we grant that it is
probable the reſt of the world adopted the
doƈtrine of the Metempſychoſis from the
Egyptians, after *they* had ſtolen it from the
Gentoo Bramins, and impoſed it as their
own, we grant a circumſtance which is not
clearly proved;—but another circumſtance
is pretty evident, and will be ſubſequently
proved, that, at the time they ſtole this
doƈtrine, they alſo purloined other fundamentals of the *Chartah Bhade Shaſtah,*
namely, *the unity of the Godhead, the immortality of the ſoul, a general and particular
Providence, and a future ſtate of rewards
and puniſhments.*

15. As a proof of the boaſted wiſdom of
of the *Egyptian* Magi, we ſhall ſee the uſe
they nobly made of *the above fundamentals :*
—they inſtituted *rites* to their two principal
fabulous divinities *Iſis* and *Oſiris,* of which
(amongſt others, truly diabolical, of their
own invention) thoſe *fundamentals,* and the
doƈtrine of the Metempſychoſis, were the
chief, and *grand myſteries ;* to which (as the
learned inveſtigator has ſhewn) none were
admitted but Kings, Princes, Lawgivers, and
Heroes, and that admiſſion not granted, but
under the moſt ſolemn oaths and ties of
ſecrecy; for " theſe were truths of too im-
" portant

" nature to be entrufted with the people,
" who, it was fuppofed, were better kept
" in fubjection by a belief in their titulary,
" and local Deities."—Thus thefe deteftable
race of Governors kept the knowledge of
the TRUE GOD from their people, as well
as thofe other *important truths*, fo neceffary for their falvation, in which thofe Magi
had been inftructed by the Bramins.—But
how are we moved to a mixture of laughter
and compaffion, when we are ultimately
told, (by the fame learned enquirer into ancient Theology) that not one of the *Egyptian* Magi, and all of the *Grecian* or *Roman* legiflators, or philofophers (*Socrates* excepted) *really believed* in ONE GOD, or the
immortality of the foul, or a future ftate of
rewards and punifhments, *although they all
taught them in their myfteries:* and in fupport of the fact, his Lordfhip produces many evidences, as well as learned arguments.
—We cannot quit this fubject without faying, that we can by no means entertain that
high opinion of the wifdom of the *Egyptians* in their legiflative capacity, which his
Lordfhip feems to do ; for by their fecreting
the being of ONE GOD, and a future ftate
of rewards and punifhments (whether they
themfelves believed them or not), they affuredly quitted the fafteft hold they had
upon the obedience of rational minds, on
whom *fuch principles, if firmly rooted,* muft

C   operate

operate more powerfully, in fecuring fubjection to government, than any others,
which the wit or wifdom *of man* could poffibly devife. It will probably be urged
againft us, that thefe doctrines are feen to
lofe their influence in ftates where they are
profeffed, and form a part of their religious
code.—If man is incorrigible we cannot
help it; but we fhould rather think, that
in thefe cafes——*they are not firmly rooted.*

16. But fuffer us, candid reader, to
change the unpleafing fcene, and, in con-
traft to *Egyptian* wifdom, to turn our eyes
towards the great Legiflator, Prince, and
High-prieft of the *Gentoos,* who, in his fcriptures, taught not only the *four great fundamentals,* of the unity of the Godhead, his
providence, the immortality of the foul, and
a future ftate of rewards and punifhments,
but alfo every other divine and *primitive
truth,* neceffary for man's knowledge in his
prefent ftate of miferable exiftence; and
thefe he taught (as elfewhere we had occafion to remark), not *as myfteries* confined to
a *felect few,* but as public religious tenets,
known and received as fuch *by all*;—and fo
forcible and efficacious was the influence
of thefe doctrines upon the people, that
they adhered ftrictly to them, and kept
them inviolate for the fpace of one thoufand
years

years (as before remarked), and until they were perverted by their own priefts, and led to new modes of worfhip, before unknown to themfelves and their forefathers. In thefe innovations on their original pure fcriptures, we will not difpute but that the Bramins might have taken fome hints for reducing the people under facerdotal dominion from the infamous political fyftems of their biethren the *Egyptian* Magi, who, it is more than probable, did, about this period, firft ftraggle into Indoftan (i. e. at the promulgation of the *Chatah Bhade*).

17. Here we cannot help obferving, that the learned author of the *Divine Legation* laboured unwittingly under two other miftakes, in fuppofing the *Hebrews* were the only nation in the ancient world who worfhipped *one God*, and in whofe government *religion* and the *magiftracy* were *united*; for by thefe the *Gentoos* were eminently diftinguifhed in the moft early known times: but of this his Lordfhip was ignorant, and therefore ftands not accountable. The labored apologies his Lordfhip makes for the *imperfect miffion* of *Mofes* may require our future notice; we fhall only remark here, the difficulty the mind has to encounter in comprehending, how any *miffion* dictated by *God himfelf* can poffibly be *imperfect?*

If

If the miffion of *Mofes* contained a *fpiritual*, as well as *temporal* allufion to the falvation of the *Hebrews*, and the fpiritual fenfe was hidden from them, it was then indeed imperfect, and the *Gentoos* fhould feem to have been *the chofen people of God*, in place of the *Ifraelites*; for to them was revealed by Bramah, with God's permiffion, not only the *real flate and condition of man*, but his doctrines alfo taught, the exiftence of *One Eternal God*, and *temporal* as well as *future* rewards and punifhments. This being the cafe, although we admit, with his Lordfhip, that " the myftery of life, and " immortality, and a future ftate; which " had been hid for ages, and from generation to generation ; was *then* made manifeft to the faints" in the gofpel-difpenfation; yet, at the fame time, we think we have undoubted authority for faying, that thefe myfteries, as before fhewn, were taught, and univerfally profeffed fome thoufands of years antecedent to that period, by a diftant, diftinct, and numerous nation, with whom indeed his Lordfhip was not acquainted ; which is to be the more lamented, becaufe, with his profound abilities, unwearied application,. and confummate learning, he would have been enabled, by a knowledge of the original tenets of *Bramah*, highly to have illuftrated his fubject, and his
perform-

performance, we conceive, would have borne
a very different afpect. For

18. We cannot help again regretting, that
fo much learned pains has been taken to
prove, that there ever exifted any nation of
people, who did not profefs, or really believe in, a future ftate of rewards and punifhments. Facts of this nature, which have
fo manifeft and dangerous a tendency to influence the minds and manners of mankind,
cannot be hid from *the learned*; but they
might eafily have been obfcured to the bulk
of the fpecies, by all controverfy relative to
them being confined to, and carried on in
the original dead languages; whereas the
contrary practice of every nation in Europe
for the laft century, by bringing thefe dangerous fubjects home to us, as we may fay,
into our native tongues, unavoidably confounds, and raifes doubts in the foul, and
leads it into a train of thinking, which
otherwife, moft probably, would never have
ftruck the imagination.

19. Infidelity treads clofe upon the heels
of fcepticifm; and notwithftanding fo much
has been faid to juftify the wife purpofes of
Mofes, " in *ftudioufly rejecting* the doctrine
" of a *future ftate* in his law to the *He-*
" *brews*;" yet the event fhewed, and the

fact

fact is confirmed by the greateſt part of
their hiſtory, that they remained without
any check upon their hearts or conduct. In
the belief of a future ſtate they were not inſtructed, and *therefore*, they naturally doubt-
ed, and could not be brought to adhere for
any time together in the belief of *One Eternal God*; nor could it be rationally thought
they would, when the *one* ſo abſolutely
and mutually depended on *the other*. The
" wiſe proviſion" (as it is ſtiled) made by
Moſes to ſupply the want of this doctrine of
a future ſtate, to wit, the menace of " God's
" viſiting the ſins and diſobedience of the
" fathers upon the children, unto the third
" and fourth generation," we have ſeen
had none effect upon either ; and he muſt
be very little acquainted with the *original*,
and continued depravity of the *human ſoul*,
who thinks it can be reſtrained from evil
by any other check than that of a confirmed belief, and expectation of *a temporal
as well as a future ſtate of rewards and puniſhments*, which brings the matter home
to the breaſt of every *individual*.

20. We ſhall now proceed with our Diſ-
ſertation on the Doctrine of the *Metempſychoſis, as a conſequent of the angelic fall*;
and we hope in the courſe of it, to point
out, and elucidate upon a rational hypotheſis,

thefis, many *important truths*; and account for, and explain fome appearances in this ftate of human and animal exiftence, which are, we conceive, utterly unaccountable, and inexplicable, without the affiftance of *that ancient doctrine.*

C 4   A DIS-

A DISSERTATION, &c.

21. THE prophets, philofophers, moralifts, and fages of all ages; whether,
moved by the infpiration of GOD himfelf,
or by other intelligent agents ; or actuated
by the mere force of their own rational
powers ; howfoever they may have differed
in other fpeculative points, yet agree unani-
moufly in this important, and interefting
one; namely, *that the human foul carries the
ftamp of original depravity, and is naturally
prone to evil.*--Deplorable as this fort of humanity is, it is rendered much more fo, by
that almoft univerfal propenfity in the fpecies, either to a total diffipation of their
time and talents ; or, employing both, in
fruitlefs ftudies, in place of devoting all his
intellectual powers, to pry into, and examine *the real ftate of his own exiftence,* for
which he difcovers an unaccountable averfion, and backwardnefs.

22. It has been wifely faid, that the fummit of human wifdom is comprifed, in this
fhort adage, MAN KNOW THY SELF ; but,
inftead of dedicating all his refearches to
this effential purfuit, *Man knows every thing
but himfelf;*——he goes on, from age to
age,

age, and from day to day, in cultivating
the arts and fciences, with a view only to
the better accommodation and enjoyment
of his prefent fojourn. With this unhappy
delufion, and with thefe non-eflential ac-
quirements, he refts perfectly eafy, and fatisfied ; *here he pitches his tent*, as if he was
never to decamp.—Man knows not who he
is, what he is, how he came by his exiftence
in this world, nor for what real purpofes he
was brought originally into it ; nor does he
feem much to concern himfelf about it, fo
long as he paffes fmoothly, and fupinely,
through it.

23. The doubts and difficulties which
man encounters, and labors under, in forming any precife judgment refpecting *the
nature and obligations of his prefent exiftence*,
we conceive to have always been the great
impeding caufes, that have ever with-held him
from deep reflection, and a proper retrofpect
into himfelf; could therefore, *that nature*,
and thefe *obligations*, be clearly afcertained
to him, the relative duties of his deftination would be alfo clear and pofitive;
and mankind would no longer infeparably
attach themfelves to the tranfient confiderations, and enjoyments of this life only.

24. How

24. How far the doctrines of the Metempfychofis tend, upon a cool and unprejudiced hearing, to clear up the doubts and
difficulties above alluded to, is the important fubject of our enquiry. In this difquifition we fhall not hefitate to affert, that the
doctrine is far from being new in this our
hemifphere; it was profeffed by our anceftors, when the fage druids led and governed their faith and politics, as the moft
learned records of our ancient hiftory
vouch, although it does not appear from
their fhewing, that it was taught by the
ancient *Britons* (for the firft *Britons* we
know nothing of) in that fimple purity,
and extent, as it was originally by the
Bramins of *Indoftan*.

25. Tender confciences have no caufe of
alarm from our reviving the confideration
of a doctrine, which in the moft early
known ages was followed by at leaft four-
fifths of the inhabitants of the earth; the
more efpecially as we hope to prove, that
this doctrine is not repugnant to the doctrines of Chriftianity.

26. Communications between the Deity
and man, either perfonally, or by his angels
or prophets, was, in early times, no uncommon event: thefe recorded facts we
muft

muſt believe, or reject and ſet at nought our own ſcriptures; and ſhall we ſuppoſe the children of the Eaſt to have been leſs the care of God, than the children of *Iſrael?* or that the whole of his creatures, howſoever diſperſed and ſeparated from each other, were not equally the unhappy objects of his benevolence and attention?——Such a ſuppoſition would arraign his juſtice and impartial diſpenſations to all his creatures : it is not becoming us to doubt the authority and divinity of *any original religious ſyſtem,* unleſs it *evidently* is repugnant to the idea of a juſt and omnipotent God.

27. To bring our Eſſay to method and perſpicuity, we muſt again have a ſhort retroſpect to the ſeveral eſſential concomitant parts of the doctrine of the Metempſychoſis, as promulged by *Bramah;* and we ſhall proceed to the diſcuſſion of *each,* reduced, as follows, under five general heads, *viz.*

First General Head.

The exiſtence of angelic beings.
Their rebellion, or fall.

Their

Their expulsion from the heavenly regions.

Their punishments.

Second General Head.

The univerſe *formed* by God, for the reſidence, ſuſtenance, and impriſonment of the apoſtate angels.

Third General Head.

Mortal organized bodies formed for their more immediate, or cloſer confinement.

Their tranſmigrations through thoſe mortal forms.

Thoſe tranſmigrations: their ſtate of purgation as well as puniſhment.

The human form their chief ſtate of trial and probation.

Fourth General Head.

Liberty given to the apoſtate angels to pervade the univerſe.

Permiſ-

Permiffion given to the faithful angelic
beings to counteract them.

FIFTH GENERAL HEAD.

The feven regions of purification, wherein the fallen angels ceafe from their mortal
tranfmigrations.

The diffolution of the univerfe, or material worlds.

28. Before we enter upon the difcuffion
of thefe five general heads, we beg leave to
be indulged in a few preparatory reflections:
firft, that it is obvious,- from the above particulars collectively confidered, one general
conclufion may be formed as the bafis of
this ancient doctrine of the Metempfychofis, viz. *That the fouls, or fpirits, of every
human or other organifed mortal body, inha-
biting this globe, and all the regions of the
material univerfe, are precifely the remainder
of the unpurified angels, who fell from their
obedience in heaven, and that ftill ftand out in
contempt of their Creator.*

29. Strange as *this fyftem* may appear in
thefe our days, and howfoever feemingly
clogged with difficulties, it is worth confideration,

deration, how far it will elucidate, and account for, many theological myfteries, and other phenomena that are annexed to this our prefent ftate of exiftence ; and which are, we conceive, otherwife unaccountable, as before hinted.——If, in the courfe of our enquiry, we advance no opinions contrary to our own *pure original fcriptures* (to which we profefs ourfelf, an unworthy, although zealous fubfcriber), nor endeavour to propagate any fyftem, but what may co-incide with *every religious Creed*, that *has been*, or *is now* profeffed throughout the known world, we are then void of offence, both to God and *man*.——Endlefs have been the difputes about religion, whilft we fee the chief contention is, Who fhall the leaft practife its precepts:—therefore how laudable is the purfuit of that man, who labors to point out *one univerfal faith*, that would infallibly reconcile all jarring principles, and unite all mankind in the bands of mutual love and benevolence. We write not to this, or that fect, or to this, or that nation, but to *mankind in general*; who feem not to advert to, or be in any degree acquainted, either with the real dignity of their original nature, or the relation in which they ftand, to their God, to their brethren, or to the reft of the animal creation.——" Let us read, let us " meditate, let us reafon, let us difpute ;

" but

" but all for the fake of Truth, which is
" the great property of mankind, confti-
" tutes all our happinefs, and therefore our
" common intereft to purfue."

First General Head,

30. In our remarks, p. 36, of our fecond part, we have given our conceptions of the fublime caufes affigned by *Bramah* for the creation and exiftence of angels; nor need we dwell long on a fact, the firm belief of which has been received by all mankind, a fingle inconfiderable fect amongft the *Jews* alone excepted.——There muft undoubtedly, and confequently have fubfifted, fome *ftriking evidence* of this great truth in the early and later times exhibited *to man*, that fhould influence and determine him to this general belief, and the propagation of it to his pofterity; which *evidence* (for caufes beft known to God himfelf) he is now, and has been for near eighteen centuries back, deprived of.

31. On recollection, we find we have been too hafty in our conclufion touching *this truth*;—a modern philofopher, more remarkable and famed for genius, and the fprightly irony of his wit, than for folidity

of

of argument, or found philofophy, and who has all his life endeavoured to laugh religion out of countenance, has been bold enough to ridicule the exiftence of angels, as beings purely ideal, and an invention of the poets; and alleges the filence of *Mofes* in proof, who, he fays, in his law to the *Jews*, nowhere mentions their exiftence; and urges alfo his filence touching *their fall*, which he infinuates is equally fabulous as their exiftence.

32. To fay nothing of the inconfiftency of this merry philofopher's drawing his negative proofs and conclufions from a book he puts no faith in, nor allows to be of any authority, we will confider the force of his reafoning; for fhould we fubfcribe to this author's affertion touching the filence of *Mofes* in the law to the *Jews*, it by no means amounts even to a negative proof of the non-exiftence of angelic beings, nor *of their fall* being only fabulous.

33. Whatfoever may have been the opinion of *Mofes* on *thofe fubjects*, it would have been more extraordinary had he made mention of them, than his filence can poffibly appear to be; as it is moft evident, that thele were matters that lay utterly out of his way, commiffioned, as he only feems

to

to be, to preach the *unity of the Godhead* to the *Jews*; a people under *the sole* protection of the Deity, their King and Governor, a fituation wherein the introduction of angelic beings would have been impertinent, and not in point to *the law* he was dictating to them.——After all, that *Moses* did believe the exiftence of angels, although he makes no mention of them *in the law*, is obvious from his 24th verfe of the 3d chap·er of *Genefis:* "So he (God) drove out " the man; and he placed *cherubims* at the " eaft end of the garden of Eden," &c. And that *Moses* was 'alfo as well acquainted with the angelic fall, we doubt not our being able to prove, in a fubfequent part of our Differtation, notwithftanding the infinuations of our modern Democritus; who, it is no wonder, fhould difcountenance the notion of the exiftence of angels, when he owns that the gofpel-difpenfation is *founded on their fall.*

34. It is not neceffary to recite the particular concurring teftimony of all antiquity to the fuppofed exiftence of angels, when we have fo much greater authorities to fupport us; the Old Teftament, throughout the whole hiftoric parts, and the gofpel of Chrift, afford us fo many ftriking inftances of thefe beings employed occafionally by GOD, either

D

ther as active inftruments againft the wickednefs of man, or as agents, faviors and com-
forters to the juft and good, that we may
with equal propriety, when we are about
it, as well deny the exiftence of God himfelf, as of his angels.

35. A belief of miniftring angels under
corporeal forms, fuffers no impeachment
from their *fpiritual nature*; for, as they are
endued by an omnipotent GOD with all
powers neceffary for the execution of their
refpective commiffions, it is no great marvel, if we conceive them capable of affum-
ing every fhape and form needful for thofe
ends and purpofes for which they are delegated; and, notwithftanding they are in
their own nature and effence fpiritual and
immaterial, yet it is no great ftrain of faith
to conclude they can occafionally affume
corporeal forms, functions, and faculties,
and diveft themfelves of them again at pleafure, as in the inftances of thofe that fo-
journed with Abraham, and Lot; and thus
CHRIST manifefted himfelf after his refurrection.——But more of this, when we
come to difcufs this fubject in its proper
place, under our fourth general head.

36. On this fundamental doctrine of exiftence of angels, and their rebellion, expulfion,

fion, and punifhment, refts not only the Metempfychofis, but the whole religion of the ancient, as well as modern Bramins; the text of *Bramah* fays, that " the ETER-
" NAL ONE, in the fulnefs of time, firft
" created BIRMAH, *Bifnoo*, and *Sieb*, then
" *Moifafoor*, and all the *Debtah-Logue*, and
" divided the *Debtah* into different bands
" and ranks, and placed a leader, or chief,
" over each: he gave pre-eminence to BIR-
" MAH, and appointed *Moifafoor* chief of
" the firft angelic band, &c."—Thefe origi-
nal tenets and principles are confirmed by our own fimilar Chriftian doctrines and be-
lief, with the difference of names only: thus the creation and exiftence of angels ftand manifefted beyond controverfy, by two of the greateft authorities of *ancient* and *modern times*.

37. Refpecting *the fall* of thefe beings, the text of *Bramah* further fays, " That
" envy and jealoufy taking poffeffion of the
" hearts of *Moifafoor*, and *Rhaboon* (the
" next in dignity to him), and of other lead-
" ers of the angelic bands, they ftood, in
" contempt of the commands of their
" Creator, threw off their allegiance, and
" drew with them into difobedience *a large*
" *portion* of their angelic brethren." The text alfo adds, " that before the expulfion

D 2   " of

" of the rebels from the heavenly regions,
" the three prime created beings, BIRMAH,
" *Biſnoo*, and *Sieb*, were ſent to admoniſh
" them, but that they continued in con-
" tempt."

38. As the goſpel-diſpenſation is allowed
by our moſt learned divines to be *founded
upon the angelic fall,* great · is the degree of
veneration which every *Chriſtian* owes to the
Gentoo ſcriptures, which taught minutely
circumſtances of that fall, more than three
thouſand years *a priori.*——The *goſpel-diſpenſation,* being undoubtedly the moſt perfect, ſublime, yet plain ſyſtem of divinity
and morals hitherto promulged to man
(when diveſted of the dreams and reveries
of its early and latter profeſſors), we cannot too highly prize the great rudiments it
conveys to us, of the love of GOD, repentance for ſin, mutual love from man to
man, and a proper faith and reverence
for that *divine being,* who was delegated
from the preſence of his GOD to preach theſe
great primitive truths as neceſſary, not only for man's happineſs here, but hereafter.

39. Yet, divine and eſſential as theſe doctrines are, and neceſſary to our ſalvation,
permit us to aſk, How can this goſpel-diſpenſation, which *ſo nearly affects man,* be
ſaid

faid with any propriety to be founded upon
the angelic fall ?—unlefs there is a nearer
relation between man and angel, than appears to have hitherto been imagined or adverted to by the profeffors of Chriftianity ?
—if man has not this nearer relationfhip,
what has he to do with *their fall?*—or how
can *that fall* ferve as a foundation for a doctrine on which his future falvation depends ?
—This (otherwife) incomprehenfible difficulty is folved only by the doctrine of the
Bramins, which teaches, that the apoftate
angelic and human fouls are one and the
fame fpirit; nor can we, upon any other
rational principle, conceive how the gofpel-
difpenfation can be founded upon the angelic fall.

40. An ingenious, fpeculative, and learned divine of our church, publifhed, in the
year 1762, a treatife, entitled, " A Pre-
" exiftent Lapfe of Human Souls *, &c."
This truly valuable performance relieves us
from much labor in the profecution of our
work, as it confirms, *from our own fcriptures,* many leading and effential points of
the Metempfychofis, as, the exiftence of
angels, their rebellion, their expulfion from

* Printed for Whifton and White in Fleet-Street,
and for Kearfly, Ludgate-Street.—By Capel Berrow,
A. M.

their

their bleſſed abodes, the cœval creation of
the angelic and human ſpirits, and the aſ-
ſociation of the latter with the former in
their apoſtacy; that their ſituation on earth
is a ſtate of *degradation* and *probation* for
that lapſe, and that *original ſin* is not that
which is erroneouſly imputed to us from
Adam, but ſprings from a much higher
ſource, *viz.* the *pre-exiſtent* lapſe of the
(human) ſpirit from its primæval purity.

41. In ſupport of this hypotheſis, the
Rev. Author exhibits many clear, ſtriking,
and convincing texts of ſcripture, as well as
the opinions of the moſt ancient and modern
philoſophers and theologians. The authorities quoted by this writer, and his ſubſe-
quent reaſoning on his ſubject are ſo full
and concluſive, that nothing can be added
by us to illuſtrate it. Therefore we beg
leave to refer our readers to the book itſelf,
(and particularly to his laſt chapter, in refutation of the ſtrongeſt objections that can be
raiſed againſt his ſyſtem), which contains
every proof and confirmation from our own
ſcriptures which we ſtand in need of to ſupport the *Gentoo* doctrine of our firſt general
head, namely, The exiſtence of angels, their
fall, their expulſion, and their puniſhments.

42. In

42. In the year 1729, an Effay was publifhed, dedicated to the then Lord Mayor,
bearing the title of an Oration, by one Mr.
J. Ilive, under four general heads, *viz.* en-
deavouring to prove, 1*ft*, The plurality of
worlds. 2*dly*, That this earth is the only
hell. 3*dly*, That the fouls of men are the
apoftate angels. 4*thly*, That the fire, which
will punifh thofe who fhall be confined to
this globe at the day of judgment, will be
immaterial.——We juft mention this *extraordinary oration* here, but we fhall fubfequently have occafion to notice it farther.

43. Before we take leave of this part of
our fubject, we will remind our readers of
what we advanced in our 4th paragraph,
where, enumerating the fundry *primitive
truths* which had forcibly been impreffed
on the mind of man, in the beginning; one
of the moft important was, the notion of
*three prime created celeftial beings, either
confounded with, or exclufive of, and fubordinate to the Deity*; thus the Bramins have
their *Birmah, Biftnoo,* and *Sieb*; the *Perfians* their *Oromazes, Mythra,* and *Mythras*;
the *Egyptians* their *Ofyris, Ifis,* and *Orus*;
the ancient *Arabs* their *Allat, Al. Uzza,*
and *Manah,* or the *Goddeffes*; the *Phæni-
cians* and *Tyrians,* their *Belus, Urania,* and

Adonis;

Adonis; the *Greeks* and *Romans* their *Jupiter Olympus, Minerva,* and *Apollo*; the Chriftians their *Father, Son,* and *Holy Ghoft*; the *Americans* their *Otkon, Meffou,* and *Atahauta,* &c. &c. And we doubt not but a fimilar doctrine might be traced amongft all the different nations of the earth, had we authentic records of their primitive religious inftitutes; it was a principle adopted by all the ancient weftern world, probably introduced by the *Phœnicians,* and confirmed to them by the *Romans.* Vide *Herodotus, Plutarch, Cicero,* on the nature of the Gods; the *Abbé Banier's* Mythology of the Ancients; *Warburton's* Divine Legation of *Mofes*; the Chevalier *Ramfay's* Difcourfe on the Theology and Mythology of the *Pagans,* &c.

44. To a notion fo univerfal·in the firft times, we think ourfelves warranted in giving the title of a primitive truth; which muft have had unerring fact, and a divine revelation for its fource and foundation, as well as the other primitive truths of the rebellion, fall, and punifhment of part of the angelic hoft, under the inftigation and leading of an arch apoftate of the firft rank; hence the *Moifafoor* of the Bramins; the *Arimanius* of the *Perfians*; the *Typhon* of the

the *Egyptians, Greeks,* &c. and **the** *Satan* of the Chriftians.—And that other *great truth,* the neceffity of a mediator, or mediators, employed either in imploring the divine mercy in behalf of the delinquent angels, or in combating or counteracting the wiles and influence of the arch apoftate, and his prime adherents;—hence the *Birmah,* &c. of the Bramins; the *Mythras* of the *Perfians;* the *Orus* of the *Egyptians;* the *Adonis* of the *Tyrians;* the *Apollo* of the *Greeks,* &c. and the *Meffiah* of the Chriftians, whofe glorious and voluntary tafk it is, to work out the reftoration of the *golden age,* by the fubduction of *the firft author of evil.*

45. From hence it is manifeft, that the notion of a golden age, fo frequently mentioned, and minutely defcribed by all the ancient philofophers and poets, was purely ideal, refpecting either any part of this material world, or any period of time fubfequent to its creation; but obvioufly could only be allufive to that ftate of beatitude and harmony which reigned in the heavenly abodes until the fall of the angelic inhabitants; for, notwithftanding the variety and confufion of opinions touching the *origin of evil,* we may confidently fay it never had exiftence, until (from the gracious root of freedom) it firft fprang up, in the bofom
of

of the firſt *grand traitor.*—As the remembrance of this celeſtial golden age of the firſt
creation of beings, muſt have been ſtrongly
impreſſed on the minds of the delinquents
at their fall, it was hence by a tradition eaſily conceived, handed down to later times,
and loſt in the ideal conceit of a golden age
in this terreſtrial globe.

46. We have already been accuſed of partiality to the doctrines of *Bramah,* but that
ſhall not deter us from *aſſerting,* what before we only hinted at, namely, that that
prophet and divine legiſlator firſt taught, by
written precepts, the pure theology of *the
unity* of the Godhead, the three prime created beings, the creation of angelic intelli-
gents, their fall, and the reſt of the *primitive truths* that were followed by all the ancient world. From this conviction it was,
that in the foregoing paragraphs, where we
had occaſion to mention the theology of the
ancients, we have given precedence to that
of *the Bramins;* and that we are not ſingular in our opinion, we could cite many authorities, but a few ſhall ſuffice : the Chevalier *Ramſay,* who has, with great ſtrength
of ·genius, and accuracy, labored to elucidate this ſubject, in the 88th page of his
Diſcourſe on the Theology of the *Pagans,*
ſpeaking of the atheiſtical tenets of *Anaxi-
mander,*

mander, fays, " *Pythagoras, Anaxagoras,*
" *Socrates, Plato, Ariſtotle,* and all the
" great men of *Greece,* oppoſed the im-
" pious doctrine, and endeavoied to re-
" eſtabliſh the *ancient theology of the orien-*
" *tals.*" Page 135 of his Diſcourſe on the
Pagan Mythology, he i.as this concluſion,
that, " as the doctrine of the *Perſians* is
" only the fequel of the *Indian* Bramins,
" we muſt conſult the one, to put the other
" in a clear light." Again, p. 39, ſpeaking of *Pythagoras,* he fays, " This philoſo-
" pher taught nothing to the *Greeks,* but
" what he learnt from *the Gymnoſophiſts.*"
—To theſe we will juſt add the ſentiments
of the very ingenious and learned Mr. *James
Howell,* in the 11th Letter of his 2d vol.
where he reports, from *Diodorus Siculus,*
" That the *Egyptians* had Kings 18,000
" years ſince, yet, for the matter of Philo-
" ſophy and Science, he (the *Egyptian)*
" had it from the *Chaldean,* and he from
" the *Gymnoſophiſts* and *Brachmans of In-*
" *dia.*"——Which country, as it is the next
neighbor to the riſing Sun, ſo the beams of
Learning (and conſequently of Religion) *did
firſt enlighten her.* Thus we have ſhewn,
that we are not ſingular in believing that
the religion of *Bramah* is the *moſt ancient,*
and conſequently *moſt pure.* For

47. It

47. It has been well remarked, that the nearer we approach to the origin of nations, the more pure we fhall find their Theology, and the reafon of things fpeaks the juftnefs of the remark ; becaufe *the period* when the angelic fpirits were doomed to take upon them mortal forms, was doubtlefs the origin of all nations ; and at that time, as the nature of their tranfgreffion and the terms of their reftoration, were frefh upon their memories, their Theology was pure, univerfal and unerring ; profeffing *one univerfal faith*, which they had as we fay from the mouth of GOD himfelf.—Surely there muft have been a time, when all nations had but *one fyftem of Theology*, or elfe it is impoffible to affign a caufe for the uniform concurrence of all people touching the *primitive truths*, we have fo often had occafion to mention ; but here the caufe is found in the rational fuppofition of *one faith* at the origin of all nations ;—and we may without deferving the imputation of too great prefumption boldly pronounce, that *until that is again the cafe*, there will be neither pure uninterrupted joy in heaven, *nor peace on earth.*——If the notion of a *terreftrial golden age* has any foundation, it can be only applicable to that feafon, which we rather think ought to be ftiled, the age of repentance and forrow, and poffibly is

the

the only fhort period and pure piety fince
the creation of the univerfe.

48. This leads us naturally to another
remark; namely, that the farther any fyftem of Theology *flows from its fource,* the
more its pure pellucid ftream is vitiated,
difturbed and rendered muddy, and unintelligible. This is verified by the ecclefiaftic
hiftory of all nations, but none with more
ftriking evidence than in that of the *ancient Bramins,* unlefs we except *our own.*
—When we compare the original, auguft,
although fimple doctrines of the unity of
the Godhead, and the three fubordinate
celeftial perfonages, *&c.* of *Bramah,* with
the later doctrines of his fucceffors in the
priefthood, how amazingly do we behold
the fublimity and purity of them mutilated
and loft! The Text of *Bramah* fays, " God
" is one, Creator of all that is.——The
" eternal One firft made *Birmah,* then
" *Biftnoo* and *Sieb,* then *Moifafoor* and the
" reft of the angelic hoft; he made his
" firft created *Birmah,* Prince of the an-
" gelic bands, and his occafional vice-
" gerent, deftined him to acts of power,
" glory, and dominion ; and appointed the
" two next created beings *Biftnoo* and *Sieb*
" his coadjutors :" and when in procefs of
time (by the defection and rebellion of
Moifafoor)

Moifafoor) God in his mercy refolved to form the material univerfe, thefe three Divine Beings became the active reprefentatives and executors of his three fupreme attributes ; his power to create, his power to preferve, and his power to change or deftroy, as their names fignify.

49. Here the people were prefented with a doctrine plain, comprehenfible, and fuited to the capacity of every intelligent being, although imprifoned under a material form; the fucceffors of *Bramah* did not indeed confound the three divine perfonages with the Godhead, but they at length did every thing elfe to cloud and obfcure every other of his *primitive truths*, until they became as deeply plunged in idolatry, and in what we may call the ufelefs parade of religion, as any people upon earth, and fo continue to this day : thus the miffion of *Bramah* was rendered fruitlefs, but the pure fpring-head of his doctrines (that is, the firft great primitive truths now under our confideration) were more fullied by the priefts of other nations, who formed monftrous copies from the fublime original of *Bramah.*

50. The *Perfian* Magi were the firft who confounded the three prime created, fubordinate celeftial beings of the ancient *Bra-*
mins

mins with the Godhead, to hide him from the vulgar; and not satisfied with this, they gave the eternal One a wife in the second person. In this domestic oeconomy they were followed by the *Egyptians, Chaldeans, Tyrians, Phœnicians, Greeks* and *Romans;* and as the *Egyptian* Magi exceeded the *Persian* in rendering these original *primitive truths incomprehensible,* so these were surpassed by the *Tyrians,* and they again by the *Greeks,* and the *Romans* outwent them all. These instances afford a striking proof of the remark we made above, that the farther any divine system of Theology flows from its original source, the more it suffers and is corrupted.

51. Thus we see the two first most essential primitive truths, to wit, the unity of the Godhead, and the creation of the three superior Divine Beings subordinate to him, as originally taught by *Bramah,* were first loaded with superstitious and idolatrous rites by his successors, after it had subsisted inviolate for the long space of a thousand years, and the sublime spirit of it utterly evaporated and lost in the various systems of the *Persian* and *Egyptian* Magi and their followers, and sunk at last into incomprehensible jargon; as any one who has leisure and curiosity may convince himself,

5   by

by confulting the authors who have exhibited the religious tenets of thefe nations.

52. Would to heaven, that that confounding incomprehenfible fpirit had ftopped, and vanifhed with the heathen priefthood! and that we ourfelves had not, by dividing that fupreme adoration, which is due alone to the ONE ETERNAL GOD, given rife to a fchifm in Chriftianity, that has fapped the very root of its fimple, exalted and divine doctrines, and proved the fource of a thoufand herefies, as well as one of the great ftumbling blocks, to the univerfal propagation of a religion, that fpeaks the finger of God in every fentence, without one fingle glance at a *Trinity in Unity, or Unity in Trinity*, an unintelligible dogma, in which the heathen leaven prevailed, and raifed a fermentation in the church of Chrift that probably will never fubfide, until God himfelf is pleafed to exert and manifeft once more his own fupremacy in power and vengeance, for the daily repeated blafphemies uttered againft his awful name; for the fpirit of man will neither regard the words of God himfelf, nor thofe of his Chrift. For,

53. " God fpake thefe words, and faid, " I am the Lord thy God, Thou fhalt have " none other Gods but me," and the congregation

gregation replies, " Lord have mercy upon
" us, and incline our hearts to keep this
" law," although they know they fhall
egregioufly break it more than once in
the courfe of the liturgy : and God himfelf, fpeaking of the Meffiah, which he
purpofed fending into the world, to promulge a new revelation of his will, fays
unto *Mofes*, " I will raife them up a PRO-
" PHET from among their brethren, LIKE
" UNTO THEE, and will put my words in-
" to his mouth ; and he fhall fpeak unto
" them all things I fhall *command him*.
" And it fhall come to pafs, that whofoever
" will not hearken unto my words, which
" he fhall fpeak in my name, I will require
" it of him."

54. When we confider the many and various declarations which dropped from the
mouth of Chrift, fo ftrongly expreffive of
his own dependent ftate and fubordination
to the will of God, how can we account for
that degree of infatuation which firft moved
the heart of man to utter and propagate the
blafphemous doctrine of his co-equality,
and co-eternity with God ? although the
fame extravagant rhapfody of faith, pronounces him *begotten of the Father*, and
confequently both *created* and *made*, if
words have any meaning. Where religion

E

is

is fhrouded under the difguife of myfteries, fymbols, allegories, hieroglyphics, and fable; they are fure and infallible criterions of that religion being fpurious, and not of divine origin. Thefe, as before remarked, were the inventions of the ancient prieft-hood and lawgivers, to cover, obfcure, and hide the TRUE GOD from the PEOPLE; and indeed they could not have concerted a more effectual and iniquitous fyftem. That religion which fpeaks not to the level of every degree of human underftanding, as well as to the heart, we will pronounce, *never came from God*; the reafon is obvious, for high and low, learned and unlearned, rich and poor, are all equal objects of his care and providence, and equally interefted in the event of falvation, which is the fole aim of the Moft High in every divine revelation of his will.

55. The religions which manifeftly carry the divine ftamp of God, are, firft, that which *Bramah* was appointed to declare to the ancient *Hindoos*; fecondly, that law which *Mofes* was deftined to deliver to the ancient *Hebrews*; and thirdly, that which *Chrift* was delegated to preach to the latter *Jews* and *Gentiles*, or the *Pagan* world. Thefe, and thefe only, bear the fignature of divine origin; for the precepts they con-

tain

tain, are plain, simple, and positive, not
disguised by mysteries, allegories, &c. but
adapted to every capacity of understanding,
although the last is so utterly mutilated and
defaced since the ascension, that Christ himself, when he descends again on earth, will
difown it, and know it not to be his; and
in Christian charity we wish he may not also disown those unhappy beings who have
been instrumental, from time to time, in
the adulteration of it, by introducing mysteries to be received as matter of faith necessary to salvation, which he never dictated, preached, or enjoined to his followers ;
as the Creed of *Athanasius*, &c. But, for
the present, we will drop a Creed, which
we believe every pious rational Christian
wishes was struck out of the Liturgy (as
well as some other articles, which also have
proved obstructions to the early universal
propagation of the gospel), and attend to
what *Christ* himself says to these subjects,
whom we think ourselves well warranted in
believing, in preference to any equivocal
expressions or sentiments, or reveries of either his apostles or disciples, or of those
who are too liberally stiled *the saints*, and
fathers of the church, whose dissentions,
dreams, and doctrines, have been wrested
by *Satan* and his disciples for a lasting foun-

dation

dation to build their extenfive kingdom upon.

56. We are here under fome apprehenfion, that we may be charged with ftepping
out of our way, and with ftumbling againft
what lies not in our path. To obviate
which, we fay, that as our view is to *re-
vive* and *re-eftablifh* the *primitive truths*
which conftituted the ground-work of the
firft univerfal religion, at the period of the
creation of the material worlds and man, it
became neceffary to ftrip them of all difguife,
myftery, and fable: in order to that, we
found ourfelves under a neceffity, occafionally to analize in part the three divine fyftems noted in our laft paragraph, not under the guife in which they now appear before us, but as they really were at their firft
promulgation; for of all the theologic fyftems that have been broached to mankind,
we think we are well fupported in marking thefe alone as *true originals*; but our benevolent view extends ftill farther, and we
flatter ourfelves (however chimerical it may
appear) mankind may be reftored again to
that *one unerring original faith*, from which,
by undue influence in every age of the
world, they have unhappily fwerved : we
are convinced, if they confulted their prefent
and

and future felicity, they would fly to embrace a rational hypothefis, that leads to fuch a bleffed iffue. And here we cannot help deeply regretting the want of that *ftupendous gift of tongues*, that our fyftem might thereby be conveyed to every corner of the habitable globe. Vain regret! fays the fceptic. Vain as it is, it is the vanity of doing good, which is the moft pardonable of all vanities. Having thus, we hope, guarded againft any imputation of wantonly deviating from our fubject, we will refume the track of our enquiries.

57. It is our purpofe to trace our divine Mediator through every text of the four Gofpels fucceffively, wherein he exprefsly declares and maintains the unity and fupremacy of God, and his own fubordination; and that in fuch terms as leaves it beyond a poffibility of being mifunderftood. Indeed, it appears every where, that he was moft anxioufly folicitous that mankind fhould be quite clear in a doctrine fo effential; and that his apoftles and difciples, who were to preach and propagate his Gofpel, fhould not be liable to error in a matter of fuch importance to Heaven and earth; and this wife precaution became the more neceffary, as they themfelves were but juft emerged

E 3 from,

from, and furrounded with, infidelity and
Paganifm.

58. We will begin with St. *Matthew*,
chap. xix. verf. 17. where *Chrift* replies to
the man who afked him the interefting queftion—" Good Mafter, what good thing
" fhall 1 do to attain eternal life?"—he faid
unto him, " Why calleft thou me good?
" there is none good but ONE, that is
" GOD." Chap. xx. verf. 23. when the
mother of *Zebedee's* children petitioned *Chrift*
that her two fons fhould fit, the one on his
right hand, the other on his left, in his
kingdom, he faid unto her, " To fit on my
" right hand, and on my left, *is not mine*
" to give, but it fhall be given to thofe for
" whom it is prepared *of my Father.*" And
verfe 28th of the fame chapter, recommending humility to his difciples, he faith,
" Even as the Son of man came *not to be*
" *miniftered unto,* but *to minifter.*" Again,
chap xxiv. verf. 36. fpeaking of the day of
judgment, he fays,—" But of that day and
" hour knoweth no man, no not the angels
" of heaven, *but the Father only.*" And
chap. xxvii. verf. 46. in the extremity of
his paffion on the crofs, he cried with a
loud voice, " My God! my God! why haft
" thou forfaken me?" than which, as nothing

thing could more powerfully denote the laft
influence of *his human nature*, fo nothing
could more forceably imply his abfolute and
avowed dependance *on his God*.

59. We fhall confider next the declarations of *Chrift*, as they ftand recorded in his
Gofpel according to St. *Mark*, chap. xii.
verf. 29. when the Scribe afked him which
was the firft of all the commandments ? *Jefus* anfwered and faid, " The firft of all the
" commandments is, Hear, O *Ifrael, the
" Lord our God is one Lord*;" and the Scribe
anfwered and faid, verf. 32. " Well, Ma-
" fter, thou haft faid the truth, for there is
" *One God*, and there is none other but
" HE;" and when he fubjoins, verf. 33.
that " the love of that *One God*, and his
" neighbor, is more than all burnt-offer-
" ings and facrifice." *Jefus* applauds his an-
fwering difcreetly, by telling him, verf. 34.
" *Thou art not far from the kingdom of
" God*," thereby confirming him in his belief of *One God only*. Chap. xiii. verf. 32.
Jefus, fpeaking of the day of judgment, is
more particular than ftands recorded in St.
Matthew, for here he declares, that " of
" that day and hour knoweth no man, no
" not the angels which are in heaven, *nei-
" ther the Son*, but the Father." Hence it
appears, by *Chrift*'s own fhowing, that one

E 4   moft

moſt important ſecret *was hid from him*,
therefore not omniſcient, and conſequently
not God, but *a diſtinɛƚ created being*. Indeed, howſoever conſcious he appears to be
of his own divine origin, yet he in no wiſe
arrogates worſhip as due to himſelf, but di-
reɛts it all to his God and Father.

60. The courſe of our enquiry leads us
next to the Goſpel according to St. *Luke*,
chap. iv. verſ. 43. where *Jeſus* being preſſed
by the people not to depart from them, ſays
unto them, " I muſt preach the kingdom of
" God to other cities, for *therefore was I*
" *ſent.*" Chap. x. verſ. 16. *Jeſus* tells his
apoſtles, " He that deſpiſeth you, deſpiſeth
" me, and he that deſpiſeth me, deſpiſeth
" *him that ſent me.*" Verſ. 21. *Chriſt*, after gently rebuking the ſeventy diſciples for
having expreſſed, with too much joy and
exultation, their ſucceſs in caſting out devils
or evil ſpirits in his name, breaks forth in
the following pathetic ſtrain of ſubmiſ-
ſive devotion, the poetic and inſpired evan-
geliſt, opening the verſe with this ſhort exordium, " In that hour *Jeſus* rejoiced in
" ſpirit, and ſaid, *I thank thee, O Father*,
" *Lord of heaven and earth*, that thou haſt
" hid theſe things from the wiſe and pru-
" dent, and haſt revealed them to babes;
" even ſo, Father, for ſo it ſeemed good
" in

" in thy fight." He then proceeds, verſ.
22. to declare to them his *delegated powers*
from his God. " *All things are delivered to*
" *me of my Father*; and no man knoweth
" who the Son is, but the Father; and
" who the Father is, but the Son, and he
" to whom the Son will reveal him." Chap.
xi. verſ. 2. when one of his difciples befought him to teach them to pray, he ſaid
unto them, " When ye pray, ſay, Our Fa-
" ther which art in heaven, hallowed be
" thy name; thy kingdom come, thy will
" be done, as in heaven, ſo on earth, &c."
Here it is worthy remark, that in ſo very
eſſential and intereſting a matter as a proper addreſs in prayer, *Chriſt* directs the
followers of his Goſpel to point their ſup-
plications and praiſes *to God alone*. Chap.
xviii. verſ. 19. records the ſame rebuke that
we have already quoted from *St. Matthew*,
with a ſmall variation of expreſſion—" Why
" calleſt thou *me good?* none is good, *ſave*
" *one*, that is, God." Chap. xxii. verſ. 42.
when *Chriſt* had ſeparated himſelf from his
difciples on the mount of Olives, he kneel-
ed down and prayed, " Father, if thou *be*
" *willing*, remove this cup from me; ne-
" vertheleſs, *not my will*, but *thine* be
" done."

61. We

61. We come now to the Gofpel of our divine Mediator and Saviour, according to St. *John*, which exhibits more numerous and ftriking declarations of *Chrift*, in fupport of the unity and fupremacy of God, and his own fubordination to his will, than all the other three put together. Chap. iv. verf. 34. *Jefus*, in anfwer to his difciples, touching his eating, fays, " My meat is to " do the will of *him* that fent me, and to " finifh *his work.*" Chap. v. verf. 19. *Jefus*, in anfwer to the *Jews*, who accufed him of breaking the Sabbath by healing the man at the pool of *Bethefda*, fays, " Verily, " verily, I fay unto you, the Son can do " nothing *of himfelf*, but what he feeth the " Father do; for what things foever he do- " eth, thefe things doth the Son likewife." Verf. 20. " For the Father loveth the Son, " and *fheweth him* all things that himfelf " doeth, and he will *fhew him* greater won- " ders than thofe, that ye may marvel." Verf. 22. " For the Father judgeth no man, " *but hath committed* all judgment to the " Son." Verf. 23. " That all men fhould " honor the Son, even as they honor the " Father, for he that honoreth not the " Son, honoreth not the Father which hath " *fent him.*" Verf. 26. to the fame *Jews Jefus* faith, " For as the Father hath life in " himfelf,

" himfelf, fo *hath he given* to the Son to
" have life in himfelf." Again, verf. 30.
" *I can of myfelf do nothing* : as I hear I
" judge, and my judgment is juft, becaufe
" I feek not mine own will, but *the will* of
" the Father, *who fent me.*" Chap. vii.
verf. 16. when *Chrifi* preached in the temple, the *Jews* marvelled, faying, " How
" knoweth this man letters, having never
" learnt?" *Jefus* anfwered them, and faid,
" My doctrine *is not mine*, but *his that fent*
" *me.*" Chap. viii. verf. 28. " Then faid
" *Jefus* unto them, When you have lift up
" the Son of man, then fhall ye know that
" I am he, and that I do nothing *of myfelf*,
" but as the Father has *taught me:*" and
verf. 42. *Jefus* faid unto them, " If God
" were your Fath :r, ye would love me,
" for *I proceedsforth*, and came *from God;*
" neither came I *of myfelf, but he fent me.*"
Chap. x. verf. 18. *Chrift*, fpeaking of the
facrifice of his life, fays, " No man taketh
" it from me, but I lay it down of myfelf.
" I have power to lay it down, and I have
" power to take it up again. *This com-*
" *mandment I have received of my Father.*"
Chap. xi. verf. 41. *Jefus*, after the act of
reftoring *Lazarus*, addreffes God in thefe
words, " *Father, I thank thee, that thou*
" *haft heard me.*" Chap. xii. verf. 27.
Chrift, after having declared to his difciples
the

the hour was come in which the *Son of man*
fhould be glorified, breaks out into this
doubtful interrogation with himfelf, " Now
" is my foul troubled, and what fhall I fay?
" Father, *fave me* from this hour!—but for
" this caufe, came I unto this hour." *Chrift*,
after declaring to the *Jews* he came not to
judge the world, but to fave it, fubjoins, verf.
49. " For I have not fpoke of myfelf, but
" the Father *which fent me, he gave me com-*
" *mandment* what I fhould fay." Verf. 50.
" And I know that his commandment is
" life everlafting; whatfoever I fpeak there-
" fore, *even as the Father faid unto me*, fo I
" fpeak." Chap. xiv. verf. 28. *Chrift*,
fpeaking to his difciples, " Ye have heard
" how I faid unto you, I go away, and
" come again unto you; if you loved me,
" you would rejoice, becaufe I faid unto
" you, I go to the Father, FOR MY FA-
" THER IS GREATER THAN I." Chap.
xvii. verf. 3. *Chrift*, in the moft folemn in-
vocation to the Deity, fays, " And this is
" life eternal, that they may know THEE,
" THE ONLY TRUE GOD, and *Jefus Chrift*
" whom *thou haft fent.*" He proceeds,
verf. 5. " And now, O Father, *glorify thou*
" *me* with thine own felf, with the glory
" which I had with thee, *before the world*
" *was.*" Chap. xx. verf. 17. in his fhort
difcourfe with *Mary Magdalen*, after his

8   refur-

refurrection, *Chrift* faid unto her, " Touch
" me not, for I am not yet afcended to my
" Father; but go to *my brethren*, and fay un-
" to them, I afcend to *my Father, and your
" Father, to my God, and your God.*" The
divine fcribe clofes this chapter with thefe
words, " But thefe things were written, that
" ye might believe, that *Jefus* is the *Chrift*,
" the Son of God; and that believing ye
" might have life everlafting." And God
of his mercy and fpiritual grace forbid, that
any of us fhould believe otherwife.

62. We are not ignorant of the reveries
of St. *Paul*, nor of the few texts in the firft
chapter of St. *John*'s Gofpel, which feem
to countenance the unintelligible and *Pagan*
rhapfodies of the *Athanafian* Creed; but we
think ourfelves well juftified in deeming
them of little eftimation, when contrafted
with the numerous *ipfe dixits* of *Chrift*, recorded in all the four Gofpels, and more
particularly by the fame Evangelift, all of
which are exprefsly repugnant to fuch a
doctrine; and if thofe texts are to be underftood in the fenfe ufually applied to them,
then this Evangelift witneffeth againft himfelf, in the many texts quoted from him in
our laft paragraph ; and he muft either ftand
felf-condemned of recording contrary doctrines, or we muft conclude his fenfe of
" THE

" THE WORD" has been mifunderftood and
mifapplied; the laft is the moft favorable
fentence that can be paffed upon this infpired writer, and is worth examining below.

63. We purpofely avoid a recital of the
many philofophical arguments, and logical
difcuffions, that have been urged both in the
early days of Chriftianity, and more modern
times, by a multitude of learned pens, in
refutation of the doctrine of a *Trinity in
Unity*, and *Unity in Trinity*, as being not fuited to every common underftanding; and
therefore have ftrictly confined ourfelves to
the lights that every one may receive from
the plain dictates of *Chrift*, who powerfully
and exprefsly enforces to his followers *the
belief* of ONE GOD, *the belief* of his own
miffion, and divine, although inferior, origin, as proceeding from God; and *the belief* of the Holy Ghoft, as the divine attribute, Spirit, or Effence of God, operating
upon all things, and on *all beings*, in the
proportion he is pleafed to infufe or fhed
upon them, and *by which Chrift* himfelf, in
proof of his divine miffion, wrought his ftupendous miracles, always directing the objects of them, " to give the glory *to God
" alone*" by the puiffance of whofe Holy
Spirit he was enabled to accomplifh them.
Thefe doctrines are fublime, yet plain, fimple,

ple, and intelligible; they bear not the femblance of myftery, but are open to a ready
faith: *Chrift* neither deifies himfelf, nor the
Holy Ghoft; the making an *attribute* of the
Deity a God, bears a glaring ftamp of Hea-
thenifm: no rational being would fay, in
an abfolute and literal fenfe, that the *fortitude*, or *chaftity*, or any other virtue of a
King, was the King himfelf, although it
is, in a relative fenfe, a part or quality of
him; nor would any man in his fenfes aver,
that the fon is the father, and the father the
fon, as one individual, when he knows the
fon muft have *proceeded* from the father,
and that the father muft· have *preceded* the
fon, and that therefore they cannot be one;
the contrary belief would be a confounding
of all ideas and things, as well as caufes and
effects, and muft neceffarily fhock all rational faith. Therefore, when *Chrift* fays,
" I am in the Father, and the Father in
" me;—I and my Father are one," &c.
he can be only underftood in a relative fenfe,
to be confiftent with himfelf; for he ever
appears particularly anxious in marking his
character, as a diftinct being from God, in
the relation of a fon to a father; and, at a
moft interefting period, he declares to thofe
who were foon after to be intrufted with the
propagation of his gofpel, " *My Father is*
" *greater than I.*"

64. There-

64. Therefore, fince God has told us, " I am the Lord thy God, thou fhalt have " none other gods but me," and as *Chrift* has alfo told us, there is *only one God*, and *one Son*, which is *Chrift*, and one *Holy Ghoft*; let us abide by, and intrench ourfelves under this ftrong evidence, and for the fake of God, let us, with one accord, ftrike out, not only the *Athanafian* Creed, but every other part of our Liturgy, which fo palpably gives the lie both to God and *Chrift*. We are aware we fhall be told that we utterly miftake the thing, for that the fame Creed teaches, that God the Father, God the Son, and God the Holy Ghoft, thofe *three Gods*, and *no three Gods*, thofe three Subftances under one Effence, thofe three Incomprehenfibles, Co-almighties, Co-equals, and Co-eternals, are but one Incomprehenfible, &c.; and to be worfhipped as ONE GOD. If, after all, this is the cafe, to what end thofe incomprehenfible, contradictory jumble of words and ideas, that have only ferved for fo many centuries to confound, perplex, and puzzle, every common as well as uncommon underftanding, and ftagger the faith of every well-difpofed Chriftian ? not adverting, that *this fenfe* of that Creed flatly contradicts the folemn declaration of *Chrift*, recited at the clofe of our laft paragraph ; for if God the Father be (as he af-

fures

fures us) greater than God the Son, then
God the Son cannot be co-equal, nor have
been co-eternal with him : the Holy Ghoft
may with propriety be faid to have been co-
eternal with God, as being the effence of
the Deity, infeparable from him, but not
co-equal, becaufe every attribute of God is
fubordinate to, and dependent on *his will*.

65. " Glory be to the Father, and to the
" Son, and to the Holy Ghoft;" to this we
fay, Amen: but let us not, like the mifguided church of *Rome, forget God,* by tranf-
ferring that worfhip and adoration to *Chrift*,
and the chofen veffel of his incarnation,
which are only due to *him*, and to his *Holy
Spirit*, his firft and great attribute, to which
Chrift eminently gives pre-eminence over
himfelf, Matth. xii. 31, 32. " Wherefore
" I fay unto you, all manner of fin and
" blafphemy fhall be forgiven unto men;
" but the blafphemy againft the Holy Ghoft
" fhall not be forgiven unto men. And
" whofoever fpeaketh a word *againft the
" Son of man,* it fhall be forgiven him; but
" whofoever fpeaketh againft *the Holy
" Ghoft*, it fhall not be forgiven him, nei-
" ther in this world, nor in the world to
" come." And in this place we cannot do
better, than to endeavor to clear the Evangelift St. *John* from the charge of contra-

diction,

diction, by urging, with all humble deference, the conception which leads us to imagine his term or phrafe " THE WORD" has been mifunderftood, and confequently mifapplied; and that his record, to be confiftent with itfelf, muft allude to *the Holy Ghoft:* and we fubmit it to the candor of every Chriftian, who, with unprejudiced heart and attention, perufes the firft chapter of St. *John's* Gofpel, whether or not every text of that chapter, which has been ufually applied to *Chrift,* may not be more juftly applied to fignify the *Holy Ghoft.* And thus the Gofpel of this infpired writer will ftand unimpeached, which otherwife remains a witnefs againft itfelf, as fhewn in our 62d paragraph.

66. The other various contradictions and evil tendency of the Creed now under confideration (firft eftablifhed by perfecution, fire, and fword), are fo obvious they call for no further comment; its origin only wants to be accounted for, which is no very difficult tafk. SATAN, finding his kingdom on earth muft fall, and come to an end, if the pure doctrines of *the gofpel* obtained univerfally, had no means left to guard againft, and prevent a cataftrophe fo fatal to his power, but exerting his influence to vitiate its pure ftream at the fountain head :

in

in order to this he moſt effectually attach-
ed himſelf and his emiſſaries to the primi-
mitive Chriſtian diſputants, and the reverend
ſaints and *fathers* of the church, as they are
called: theſe he well knew had not tho-
roughly ſhook off from their hearts the impreſſions of the *Grecian* and *Roman* mythology and *Polytheiſm*; on this knowledge he
founded his hopes, and by the event ſhowed
he was no bad politician, for his ſuccefs was
anſwerable to the moſt ſanguine wiſhes of
his bad ſoul, and he ſoon had the malicious
joy of beholding *three gods* ſtart up in the
Chriſtian ſyſtem, in violation of the doctrine
of their divine Leader, who had ſo often
preached to his followers there was but
ONE. It is well known the advantages *Sa-*
tan and Mahomet, and his ſucceſſors, took
of the Polytheiſm introduced into the Chriſtian faith, not only to the downfal and deſtruction of the ſeven churches of *Aſia*, and
the empire of the *Romans*, but alſo to the
obſtructing the univerſal progreſs of Chriſtianity; and we may, with juſt boldneſs
ſay, that had it not been for *that opening*
given to that enterpriſing enemy of our
faith, neither *Mahommed as a prophet*, nor
the Koran as a religion, would ever have
had exiſtence, but the pure doctrines of
Chriſt would have overſhadowed the face
of the earth, and its inhabitants pro-

. bably,

bably, at this day, have been of one only *univerfal church*, unmixed with fchifms, fects, or feparations, to the faving of millions of fouls, and del ges of blood. The ground-work of *Mahommed's* fcriptures was the pure unity of the Godhead. (Koran, chap. iv.) " Surely God will not pardon the " giving him *an equal*; but will pardon any " other fin, *except that*, to whom he plea- " feth : and whofo giveth a *companion* unto " God, hath devifed a great wickednefs." Again, " Say not there are *three gods*; for- " bear *this*, it will be better for you ; God " is but ONE GOD." And upon the efficacy of this divine principle we may conceive, that God permitted the fo amazing and rapid, as well as extenfive progrefs, of *Mahommed's* Koran.

67. Another ftumbling-block to the univerfal propagation of *Chrift's* gofpel, is the fuppofed fupernatural mode of his *conception* and *incarnation*; which fuppofition has afforded a handle to the enemies of Chriftianity, to ftamp it with the imputation of prieft-craft, the fact being only recorded by two of the evangelifts, *Mark* and *John* being entirely filent on the fubject ; and *Chrift* himfelf, in all that ftands recorded of him, gives not the fmalleft intimation of his miraculous or fupernatural conception. Herein

in our free-thinkers outdo *Mahommed*; for, in the xixth chapter of his Koran, he accedes to the fact, and condemns the *Jews* for their difbelief; but we imagine the objectors might, fomehow or other, have arrived at the knowledge, that the miraculous conception of a virgin was a very ancient piece of *Pagan* prieſt-craft; it was firſt introduced by the adulterers of *Bramahs Shaf-tah*, and afterwards adopted by the compilers of the *Viedam*, in the perfon of their *Viſtnoo*; and from this origin might poſſibly defcend to later times. Be this as it may, it is moſt certain, that the ſtupendous example, life, miracles, and doctrines of *Chriſt* ſtood in no need of a myſtery of this nature to prop and give it weight and evidence; and therefore, by adding an incumbrance it did not want, rather weakened, than ſtrengthened the whole fabric of Chriſtianity. Had this myſtery been a neceſſary article of faith to falvation, moſt aſſuredly *Chriſt* himfelf would have given fome intimation of it to his followers: we do not find the miſſion of *Elijah* (who was inveſted by God with powers on earth near equal with *Chriſt*), nor any other of the infpired prophets ſtand impeached, becaufe his or their *conceptions* were according to the natural courfe of generation, then why fhould that of *Chriſt?* So that the objectors gain nothing in the conteſt, fuppoſing we fhould .

give

give up the argument to them: although the conception and birth of *Chriſt* may in one indiſputable ſenſe be truly termed miraculous! when we ſee ſuch an abundant portion of the ſpiritual eſſence of God in *Chriſt*, was thereby ſubjected by his permiſſion to the fleſh, for the ſalvation of mankind; but we truſt we ſhall not offend, when we ſay, the event would not have been leſs miraculous, nor efficacious, had it happened according to the uſual courſe of nature.

68. God forbid it ſhould be thought, from the tenor of theſe our diſquiſitions, that, with *Hobbes, Tindal, Bolingbroke,* and others, our intent is to ſap the foundation, or injure the root of Chriſtianity. Candor and benevolence avert from us ſo uncharitable and ill-grounded an imputation! On the contrary, our ſole aim is *to reſtore* its purity and vigor, by having thoſe luxuriant injurious branches and ſhoots lopped off and pruned, which have ſo obviouſly obſtructed, ſtinted, and prevented its natural, univerſal growth and progreſs; and as we have aſſumed to ourſelves the title of *the reformed church,* by judiciouſly and piouſly abjuring *ſome* of the impious, idolatrous extravagancies and tenets of the church of *Rome,* let us boldly, *in the cauſe of God and his ſupremacy, uniformly* deſerve the character we have aſſumed.

69. From

69. From all that has hitherto been advanced (fupported with what will occafionally follow), three moft important truths may be clearly gathered. Imprimis, that the FIRST and LAST revelation of God's will, that is to fay, the *Hindoo* and the *Chriftian* difpenfation, are the moft perfect that have been promulged to offending man; fecondly, that the FIRST was to a moral certainty the original doctrines, and terms of refloration, delivered from God himfelf by the mouth of his firft created BIRMAH to mankind at his firft creation in the *form of man*; and that, after many fucceffive ages in fin, and every kind of wickednefs, GOD, in his tender mercy, reminded mankind of *their true ftate and nature*, of their *original fin*; and by the defcent of BRAMAH, gave to the *Hindoos the firft written* manifeftation of his will, which (by the common fate of all oral traditions), had moft probably, from various caufes, been effaced from their minds and memories: Thirdly, that every intermediate fyftem of religion in the world between that of BRAMAH and CHRIST are corruptly branched from the *former*, as is to demonftration evident, from their being founded on, and partaking of, with more or lefs purity thofe *primitive truths*. Vide 3d and 4th paragraphs.

70. Let

70. Let us next fee how far the fimili-
tude of doctrines, preached firft by *Bramah*,
and afterwards by *Chrift*, at the diftinct period of above three thoufand years, corro-
borate our conclufions; if they mutually
fupport each other, it amounts to proof of
the authenticity and divine origin of both.
Bramah preached the exiftence of ONE ON-
LY, ETERNAL GOD, his firft created angelic being, BIRMAH, *Biftnoo, Sieb, and Moifafoor*; the *pure* gofpel-difpenfation teaches
ONE ONLY, ETERNAL GOD, his firft begotten of the Father, CHRIST; the angelic beings, *Gabriel, Michael*, and *Satan*, all thefe
correfponding under different names, minutely with each other, in their refpective
dignities, functions, and characters: *Birmah* is made prince and governor of all the
angelic bands, and the occafional vicegerent
of the *Eternal One*; *Chrift* is invefted with
all power by the *Father*; *Birmah* is deftined
to works of power and glory, fo is *Chrift*;
Biftnoo to acts of benevolence, fo is *Gabriel*;
Sieb to acts of terror and deftruction, fo is
Michael; the Holy Ghoft is exprefsly figni-
fied in *Brum*, the Spirit or Effence of GOD,
abundantly difplayed in all the operations
and behefts of the Eternal ONE. The
Shaftah of *Bramah* records the rebellion of
a portion of the angelic hoft, and their expulfion from heaven; the fact is alfo inculcated

cated by the gofpel; *Moifafoor* is reprefented as a prime angel, and the inftigator and
leader of the revolt in heaven, fo is the *Satan* of the gofpel; *minifiering angels*, or the
interpofition of the heavenly beings in human affairs, is a principle of *Bramah's* Shaftah, fo it is of the gofpel-difpénfation; the
neceffary duties of *repentance, good works,
univerfal love, and charity*, are indifpenfably
enjoined in the Shaftah, fo they are in the
gofpel inftitutes; but in a more forcible, elaborate, and eminent degree, as being the
laft and moft perfect miffion that God in his
mercy delivered to man. The immortality
of the foul, and its future ftate of rewards
and punifhments, are fundamentals of the
Shaftah, fo they are of the gofpel; that
man is here in a *ftate* of *purgation, punifhment*, and *trial*, is alfo a fundamental of the
Shaftah, fo it is of the gofpel, fupported by
the opinions of the moft learned divines and
philofophers. That man is doomed to *this
ftate*, for an unhappy LAPSE in a PRE-EX-
ISTENT ONE, is another fundamental of the
Shaftah, and is evidently implied in the gofpel. See the Rev. Mr. Berrow's Treatife
on that fubject before alluded to in our 40th
paragraph. The neceffity of *mediators* between God and man, and voluntary facrifices for the tranfgeffions of the latter in the
perfons of *Birmah, Biftnoo*, and *Sieb*, and
others

others of the faithful angelic hoſt, are doctrines of the Shaſtah; and are all fully com-
priſed in the goſpel, by the ſole voluntary
ſacrifice of CHRIST, our conſtant *Mediator.*
That there is an intermediate ſtate of *puniſhment* and *purification* between death and the
perfect reſtoration of the human ſoul, is a
poſitive tenet of the Shaſtah, and is countenanced by the goſpel, notwithſtanding the
church of *Rome* makes ſo bad a uſe of the
firſt, in their ſyſtem of purgatory. God's
general providence over his whole creation,
is an expreſs doctrine of the Shaſtah; and
his *particular providence* over individuals is
obviouſly *implied,* from its doctrine of the
viſible, or inviſible miniſtration and inter-
poſition of the angelic beings in human affairs; theſe are alſo fundamental dogmas of
the Chriſtian ſyſtem.

71. The compariſon might be extended
to a much greater length, but the above,
we think, will ſuffice to prove, that the
miſſion of Chriſt is the ſtrongeſt confirmation
of the authenticity and divine origin of the
Chartah Bhade Shaſtah of Bramah; and that
they *both* contain all *the great primitive
truths* in their original purity that conſti-
tuted *the firſt* and *univerſal religion;* and that
the very ancient ſcriptures now under our conſideration, exhibit alſo the ſtrongeſt conviction

tion of the truth of the celeftial origin of *Chrift's* miffion. Yet the former is the fyftem of divinity and ethics which the Critical Reviewers have indifcriminately (as a fpecimen of their candor, erudition, and penetration) ftigmatifed with the opprobrious epithets of " *nonfenfe, rhapfodies,* and *abfurdities;*" and in proof of their *profound judgment,* they unfaithfully took the liberty of re-printing our fecond part, *without* the errata prefixed to the 1ft page, by which defigned omiffion, they indeed circulate nonfenfe enough *of their own making*; but, requefting our readers pardon for beftowing fo many lines upon a matter fo little worth our notice, we will purfue our fubject.

72. In two points of doctrine the Hindoo and the Chriftian fyftem differ (but the one in mode only), 1*ft,* The punifhment of the damned, or thofe fouls that fhall remain reprobate at the diffolution of the univerfe, or expiration of their *term of probation.* 2*dly,* The refurrection of the fame body. Touching the firft, *the Shaftah* teaches, that thofe reprobate fpirits fhall be caft out, and languifh *for ever in intenfe darknefs,* in a particular region prepared for them; *the Gofpel,* that they fhall perifh everlaftingly in *actual fire.* Without difcuffing the point how, or by what mode of

action

action fire will operate on spiritual beings;
we will only say, that possibly the latter sentence may act more *in terrorem*, than in the
other; not that we think there is a pin to
chuse between them, nor that the matter
of difference is of much importance, whilst
they both agree in the fundamental point,
that those unhappy delinquents will be given
over to everlasting punishment.

73. Touching the second, which is a
matter of deeper concernment to be clear
in, the Hindoo system teaches, that the
corporeal part, or prison of the soul or spirit, being composed of the four elements,
each again receives *its part* at the dissolution
of the body, or death; and that the spirit,
according to its *merits* or *demerits*, is either
conveyed to the first region of purification,
or punished for a space, and doomed to enter and animate another corporeal form, body, or prison, that shall be prepared for its
reception. The Christian system, without
giving us any lights touching the state or
existence of the soul or spirit, during the
long intermediate space between death and
the day of judgment, says, that at that day
the graves shall give up their dead, and that
there shall be a *resurrection of the same body*,
to which its soul shall be re-united, and both
receive judgment. By both these systems
the

the doctrines of future judgment, rewards and punifhments, are clearly revealed to us, but with this difference, that the Hindoo dogma pronounces, as we may fay, a *daily judgment* of the foul (for multitudes are fubject to death each revolving fun), as well as a final one, and the Chriftian poftpones it to the day of refurrection, leaving the foul during the intermediate ftate to exift——the Lord knows where. The refurrection of the *fame body* is a doctrine obvioufly repugnant to the Hindoo fyftem.

74. The refurrection of *Chrift*, or the re-union of his fpirit to the body on the third day, is a ftupendous proof of his divine miffion, for he had *before declared*, " He had power to lay down his life, and " had power to take it up again; for that " commandment (or power) he had receiv- " ed from the Father." But this fingle inftance, peculiar to *Chrift*, does not, we conceive, countenance the general doctrine, as ftated above, which is far from being univerfally believed or received; many learned pens have been drawn againft it, and many texts of fcripture urged in oppofition, befides unfurmountable arguments and difficulties that we have to encounter, which ftagger the ftrongeft faith; fuch as the ftate and exiftence of the foul during the fpace above

hinted

hinted at; the confideration that matter, of which the body is compofed, being in its nature paffive and inactive, cannot be the object of either rewards or punifhment. But the *fpirit alone*, which is the active, deferving, or offending part, can be the only object of judgment; the *non-identity* of the body (if we may be allowed the expreffion), which continues not the *fame body* one hour together, will have its full force on every rational mind, notwithftanding the fpecious cafuiftry of a *Liebnitz* and *Locke* to invalidate the objection. How far the Metempfychofis of *Bramah* will folve thefe problems, and how far that doctrine will be fupported by the gofpel-difpenfation, will appear when we come clofer to that main fpring of all our movements.

75. From what has been advanced in our 70th, and part of our 71ft paragraph, we find that Chriftianity is, *bona fide*, *as old as the creation*, although in a very different fenfe from that of the libertine freethinker, who publifhed, fome years fince, a labored treatife to undermine the gofpel-difpenfation, under that title : yet, let us not, although it fprings from a truly learned and pious zeal, pretend *to prove*, that " the want " of univerfality is no objection to the Chri-" ftian religion," by bringing *a chain of events,*

events, taken upon truft, from a fpurious eaftern fcripture, as applicable to the conception, birth, miracles, and death of *Chrift,* that are utterly deftitute of true chronology to fupport it, left it fhould give a handle to freethinkers of the complection juft mentioned to fay, that the Chriftian fyftem is only a copy of an *eaftern fable,* as one of the Popes of the church of *Rome* is recorded to have faid, or fomething like it. That the circumftances attending the walk of *Chrift* on earth have been tranfmitted to the Eaft we do not difpute, but that they could ftand recorded in an eaftern fcripture, which was compiled fome thoufands of years before *Chrift's* appearance in *Judea,* is not poffible : the facts could not be before they had exiftence. But the misfortune is, that in difquifitions of this nature we are generally too apt *to prove too much,* and thereby hurt the caufe we are laboring to defend. Had the learned and revered fupporter of Chriftianity whom we allude to above, extended his view, and been acquainted with, the original *Chartah Bhade of Bramah,* he would have found that it is a fundamental doctrine of that fcripture, that the angelic beings, prior to the *Kolee Joque* or age of corruption, frequently defcended to the earth, and voluntarily fubjected themfelves

to

to undergo the eighty-eight tranfmigrations
to animate the form of man, thereby to
guard him from a fecond feduction of *Moifafoor* or *Satan*; that even *Birmah*, *Biftnoo*,
and *Sieb*, did not exempt themfelves from
thofe voluntary facrifices.

76. This being premifed, it is no violence
to faith, if we believe that *Birmah* and
Chrift is one and the fame individual cœleftial being, the firft begotten of the Father,
who has moft probably appeared at *different*
periods of time, in *diftant* parts of the
earth, under *various* mortal forms of humanity, and denominations : thus we may very rationally conceive, that it was by the
mouth of *Chrift* (ftiled *Birmah* by the eaft-
erns), that God delivered the *great primitive
truths* to man at his creation, as infallible
guides for his conduct and *reftoration :* but
the purity of *thefe truths* being effaced by
time, and the induftrious influence of *Satan*, affifted by the natural unhappy bent of
the human foul to evil, it became neceffary
that they fhould be given on *record* to a nation that was moft probably at that period
much more extenfive than we can at prefent
form any idea of ; and it appears as near to
demonftration as a circumftance of this nature can admit of, that it was owing to this
divine

divine revelation delivered *to them*, that this people acquired so justly that early reputation for wisdom and theology, which the whole learned world has ascribed to them: but this by the bye.

77. The *same causes* subsisting, the above *truths* soon lost *again*, their original purity and simplicity, and a multitude of different *religious systems* were propagated through the world, having more or less (as intimated paragraph 3d) of *these truths* for a basis, according to the bent and genius of men, and talents of the first impostors that broached them, excited and furthered possibly, also, by the adventitious circumstances of air, soil, climate, situation, regimen, &c. By this deviation, wickedness continued to gather increase through every region of the earth, but still the mercy and forbearance of God was not exhausted; for in the fulness of time, *as his last grace*, he *once more* delegated his first begotten son, under the mortal form of JESUS, to *restore these truths* to their full primitive lustre, and pitched upon *Judea* as a proper center from whence the beams of the *Sun of righteousness* should be scattered, and spread over the face of the whole world. How the universality of this intended stupendous blessing was prevented, we have already shewn in

part, and ſhall more fully hereafter; obſerv-
ing that the genuine ſcriptures of *Bramah*
and *Chriſt* have ſhared the ſame fate, mutilated and betrayed by thoſe who were appointed the guardians and ſupporters of them.
We ſhall cloſe this paragraph with a ſug-
geſtion that appears to us moſt probable and
rational, *viz.* that *every individual* of the
angelic beings who have occaſionally viſited
the earth, under the mortal form of humanity, either by ſpecial voluntary licence, or
ſpecial appointment of God, for the example, defence, admonition, comfort, and
correction of mankind, have *each* aſſumed
different forms and names, at different ſucceeding times, in different regions; in ſuch
wiſe as *Elijah* and St. *John* the Baptiſt is
ſuppoſed by ſome to have been one and the
ſame ſpirit, from the intimation of the prophet *Malachi.* (Vide part the ſecond, pages
71 and 72.)

78. In our laſt paragraph we promiſed to
ſhew more fully how the bleſſings of the goſpel were converted into a curſe, as the prophetic ſpirit of *Chriſt* foretold it would be,
from his obſervation of the general corruption and incorrigibility of the human ſoul;
for otherwiſe it would not have been poſ-
ſible that his plain dictates could have been
miſtaken, or perverted to any other purpoſes

pofes than he benevolently defigned them :
but he had hardly left his followers to themfelves, than religious diffentions took place,
that blafted all his hopes, and rendered his
miffion of none effect ; fo that, within the
fpace of a very few centuries, and almoft as
foon as they had affumed to themfelves the
general name of Chriftians, he faw, with
heart-felt grief, his plain, fimple, and divine doctrine fplit into more jarring fects
and fchifms than any religious fyftem had
fuffered fince the creation.

79. *Chrift* had preached, as effential pre-
liminaries to the falvation of his followers *in
a future life,* peace, charity, and mutual
love *in this.* But the differing fects of Chriftians thought it more available to whirl
damnation at each other's head; and in
place of thofe godlike virtues, to fubftitute
hatred, revenge, and perfecution ; fome
conftrued particular texts of fcripture lite- .
rally, others allegorically, others fymboli-
cally ; and fome broached, as Chriftian doctrines, diabolical fyftems, which rafhly favored of that Paganifm from which they
had been fo lately reclaimed and converted;
and each thought themfelves warranted *by
thofe very fcriptures of peace,* to cut the
throat, for God's fake, of every one who did
not fubfcribe to their opinions : witnefs the

ever memorable and bloody contests between the early bishops of the church, about
the establishment of the *Athanasian* Creed,
and the contention for supremacy between
the *Greek* and *Latin* churches, which came
to a drawn battle at last; as also in later
times, the unchristian and inhuman difputes between the Romanists and Prote-
stants, each exerting their infernal spirit of
persecution, as power afforded them the
means; a contest in which deluges of blood
have been spilt, and are spilling to this
hour, infomuch that we may justly aver,
lamentable as the truth is, that there exists
not upon the face of the Christian world,
more than ONE SECT of mankind, who
preserve *any appearance* of having a true
claim to the title of Christians. Here our
readers cannot be at a loss to know, that we
mean that respectable body of people, commonly, although ludicrously, stiled QUA-
KERS, a people that in their principles and
practice do honour to primitive Christiani-
ty and humanity. But, to resume the
thread of our subject, and analize in few
words (as necessary to our main view) the
causes, nature, and progress of the last-
mentioned contest between Christians (no-
minally so) originally of the same church,
although an idolatrous and superstitious one:

8o. After

80. After the feparation of the *Greek*
and *Latin* churches, the laft fupported her
fupremacy in the Weft for fome ages; at
length avarice and tyrannic exactions (and
partial favor fhewn to one fet of monks in
the collection of thofe exactions), in the
Pope; fpiritual pride, refentment, revenge,
and an affectation of fingularity in the brcafls
of *Luther* and *Calvin*; and luft and wrath
againft the Pope in the heart of our Harry
VIII. brought about *a partial Reformation of the Chriftian church.* Thus God
fometimes works out his purpofes *of good,*
by moft *evil* tools. This defertion gave a
" perilous gafh to the body of the church
" of *Rome,* and many a profitable limb was
" lopt off," and loft, never to be recovered.
But *Luther* and *Calvin,* not according to
the principles and modes of Reformation,
became the leaders of two oppofite religious Proteftant factions, with about an
equal number of profelytes, who foon began
to harbor as mutual and cordial a hatred,
and unchriftian-like animofity againft each
other, as they both bore to their mother
church of *Rome :* then *bifhops* and *no bifhops*
proved the fource of frefh. bloody, and
cruel contefts. Spiritual pride, joined to
temporal political maxims, have kept alive
an unceafing rancour in the hearts of thofe
two Proteftant fects, that muft ever keep
them

them afunder, although nothing is eafier to
be effected than a union, were it poffible
to bring them back to Chriftianity, from
which they have *both* fwerved in principle
and practice; whilft *Rome* is not without
her hopes from thefe divifions, and waits a
favorable conjuncture to re-unite them to
the bofom of her church, either by force,
or fraud, or both; an alarming event!
which poffibly may not be fo far diftant as
fome fondly imagine. But the feuds and
differences between the *Lutherans* and *Cal-
vinifts* hurt the caufe of *Chrift* ftill more
deeply; for many of each perfuafion, obferving the eafy fuccefs of thofe leaders, and
how glorious and profitable it was to become the head, the *primum mobile* of a fect,
deferted again their colours, and fetting up
for themfelves, formed innumerable *fubdivifions of faith*, under various *independent
denominations*; and each leader had his followers. Thus old herefies were revived, and
new ones inftituted, and fanaticifm of every
abfurd and extravagant fpecies had a quick
and dangerous growth; each fect audaci-
oufly affirming, from the fame fcriptures,
that theirs, and theirs only, was the true
orthodox fai h, and the right road to falvation: yet, with fuch doctrines, they brought
the head of a good, moral, and pious, but
mifguided

mifguided Prince, to the block, and over-
turned the conftitution of a kingdom.

81. Such is the whole prefent ftate of
Chrift's church *militant* here on this weftern
earth; and the above, added to fome *before
noted*, are the reproachful fatal caufes that
have obftructed and utterly choked the
univerfal growth and progrefs of the gofpel;
and hence we are urged, by a fpirit of true
benevolence to mankind, to promulge the
following reflections :

82. During our non-age, we naturally
receive and adopt the notions and principles
inftilled by our parents and teachers; but
when man arrives at maturity, he will as
naturally affert his great privilege of reafon,
and think for himfelf. But what muft be
the confufion and perplexity of his reflections and ideas, when he begins the neceffary inquiry after TRUTH, in fo effential a
matter as the worfhip of his GOD ? when
he finds, we fay (in what is vainly and fal-
lacioufly called a Chriftian country), every
Chriftian church divided againft itfelf, and
the profeffors of Chriftianity purfuing each
other with concealed or open execrations,
malice, and all uncharitablenefs, that mifguided zeal, temporal interefted views, or
enthufiaftic rage can poffibly dictate. Thus

G 4 circum-

circumftanced, *a thinking being* has no re-
fource, but *either* totally to abjure Chriftianity, *or* to endeavour to work out his own
falvation, according to the lights which
pure fcripture, and his own unbiafed *reafon*
affords him, without adhering to any one
Chriftian church or fyftem whatfoever as
now profeffed in any part of the world, as
they have *one and all* proved defective, and
inefficacious to cement the bands of mutual
love, charity, forbearance, and peace a-
mongft men; which relative duties are the
quinteffence, the *fine qua non* of the gofpel-
difpenfation. But——as the *different* inter-
pretations of the fame fcriptures have been
the great, the mifchievous caufe of the numerous jarring fects of Chriftians (the leaders of each drawing a miffive weapon from
the fame text); and as the fatal effects of
thefe fects and fchifms in Chriftianity have
been truly diabolical in every inch of *Europe*
(infomuch that a ftander-by might be well
excufed if he was induced to think the Devil
himfelf had been the author of it, in place
of God), we muft go farther, and utterly
reject all that has been written by the apoftles and difciples, and every paraphrafe,
expofition, and vifionary doctrine that has
been tortured from them, *except* the exprefs
declarations and *doctrines* which fell from
the mouth of *Chrift himfelf*, as they ftand
recorded

recorded in the four Gofpels: by thefe let us abide, be thefe the *ſtandard of our faith*, and ſheet anchor of *our hope*, and thefe *only*. His language is plain, his words cannot be *miſ-interpreted*, nor perverted to different meanings; he ſpeaks to the level of every underſtanding, as well as to the heart, and cannot be miſunderſtood. To this it may be objected by freethinkers, that herein we are ſtill at no certainty that thefe goſpels were penned after *Chriſt*'s aſcenſion; that poſſibly thoſe his declarations and doctrines may not have been faithfully recorded; that we ſtill take them upon truſt, &c. To this we anſwer, and lay our appeal to the *doctrines themſelves*; then let every one who doubts knock at his breaſt, and ſay, if he can, from the *conviction* of his own heart, that ſuch doctrines, conſidered as a ſyſtem of theology and ethics, are not of divine origin. Let this be the text, and ſceptics will no longer have exiſtence.

83. *Oh Man! Oh Chriſtian!* Emperors, Kings, Princes, Potentates, and Powers; Rulers, and Leaders, under whatſoever denomination of Chriſtians you have continued to diſgrace thofe *originally reſpectable names*, whether Papiſt or Proteſtant, Lutheran or Calviniſt, &c. &c. no longer ſuffer to be *ſeverally* applied to you that prediction

diction which *Chrift* applied to the *hardened Jews*, refpecting his perfecuted apoftles,
" Yea, the time cometh, that whofoever
" *killeth you*, will think he doeth God fer-
" vice;"——no longer, we fay, adopt fuch
an impious doctrine and fuppofition (for
herein you are worfe than the *Jews*, for
you *pretend* to believe in *Chrift* and his
doctrines, which they did not) but mutually labor to re-eftablifh peace on earth, and
harmony in heaven, by reftoring *once more*
the true fpirit of thofe *primitive truths*,
which were, as the *firft* and *laft* grace of
GOD, delivered to you at your creation originally by BIRMAH, and fubfequently by
CHRIST, *the one and the fame individual, firft
begotten of the Father*, as before fuggefted.
Our candid reader will now fee the neceffity
we were under of analifing the *modern Chriftian tenets and practice*, and of expofing the
fatal innovations that brought it firft into
difrepute, and that ftill continue to obftruct
its univerfality : we are fenfible that we
hereby lay ourfelves open to the cenfure of
fuperficial thinkers, who will be ready e-
nough, although unjuftly, to accufe us of
Deifm, according to the common accepta-
tion of the phrafe; but, as we think we
have as indifputable a right as Dr. *Clarke*
or others, to extend or give *a new* fignification to the word *Deift*, fo we pronounce,
that

that a man may, with ftrict propriety, be
an orthodox Chriftian Deift ; that is, that he
may, *confiftently*, have a firm faith in *the
unity of the Godhead, and in the pure and original doctrines of Chrift.* In this fenfe alone
we glory in avowing ourfelf—A CHRISTIAN
DEIST.

84. Having thus fubmitted to our intelligent readers all that we thought neceffary
to the elucidation of our Firft General
Head, to wit, the exiftence, the rebellion,
the expulfion and punifhment of the apoftate angels, according to the minute hiftory of that great and fatal event, given in
the *Chartah Bhade of Bramah,* from which
all antiquity borrowed their conceptions of
this effential piece of knowledge, and which
alfo ftands confirmed by the gofpel-difpenfation ; and having likewife, occafionally,
as we purpofed, drawn fome (we hope)
ufeful and moft neceffary conclufions and
doctrines, from the comparifon between
thofe two divine fcriptures, the courfe of
our purfuit leads us to the inveftigation of
our Second General Head, *" The creation of
" the univerfe,* for the reception and refi-
" dence of the expelled angels, after their
" emerging from the *Onderah,* or place of
" *intenfe darknefs,* into which they had been

3   " precipi-

" precipitated, upon their expulfion from
" heaven."

SECOND GENERAL HEAD.

85. The eternity, or non-eternity of
matter (a queftion which exercifed the
brains of *Plato*, *Ariftotle*, *Epicurus*, and
others of the ancients and moderns to little
purpofe), is a fubject, the difcuffion of
which would be foreign to our defign; but
the eternity of the *world*, which fome philofophers have held as a principle deduced
from the pofition of the eternity of matter,
is furely one of the greateft, of the moft
daring, and inconfiflent extravagancies of
the ancients; a conclufion, that is neither
fupported by found philofophy, reafon, or
probability. Nor is it lefs extravagant in
man, to fuppofe, that this world, and all
that is in it, was made for him; that is, if
we confider him in the light in which he
feems (by the whole tenor of his actions) to
view himfelf, the mufhroom of a day. And
indeed it fhould alfo feem, that man, from
his blind and thoughtlefs eftimation of the
world, was likewife perfectly convinced,
that he himfelf *was made only for it*. With
this grovelling conception of his nature and
origin,

origin, it is no wonder that his purfuits fhould be adequate, and difgrace his intellectual faculties. Man is a free agent, and *may fay* whatfoever he pleafes to amufe himfelf; he may plume himfelf in afferting the immortality of his foul, his fuperior form, and intellectual powers, in comparifon with the reft of the animal creation: he *may alfo fay*, that he looks up to a life beyond this, a future life of rewards and punifhments;—but we maintain againft him, that he neither *believes* the one or the other; facts ftare him in the face and refute him, his daily practice contradict his words, and prove his attachments and views are folely limited to, and circumfcribed by the folicitudes and fenfual indulgences of *this world*, which, with all its annexed appurtenances, he arrogantly and prefumptuoufly conceits was made for his ufe and—abufe. Strange and irrational conceit, for a being thus circumftanced!

86. In combating and difavowing the poffibility of man's firm faith in the *primitive truths* juft above fpecified; we think we pay the higheft, the moft favorable compliment and conftruction to his underftanding and conduct, that is in our power; for if he really and truly *believes*, and ferioufly thinks himfelf entitled to hold that fuperior

rank

rank in the fcale of terreftrial beings, by virtue of his fuperior intellectual powers and faculties, and ftill degrades and debafes himfelf, by the perverfion of thofe bleffings, below the level of the brute; fo much the more deplorable is his ftate: nonbelief affords fome plea, as faith is not always within the compafs of our reach; but to fay we *truely believe*, and ftill perfift in evil, leaves us without excufe : therefore we repeat, that our judgment is more favorable to man, when we pronounce, *He does not believe*, than to fay *he does*; and the only apology that can be framed for him, either in the one cafe, or the other, is *the ignorance* he ftands in of *his real ftate on earth*, and the nature of his relative obligations *as man,* which we now purpofe to *elucidate*, for his prefent benefit, and his future felicity. In the profecution of this our benevolent purfuit, we again invoke the affiftance of that Being, WHO CAN ALONE ENLIGHTEN US.

87. We have fhewn, that man cannot rationally or confiftently flatter himfelf, that this world was made for him only, upon the footing of his *commonly fuppofed* exiftence. In truth, did not a vain pride and partiality obfcure his reafon and his optics, he would perceive, that the world was made for the fly, as much as for him; the former

mer

mer poffeffing every fenfual enjoyment fuited to his rank in the fcale of beings, in as
full perfection as mere man can boaft of :
but——if he extends his profpect, looks
higher, and conceives of himfelf, as he truly
is (according to the fcriptures of *Bramah)*
one of thofe very identical cœleftial fpirits
that were banifhed heaven, he may then erect
his head, and without offence either to
modefty or probability, think the world, and
every comfortable production of it, *was
made for him*, as moft affuredly it was.
Here we difcover a moft noble caufe, worthy of THE ETERNAL ONE, for fo ftupendous a creation, as that of the univerfal
planetary fyftem : the angels had finned,
they were degraded, they were fallen; but
—ftill they were angels, and immortal!
and had borne a glorious rank in heaven!
and it affords the higheft illuftration of
God's mercy, that when he was moved to
mitigate their punifhment, and give them
an opportunity of regaining their loft fcats
in a *ftate of probation* ; that he, with fuch
infinite powers and wifdom fhould conftruct
fo wonderful an edifice as this world for
their reception and refidence, befitting a
race of cœleftials, although in a ftate of degradation; for fuch undoubtedly was the
face of the commonly called antediluvian
earth,

earth, when a fecond defection made T H E
E T E R N A L ONE juftly determine it was too
good for them ; and was provoked to leave
it at the deluge, or fome other equally
tremendous fhock, as we now find it.

88. How the angelic beings, deftined to
inhabit the other regions or planets of the
extended univerfe, continued to deferve this
exalted grace of their Creator, or what
changes they may have juftly undergone,
GOD only knows; but refpecting this our
globe, *bad as it is*, we may (without any
breach of Chriftian charity) aver, it is ftill
abundantly better than we merit ; and fhould
it grow worfe and worfe, and lefs comfortable, (which appears to have been the cafe
for fome centuries back in every region of
the earth, by remarkable variations of feafons, frequency of earthquakes, ftorms,
inundations, &c. &c.) ftill the juftice of
God ftands unimpeached, by the increafe
of fin, and continuance of reprobation. After all, in this world of natural evils, *rational man*, if he looked up to his divine
Origin, and moved confiftently thereto,
might fpin out, in a very comfortable exiftence, *his deftined term of probation*, and
fecure to himfelf felicity here and hereafter ;
fo that in truth it is no bad world, but as
we

we ourfelves make it fo; and blind, infatuated Man, as if he thought the *natural
evils* of this world were not fufficient,
feems refolved to exert · thofe intellectual
powers that were given him for very different purpofes, to make up the deficiency by
the addition of *moral ones* ; thereby exceed-
ing the meafure of his punifhments to a degree that God never intended he fhould fuffer. But to illuftrate farther the tenor of
our four laft paragraphs by way of expofition on the text of *Bramah.*

89. Learned philofophers and divines
have been deeply puzzled and perplexed,
how to reconcile the juftice of God with
the creation of a rational being *out of nothing*, or from matter, yet fubject to natural and moral evils; and apparently, from
every confideration of his exiftence (from
the cradle to the grave viewed under the
moft favorable afpect), placed here in a ftate
of fucceffive punifhments which he cannot
poffibly *as mere man* have deferved, by any
adequate tranfgreffion committed during
his prefent ftate of exiftence; for his punifhments commence with his birth, and
purfue him through infancy, periods during
which neither his corporeal or mental powers can be fuppofed capable of tranfgreffion

H   or

or fin. Thus the juftice of God muft ever
ftand arraigned, if the pofition *refts there*;
but—the very confideration *that God is and
muft be juft*, tells us that cannot be the fact;
and that therefore there muft have been a
prior, fome anterior caufe, for fuch (otherwife unmerited) punifhments. But when?
where? The anfwer is obvious and indifputable——in fome antecedent ftate of the
foul's exiftence; this truth, natural reafon
and the laws of common juftice convince us
of, without the affiftance of the many texts
of fcripture advanced by the ingenious Mr.
Berrow to prove the *pre-exiftent lapfe of the
human foul:* to which we may add an argument drawn from the immortality of the
foul; for if the foul is immortal, ánd neceffarily exifts in a feparate ftate after the
diffolution of the body, it muft have neceffarily exifted *fomewhere* before its union to
it, unlefs we fuppofe God is employed in a
daily, we may fay hourly, creation of fouls;
an opinion not lefs extravagant than the
fuppofed eternity of the world, an opinion
that would ftill leave the juftice of God in
the fame predicament liable to impeachment.

90. Although a pre-exiftent ftate, and
lapfe of the human foul, are doctrines that
have

have been avowed by all antiquity, and by many learned moderns (fee the authorities produced by the Reverend Mr. *Berrow*), yet a difficulty remained of what nature that ftate and lapfe was? This embarraffment can only be accounted for by mankind having, in procefs of time, utterly loft the remembrance of thofe *pr.mitive truths*, which clearly laid open to him *his real ftate and nature*, both in his prefent and pre-exiftent ftate. Some have endeavored to folve the difficulty, by fuppofing that man was created *to fill up the vacant feats* in heaven, and that his lapfe or crime was, *his wickedly affociating with the apoftate angels*, in place of aiming at the poffeffion of their feats : but this round-about fuppofition leaves the difficulty juft where it found it, and gives an opening ftill to arraign the juftice of God. But Mr. *George Ilive* came moft certainly nearer the mark (howfoever he came to hit it), in pronouncing " that the fouls or fpi-" rits of men are the identical apoftate an-" gels themfelves," without knowing that he was fupported in fuch a conclufion by the moft ancient divine fcripture that had been delivered to the inhabitants of this globe : here then we are to look up for the pre-exiftent ftate and lapfe of the human foul, *the original fin* in the *angelic fall*, typified by *Mofes* in his hiftory of the *fall of man* ;

H 2   and

and hence is every one " born in fin, the " children of wrath," and hence only is the juftice of God reconcilable with his creation of man at all; a creation, which by this hypothefis highly exalts and illuftrates, not only his JUSTICE, but his MERCY.

91. And here, candid reader, fuffer us, from the feelings of a general philanthropy that warms our bofom, to congratulate our fellow-creatures upon the reftoration and recovery of this great, this effential, this divine truth, fo long loft to our remembrance. A *primitive truth*, which enlightens mankind with the knowledge of their *real ftate*, the true relation in which they ftand towards their God and Creator, and the relative duties which they owe to the fpecies in general, from all which they have deeply and dangeroufly fwerved for a feries of ages paft, from ignorance of their *original dignity*, *original fin*, and the nature and terms of their earthly fojourn: to that ignorance alone (and to the ready bent of the human foul to evil in confequence of it) muft be afcribed the fmall efficacy which the preaching and doctrines of *Chrift* has had upon the world; the feed was good, but fown in unprofitable ground, and although it was not poffible to inculcate the neceffary doctrines of *the love of God*, and

of

of our neighbor *as ourselves*, in stronger terms than *Christ* enforced thofe duties; yet men still perfevere in plundering, oppreffing, perfecuting, and butchering one another without mercy, in open violation of all that is good or holy. The truth is, *man knew not himfelf*, nor the relation he stood in to his God and neighbor, although, had he diligently fearched the fcriptures, he would therein have found full fatisfaction in both, either exprefsly, or by plain and direct implication. *David* feems to have been very clear in his conceptions touching his own pre-exiftent ftate, as well as that of his *Ifraelites*, when he pathetically addreffes his God in thefe words of his xcth pfalm, " Lord, thou haft been *our* refuge, " from one generation to another, *before* " *the mountains were brought forth, or even* " *the earth and the world were made.*" Now, as all mankind are unanimous in opinion, that there was no creation of beings prior to the creation of the *earth and world* (or the univerfe) but that of the angels, fo it is plain he could allude to no other; the inference is obvious—*David* and the *Ifraelites* were the apoftate angels. And in truth that moft remarkable, and feemingly incomprehenfible favor and partiality which God in a long feries of events manifeftly fhewed to that race of people, can be only

accounted

accounted for, by their having been one of *the leaſt* offending of the angelic tribes, drawn off from their allegiance, not by the pride and malice of the heart, but probably from the influence and impulſes of a divine love and friendſhip for ſome of the other re⹁ volted tribes : thus the ſuppoſed *partial favor* of God *to that people* no longer remains a charge againſt our eternal IMPARTIAL JUDGE, nor that he ſhould not have, from the ſame cauſe, his *choſen* and *elect* of other nations. And here we cannot help entering into a ſhort expoſtulation with mankind upon their univerſal evil treatment of that once favorite people of God, the *Jewiſh* race, who are the common butt of oppreſſion in all nations; we brand them with the epithets of *fraudulent* and *infamous,* whilſt the cruel hardſhips every ſtate impoſes on them, lays them under a fatal neceſſity of perpetrating vices for their own defence and ſecurity, and to retaliate in ſome meaſure the injuſtice they everywhere labor under.——Religion and humanity would think and ſay, it is enough that they are outcaſts, and ſcattered over the face of the earth, without rule or domain; let us not therefore burden them with greater grie⹁ vances than they can, or than God intended they ſhould, bear :——had thoſe who profeſſed themſelves Chriſtians, been truly

ſo,

fo, it is more than probable there would not at this day be one *Jew* exifting in the world. But what encouragement can any of that tribe have to forfake his errors, or enter into the fold of Chriftianity, when they fee themfelves from age to age op-preffed, hunted, and their fubftance de-voured by the *Chriftian wolves* of every ftate, in direct violation of the gofpel they profefs.——Although God has been pleafed to difperfe them, we are told *on good autho-rity* he has not abandoned them; and we know not how far the evil treatment of that people may have been, and ftill is, one (amongft many others) of the great caufes of the calamitous figns of God's difpleafure, in his fignal vifitations for a long feries paft to every Chriftian ftate under one tremendous form or other; for we think, refpecting the evil ufage of that forlorn unhappy race, no ftate in Chriften-dom is exempt.

92. Having thus, we truft, fuccefsfully fhewn to the higheft moral certainty, that the univerfe was conftructed by God for the reception, refidence, and fuftenance of the apoftate angelic tribes; and that mankind are the very identical remains of thofe un-purified fpirits, who have not as yet re-gained their loft feats, we haften to the con-

clufion

clufion of this our Second General Head, requefting only that our candid reader will accompany us in the contemplation of that fublime picture of the human fpecies, as drawn by our great mafter of reafon and nature, *Shakefpeare*, from the mouth of his *Hamlet*——" What a work " is man! how noble in nature! how infi-" nite in faculty! in form and moving how " expreffive and admirable! in act like an " angel! in comprehenfion like a god!" ——Now fay, reader, can fuch a being be aught lefs than angel? Surely no.——Angel he muft be, and an apoftate one, or we pronounce he is——nothing. Indeed there are many movements and emotions of the human foul, that are utterly inexplicable but upon this hypothefis, as, fudden and inftantaneous violent love, friendfhip, antipathy, diflike, hatred, &c. *at firft fight*; which can only fpring from a fympathetic fenfation of the fpirit's prior knowledge or intimacy in their angelic pre-exiftent ftate. *One* of the great comforts of a departing foul in death, and of thofe that furvive, who are mutually dear to each other, is the hope, that their fpirits will foon be re-united, in a future ftate of lafting blifs, which here is only imperfect and tranfitory: but fuch hope is obvioufly ill-founded, unlefs built upon this hypothefis. We hope and pray

for

for *a reſtoration* (Reſtore us, O Lord, that
are penitent)——What reſtoration ? What
can we be reſtored to, *as man ?* what as
mere man have we loſt ?——Nothing; but
as apoſtate angels, we have loſt much indeed, and may with propriety both hope
and pray for a reſtoration, otherwiſe we
pray and hope for——we know not what.
We are told, " that there is more joy in
" heaven for one ſinner that repenteth,
" than for ninety-nine that are juſt ;"——
what relative concern can the angelic beings
have for *man,* *merely as ſuch,* that his repentance ſhould occaſion ſuch an extraordinary effect ? None ſurely that with propriety can be conceived; but—when we look
up to our hypotheſis, and view *the ſinner* in
the light of *one of their brethren* reſtored,
whom they had reaſon to fear was eternally
loſt to them, then the exceſs of joy is natural, and ſtands well accounted for.——Reſpecting the various ſpecious arguments
that have been ſtarted againſt the pre-exiſtent ſtate and lapſe of the human ſoul, particularly that of the ſoul's *not being conſcious*
of ſuch a ſtate, we again refer our readers to
the labors of the reverend and ingenious
Mr. *Berrow,* who has fully refuted *that,*
and every other objection that can be raiſed
to that doctrine; to which we will juſt
add,

add, that the foul of every thinking being would be foon confcious of that great and effential truth, if man would be brought to reflection, and *fink deeper into himfelf.*

THIRD GENERAL HEAD.

93. We are now arrived at our Third General Head, the *Metempfychofis of Bramah,* from which we have been kept back by fundry, yet neceffary digreffions, and difcuffions of many interefting objects and points of doctrine, which ftarted up upon us in our way, and retarded our fpeedier paffage; although hereby we may appear to fome deferving the cenfure of prolixity, yet we truft it will be acknowledged in the end, that without them our aim and endeavors would not have been attended with *that general utility* which we flatter ourfelves they now affuredly will.———Before we fubmit our own fentiments to the world on a doctrine fo little attended to in modern times in this our hemifphere, it becomes neceffary (to fave our readers the trouble of turning back to our fecond part, p. 49, &c.) that we recite the texts of *Bramah,* who firft, by divine authority, promulged that ancient fyftem

ſtem.———" And THE ETERNAL ONE
" ſpake again unto *Biſtnoo*, and ſaid, I will
" form mortal bodies for each of the delin-
" quent *debtah* (or angels), which ſhall for
" a ſpace be their priſon and habitation, in
" the confines of which they ſhall be ſubject
" to natural evils, in proportion to the de-
" gree of their original guilt.———The bo-
" dies which I ſhall prepare for the recep-
" tion of the rebellious *debtah*, ſhall be
" ſubject to change, decay, death, and re-
" newal, from the principles wherewith I
" ſhall form them ; and through theſe mor-
" tal bodies ſhall the delinquent *debtah* un-
" dergo alternately eighty-ſeven tranſmi-
" grations, ſubject more or leſs to the con-
" ſequences of *natural* and *moral* evils, in a
" juſt proportion to the degree of original
" guilt, and as their actions through thoſe
" ſucceſſive forms ſhall correſpond with the
" limited powers which I ſhall annex to
" each ;—and this ſhall be their ſtate of
" *puniſhment and purgation.*—And it ſhall
" be—that (after paſſing the eighty-eight
" tranſmigrations) the delinquent *deb-*
" *tah*, from my more abundant favor,
" ſhall animate the form of mhurd (man)
" ———and *in this form*, I will *enlarge their*
" *intellectual powers*, even as when *I firſt*
" *made them free* ;—and this ſhall be their
" chief ſtate of TRIAL and PROBATION."

94. As

94. As the foregoing doctrine of *Bramah feems* glaringly to clafh with *Mofes*'s hiftory of the *creation of man*, it is previoufly neceffary to account for this *feemingly* great difference; for they *appear* to agree only in one circumftance, namely, that man was the *laft work* of the material and animal creation. By this difcuffion we purpofe to avoid the imputation of flighting *a fcriptural detail* that has for a fucceffion of ages been received as orthodox by both *Jews* and *Chriftians*; a detail, that by being taken literally and mifunderftood, has proved the · fource of many egregious and fatal errors, highly injurious to God's juftice and clemency; the moft enormous of which is, that infatuated belief, that a race of *unoffending* beings fhould *ftand accurfed* for the guilt and difobedience of *one man* and *one woman*.

95. The miffion of *Mofes* may without offence be confidered as a very imperfect one, fo defigned by God himfelf; not only for that it was limited to one tribe of beings particularly favored of God, but alfo as it is totally filent upon all the *primitive truths* but one, *viz.* THE UNITY OF THE GODHEAD. This divine truth he was fpecially commiffioned to declare to his people, as well to refcue them from the idolatrous

fuperfti-

fuperftitions of the land he led them from,
as from thofe of the promifed land he was
leading them to. As *Mofes* was allowed to
be moft profoundly fkilled in all the learning of the *Egyptians*, and confequently in
that of the *Bramins* (which had been perverted by thofe Magi, as before fhewn, to
myfterious purpofes), we cannot fuppofe
him to have been ignorant that the *other
primitive truths* had *been already revealed*,
and that in fulnefs of time they would be
confirmed to mankind; but he alfo knew
that was a tafk referved for a more exalted
being than himfelf; therefore we are not to
wonder that he is utterly filent on thofe
heads of falvation.

96. Refpecting *Mofes's* fhort narration
of the creation and fall of man, it fhould
feem, if taken literally, to be a matter foreign to his commiffion; but on a nearer
view, and confidered as *typical of the angelic fall*, it carries a very different and effential afpect; and if not typical, it is moft
certainly laughable. We cannot, without
violence to our conceptions of the wifdom
of God, fuppofe, that he would propagate the
human fpecies by a horrid inceftuous union,
which pure human nature ftarts at, and
which by his Holy Spirit ftands condemned
in his gofpel-difpenfation; for thus mankind

kind *muſt have increaſed*, if propagated according to the literal ſenſe of *Moſes*, from *one man and one woman*; ſo that it is ſelf-evident he never intended it ſhould be taken literally, but as typical of a prior and much greater event: nor have we the ſmalleſt doubt but that, in the days he penn'd it, the allegory was well and commonly underſtood by all; and we think we ſhall be able, without much difficulty, to prove to a demonſtration, by analiſing this allegory, that it affords the fulleſt confirmation of the truth of the Bramanical doctrines of the creation of man, that man can be no other than the apoſtate angels, and that the Metempſychoſis is a well-founded truth, neceſſarily reſulting from theſe premiſes; and we ſhall alſo ſhew, that *Moſes* was well acquainted with thoſe doctrines; nay it is more than probable that he himſelf was the very identical ſpirit, ſelected and deputed in an earlier age, to deliver thoſe truths free from allegory, under the ſtile and title of *Bramah*, as before intimated. But to our proof, from *Moſes*'s narrative.

97. *Eve* is beguiled by the ſerpent, ſhe eats, and tempts *Adam* to do the like, and thereby both become guilty of the ſin of diſobedience againſt an expreſs law and order of their God and Creator: *Satan* is
tempted

tempted by *Evil, the affociate of his bofom.*
The *ferpent* reprefents the infidious arguments
and wiles of *Satan* to engage the angelic tribes
to become affociates in his revolt and rebellion, which it may be very naturally fuppofed were fimilar to thofe made ufe of by the
ferpent to Eve. *Paradife* marks the beauty
of the original earth, and the garden of
Eden is the fymbol of *heaven*; *Adam and
Eve* for their difobedience are driven out of
Eden, and *Satan and his affociates* are banifhed from heaven for their rebellion. The
gates of Eden are fhut, and guarded on
every fide by angelic powers, to prevent
the re-entrance of *Adam and Eve* and their
pofterity; the heavenly regions are impervi-
ous to *Satan* and his *confederates.* The
curfe of forrow, labor, and death, are entailed upon *Adam* and *Eve*, and their pofterity; wherein is figuratively fhewn the original fentence, doom, and punifhment of
the *apoftate angels* in their mortal fojourn on
earth. *Mofes* introduces God curfing the
ground for their fakes, allufive of the change
brought about in this globe at the deluge,
&c. occafioned by the *fecond defeEtion* of the
apoftate angels in their ftate of probation.
The brutes being the elder brothers of the
creation, and prior to the formation of man
(the doEtrine both of *Bramah* and *Mofes)*,

.5   fhews

fhews them to have been a preparatory creation for future purpofes ; and *Mofes* tacitly
coincides with *Bramah* as to the intended
ufe of this prior animal creation ; otherwife
man, who is evidently fuperior in form and
intellect, would, upon a rational fuppofition,
have been the firft object of all animal creation. God's being faid by *Mofes* to have
breathed the breath of life into all his animal
creation, is a happy figurative illuftration of
that paffage in *the Shaftah* (part 2. pag. 59),
where " the ETERNAL ONE fpake again,
" and faid——Do thou BIRMAH (the firft
" created, the *Chrift*), arrayed in my glo-
" ry, and armed with my power, defcend
" to the loweft boboon (region) of punifh-
" ment and purgation, and make known
" to the *rebellious debtah* the words that I
" have uttered, and the decrees which I
" have pronounced againft them, *and fee*
" *that they enter into the bodies that I have*
" *prepared for them.*——And *Birmah* ftood
" before the throne and faid, ETERNAL
" ONE, I have done as thou haft com-
" manded.—The *delinquent debtah* rejoice in
" thy mercy, confefs the juftice of thy de-
" crees, avow their forrow and repentance,
" *and have entered into the mortal bodies*
" *which thou haft prepared for them.*"

98. The

98. The perfonages which *Mofes* calls by the names of *Abel* and *Cain*, faid to be the immediate defcendants of *Adam* and *Eve*, are obvioufly types of *good* and *evil*, or vice and virtue, that were to guide and govern the actions of the human fpecies, in the courfe of their trial, from generation to generation. In the murder of *Abel* by *Cain*, *Mofes* prophetically points out (what his knowledge of *the race* then made clear to him), that *vice* would totally fubdue and deftroy *virtue*; a prediction that is now, we fear, very near being accomplifhed, as fhe may be too truly faid to be at the *laft gafp*, and on the verge of *expiring*. By fin, our fcriptures fay, death entered into the world, that is by the fin of *Satan*, not of *Adam* (vide the Rev. Mr. *Berrow*), and as in *Satan* (not in *Adam*), all men die, that is, are fubjected by fentence to death, fo in *Chrift* (deftined to confirm to mankind the *primitive truths of falvation*) fhall all be made alive, " a confummation devoutly to be wifhed," but of which we have yet *no figns* or *tokens*. Why *Mofes* has made woman the fubftitute of evil, is not very clear, unlefs from his profound wifdom and knowledge of human nature, we fuppofe he had obferved, that no object had fo powerful an influence to feduce man from his duty and allegiance, as woman; and from thence he poffibly

I   thought

thought her the fitteft fymbol he could ufe
on that occafion, without (we dare fay) in-
tending it fhould be taken as a general reflection upon the fex.

99. It is here worth noting, that the
creation and propagation of the human form
according to the fcriptures of *Bramah*, are
clogged with no difficulties, *no ludicrous unintelligible circumftances* or *inconfiftencies.*
GOD previoufly conftructs mortal bodies of
both fexes, for the reception of the angelic
fpirits proportioned to their number, which
were to animate or give life to thofe as yet
inanimate machines, and thefe were all
doomed, without exception, to pafs through
many fucceffive tranfmigrations in thefe
mortal prifons, as a ftate of punifhment and
purgation, before they received the grace of
animating the human form, which was to
be their chief ftate of probation and trial:
thus it is rationally fuppofed, that multitudes of them might arrive at the fame period to that fuperior degree; and that male
and female forms, by the *inftantaneous fiat*
of the DEITY, were ready for their reception. Thus the propagation of the fpecies
went naturally on, as well as that of the
other animal forms. Refpecting the number of angelic beings firft created by GOD,
the fcriptures of *Bramah*, the Old Teftament,

ment, and *Chrift*, are filent, confining
themfelves to the fact only; but if we form
our calculation and judgment upon the
multitude of organized mortal bodies in the
world, we muft conclude the original creation to have been amazingly immenfe!
when we fuppofe, that only a portion of
them rebelled, ufually fuppofed (but upon
what foundation we know not) to have
been about one third. Be this as it may,
it is a fpeculative point of little import to
us, it being as eafy to Omnipotence to create
many hundred thoufands of millions as
one.

100. We now flatter ourfelves that we
have fully proved, to the conviction and fatisfaction of our intelligent and unprejudiced reader, that *Mofes*'s hiftory of the *creation and fall of man*, was *purely typical of
the angelic fall*, and made ufe of by him *figuratively* to denote that great and prior
event with its fatal confequences; and at
the fame time to point out *the fecond defection* of thofe unhappy delinquents, after
they had been placed by the grace and favor
of GOD in a fufferable probationary ftate,
beyond their merits or juft expectation : alfo to give a ufeful and neceffary admonition
to his people, that *temptation was no plea*

for

for fin and difobedience. As to the actors
Mofes employs, under the denominations of
Adam, *Eve*, *Cain*, and *Abel*, it is plain they
never had any *real perfonal exiftence;* it is therefore evident that *the creation of man,* according to the fcriptures of *Bramah,* is the
only real and *original* one; and that man
was not, as fome have advanced, coeval
with the angelic creation, but fubfequent to
their fall. *Mofes* appears to us to have had
an under plot (if we may be allowed the
expreffion), in the circumftantial hiftory he
gives of the defcendants of his fuppofed
Adam and *Eve;* he politically faw, that for
the prefervation of the religion and morals
of his people, it was abfolutely neceffary to
keep them a feparate nation as much as poffible : to effect this he thought nothing
would more powerfully conduce than rai-
fing the ideas of their own dignity, put in
comparifon with the nations around them ;
they already had ftupendous proofs of their
being a chofen race peculiarly favored of
God, and *Mofes* traces their genealogy to as
diftant a root as poffible, and carries it up
to his typical creation of the firft man and
woman: thofe who know what influence
this vanity of *the antiquity of nations* has in
modern times, will applaud the fagacity of
Mofes. And here we cannot help regretting
that he has not left us his opinion of *the age*

of

of the univerfe; he has left it pretty clear, that the creation of *that* and *man* were nearly coeval, but there he has left both to exercife our fruitlefs guefles. On this fubject we will only add, that the ancients *may have exaggerated*, but he *that dreams with the moderns*, that the world is not yet fix thoufand years old, may very eafily acquire faith fufficient to believe the grofleft of abfurdities, or, with fome of the ancient philofophers, that the heavens are made of brafs or iron. Having fulfilled our engagement refpecting that ancient typical *Mofaic* hiftory of the creation and fall of man, we proceed with our fubject.

101. We have feen a noble and exalted caufe for the formation of the material univerfe, in which we behold man placed in the fupreme degree over all animated mortal beings; but—ftill we obferve many myriads of thofe beings, formed with no lefs ftupendous wifdom and art, and endued (although in an inferior proportion) with the fame rational intelligent faculties as himfelf, concerning whom we feem to be utterly at a lofs; nor is there any abftrufe point, in which the learned of all ages have been more divided than touching the ftate and nature of the *brute creation*. The pride

I 3   of

of man fhudders at claffing them with himfelf, yet his confcious reafon, on reflection,
in fpite of himfelf, checks his prefumption.
Thus the inimitable and philofophic *Prior*
fweetly fings to our purpofe:

" By what immediate caufe *they* are inclin'd,
" In many acts, 'tis hard I own to find;
" I fee in *others*, or I think I fee,
" That ftrong *their* principles and ours agree:
" Evil, like us they fhun, and covet good,
" Abhor the poifon, and receive the food;
" Like us they love or hate, like us they know,
" To joy the friend, or grapple with the foe;
" With feeming thought, their actions they
    " *intend*,
" And ufe the means proportion'd to the end;
" Then vainly the philofopher avers,
" That reafon guides our deeds, and inftinct
    " theirs;
" How can we juftly different *caufes* frame?
" When *the effects* intirely are the fame;
" *Inftinct* and *reafon* how can we divide?—
" *'Tis the fool's ignorance, and the pedant's pride.*"

102. It is *amufing* to trace the different
and bewildered fentiments of mankind on
this fubject; but if it was *otherwife*, yet it
is neceffary to the execution of our plan.—
The *Cartefians* maintain that brutes have no
intelligent foul, but are mere machines, and
unfeeling pieces of clock-work; and indeed,

7   by

by the treatment they receive in the world,
it fhould feem that mankind in general
were difciples to that inhuman and ftupid
doctrine :—However Meff. *Yvon* and *Bouil-
let* refute the *Cartefian* hypothefis, by ma-
fterly indifputable philofophic arguments,
and prove that brutes have a rational intelligent foul, and then—leave that foul to
perifh with the body. Some have imagined
the *fouls* of brutes to be *material*; flat nonfenfe in *terms*, as well as in *philofophy.*
Ariftotle, who fuppofed the fouls of brutes
to be *fubftantial forms*, is not a whit more
intelligible. *Cicero*, who, great as he was,
poffeffed a portion of that pride and vanity
which flefh is heir to, made no fmall con-
ceffion, when he fays, " In 'every effence
" that is not fimple, but compounded of
" parts, there muft be fome *predominant*
" quality; in man 'tis *reafon*, in brutes it
" is——*fomething like it.*" A late performance, faid to be a tranflation from the
French, makes all animal life, not man excepted, a *Jeu D'Efprit*, or an amufement
of the Deity, and for no other end or purpofe. Thus brutes reafon upon brutes,
fays *Voltaire.* Another well-intended and
ingenious late performance gives to the fouls
of brutes immortality, and a future life of
rewards and punifhments, and takes its
proofs from fcripture, but is utterly at a

I 4   lofs

lofs to account for the predicament in which they ftand on earth, liable as they are *to mifery*, without the authors being able to conceive by what mode of tranfgreffion they could poffibly *deferve it*; touching which we hope to fatisfy his doubts and curiofity. Another divine, in a late treatife upon the general deluge, boldly cuts the matter fhort at one ftroke, as *Alexander* did the *Gordian* knot. He fuppofes, " that as the brute " creation was made folely for man's ufe, " and that when they could be of no fur- " ther fervice *to him*, they became *ufelefs* in " the creation, and fuffered *as matter* in the " general deluge, and it became *requifite* " they fhould perifh together—as it cannot " *be fuppofed* they were punifhed on their " *own account*."—Here, reader, you have a choice fpecimen of *clofe reafoning* exhibited to you; and a *ftriking* inftance of God's *juftice* and *clemency !* delivered by a fervant of the MOST HIGH !—*Montaigne* thinks more honorably of the brute creation; " What kind of fufficiency," fays he, " is " there in us, which we do not obferve in " the operations of the animals ?" To which he afcribes deliberation, thought, and conclufion; and from thence gives the fuperiority to beafts over man, infomuch as the works of nature excel thofe of art. He goes further, and pronounces the animals *free agents*,

agents, as well as mankind ;—" I fay there-
" fore, that there is no appearance of rea-
" fon to fuppofe that the beafts fhould, by
" a natural and forced inclination (inftinct),
" do *the fame* things that we do by our
" *choice* and endeavor; we ought from *like*
" *effects* to conclude *like faculties*, and from
" *richer effects, richer faculties*; and by con-
" fequence to confefs, that *this fame reafon,*
" this *fame method* by which *we operate*, is
" common alfo to the animals, or fome
" other *that is better."* The whole reafoning on this fubject of that acute but irregular writer, is worth perufal, as it lies
fcattered through his apology for his learned friend *Raymond de Sobonde.* This induftrious author feems quite clear as to the
pre-exiftent ftate of the human foul :
" Death," fays he, " is the beginning of
" *another life*; fo did we weep, and fo
" much did it coft us, *to enter into this;*
" and *fo did we put off our former veil,*
" when we entered the prefent ftate." And
by the courfe of his reafoning juft above re-
ferred to, it fhould alfo feem, that he favored
the fame opinion of the brute foul, as well
as the doctrine of the Metempfychofis.—
Our learned and philofophic *Baxter* (in his
Treatife of the Nature of the Soul), after
proving that the foul neceffarily lives after
its feparation from the body, proceeds and
adds,

adds,—" As man is a being compounded of
" *spirit* and *matter*, the *laft* an impeding
" and obftructing caufe on the activity and
" perfection of reafoning in the *firft*, as the
" the miniftering organs of the *laft* may
" happen to be maimed, defective, or dif-
" ordered; and as a feparation of the union
" leaves the *firft* difengaged and at liberty,
" it is a rational fuppofition, that either the
" foul is in an abfolute ftate of feparation
" from *all matter*, or (when it fhall pleafe
" our infinitely wife Creator) *re-united* to
" matter of a more *favorable kind*, that
" fhall be lefs obftructive to our immaterial
" powers.—Omnipotence admits of no li-
" mitation, fouls may be united to fyftems
" of matter, according to the purpofes of
" infinite wifdom, that will be vaftly more
" advantageous, and the union with them
" more pleafing, than with our prefent bo-
" dies ; our prefent union being equally in-
" conceivable, although we cannot but be
" confcious of the fact, however unac-
" countable by our limited conceptions."—
Again, " Men who hold the immateriality
" of the foul, need not be embarraffed how
" to difpofe of the *immaterial fouls* of
" brutes, or be concerned what powers they
" may have after the diffolution of their
" bodies, but leave all to the Being that
" made them."—" It is to be obferved,
" that

" that the activity of the human foul is of
" two kinds, that which is exerted in the
" fpontaneous moving the limbs, and that
" power whereby we turn back our percep-
" tive capacity to our paft perceptions, fo
" as to compare them together: the per-
" ceptivity alfo of it is twofold, for it is
" percipient of the action of matter upon
" itfelf, and percipient of its own internal
" operation in thinking. Brutes have the
" firft of thefe powers, but want the fecond
" altogether, which conftitutes the *diftinc-*
" *tion* between man and beaft; they who
" run the parallel between the human foul
" and that of the brutes farther, fuppofe
" ftill the fame powers in both. But furely
" rationality muft be found in fome powers
" which the brutes *as fuch* have not. This
" argument therefore does not prove the
" activity of the brute foul when feparat-
" ed——*although, if any one could prove it,*
" *he would do no differvice perhaps to philo-*
" *fophy.*" Again, " It is felf-evident, that
" the wide-extended univerfe, though
" ftretched beyond imagination, with all
" the wonders of wifdom and power in it,
" is folely defigned for the fake of intelli-
" gent beings, *to train them up* for a ra-
" tional eternity."—That the general fentiments of this truly pious and learned divine
fupport the probable doctrine of the Metemp-
fycholis

fychofis is fo plain, it hardly needs pointing out to the obferving reader; therefore
we fhall only add, that if *the act of dream-
ing* proves (as he afferts it does) the feparate
exiftence and active percipient powers of
the human foul, after the diffolution of the
body, it equally proves the brute fouls to be
endued with the fame powers—for undoubtedly—they dream. Unwilling as we are
upon any occafion to diffent from the reafoning of this truly great and good man, yet
we find ourfelves under that neceffity, when
he fays, " the human foul is form'd at firft
" without knowledge or experience, but
" hath the power of attaining both.———
" Brutes are *incapable of improvement*, fi-
" nifhed in their *fpecific perfection* all at
" *once.*" So ftrange a pofition as the foregoing, could proceed only from non-atten-
tion to the progrefs of the intelligent faculties in both fpecies from their ftate of infancy, or—from thofe feelings of human pride
that will fpring up in the beft heart, when
the fuppofed dignity of his fuperior nature is
brought into competition.—The fentiments
of the ingenious Mr. *Berrow* (fo often re-
ferred to) upon the brute creation, may be
clearly gathered from his own words, which
we fhall prefent to our readers, as a curious
and uncommon fpecimen of *unprejudiced
reafoning* in a Chriftian divine.———" If it
" fhould

" fhould be urged, that the affigning fouls
" to one part of the brute creation, will re-
" duce us to the neceffity of fuppofing the
" *like* to actuate the moft minute fpecies of
" vital nature alfo ; I fhall only remind the
" fpeculative and philofophic part of man-
" kind, that there is difcernible, by the
" microfcopic eye, as exquifite a due pro-
" portioned difpofition of organs, fibres,
" &c. (the more amazing in proportion as
" they are more minute) in the one as in
" the other——That, again, the foul has
" the power of *felf-contraction*, to an *infi-*
" *nitefimal degree*, as well as that of *felf-*
" *dilatation*——That fuppofing, in the next
" place, every organized body, as well in
" the brute as in the rational, to be an al-
" lotted *temporary* prifon for a *pre-delinquent*
" foul *(an hypothefis, than which there can-*
" *not I think be one more rational)*, it is eafy
" to conceive how and why *fome* may be
" made here prifoners *more at large* as we
" fay, and entrufted with privileges and
" faculties more numerous, extenfive, and
" exalted than others : and that, laftly, it
" is impoffible to fay into how many differ-
" ent kinds of vehicles *a foul may tranfmi-*
" *grate*, ere its *plaftic faculty* be refined
" enough to *inform one*, wherein to perform
" the functions of an *intelligent* and rational
" life."

"life."——Here we fee a learned divine, to the honor of the church of *England*, fcruples not to avouch, without referve, one moft material part of *Bramah*'s doctrine of the Metempfychofis; and it is a pity he was not further enlightened; he then would not (with many others of the learned) have been drove to the fubterfuge of making a new creation to animate and actuate all' mortal forms, when there were a race of angelic delinquent beings ready made to his hands.——Having thus thrown together, under one paragraph, the different fentiments of mankind touching the ftate and nature of the brute creation, we will next proceed to confider *their ufe*, and the intent of their creation; a matter in which we fhall not find mankind fo much divided, but on the contrary (the bulk of them at leaft) pretty unanimous.

103. Man's prefumption in fuppofing the brute creation was intended *folely for his ufe*, may be afcribed to two caufes: the firft his pride, or natural unbounded *thirft of power*; an intellectual *faculty* he picked not up here, but brought with him from above, from his pre-exiftent angelic ftate : *there* it had proved his bane, and here, having not immediately the governing powers of heaven

ven to combat againſt, to keep his ruling
paſſion in action, he exerciſes it, not only
on the unoffending brute creation, but on
his own ſpecies.———The ſecond cauſe we
conſider as a plea and ſanction taken from
the 26th verſe of the firſt chapter of *Geneſis*,
where *Moſes* ſays, that " God ſaid, Let us
" make man in our image, after our like-
" neſs ; and *let them have dominion* over the
" fiſh of the ſea, and over the fowl of the
" air, and over the cattle, and over all the
" earth, and over every creeping thing that
" creepeth upon the earth."———To combat the *firſt cauſe*, would prove a labor
truly Herculean, without the ſmalleſt chance
of victory, and therefore we avoid the battle ; and touching the ſecond, we might
avail ourſelves of the demonſtrative proofs
already ſtated, that the *Moſaic* hiſtory of
the creation of terreſtrial animals was purely typical ; but we will wave that juſt privilege, and examine the fact, as it literally
ſtands ; premiſing, that man has no right
to chuſe his texts, but if he thinks to benefit himſelf *by one*, he ought to acknowledge the force and efficacy *of another*, and
abide with equal ſtrictneſs by both ; that he
has not preſerved this equity towards a *more
expreſs* dictate of this ſcripture is certain;
for, verſe 29th of the ſame chapter, " God
" ſaid (to man), Behold, I have given you
" *every*

" *every herb* bearing feed, which is upon
" the face of all the earth, and *every tree*,
" in the which is the fruit of a tree, yield-
" ing feed: to you it fhall *be for meat.*"
Which words convey a palpable although
tacit interdiction of all other food: but more
of this hereafter, when we have no doubt
of proving indifputably that the breach of
this pofitive injunction, or rather this *firft
law* of nature, has been one of the great, if
not chief fource of phyfical as well as *moral
evil.* We now return to our more immediate fubject.

104. That the brute creation was defigned to be fubfervient to, or made for the ufe
of man, is a conceit incompatible not only
with the juftice of God, but alfo his wifdom; and that, therefore, the ufurped
fenfe of the phrafe, " Let them have do-
" minion," (on which fo much ftrefs has
been laid) is not well-founded, and implies only, Let them have pre-eminence,
predominance, fuperiority, in *intellectual
faculties over the reft of the animal creation.*
Thus *Bramah*, " And in this form I will
" enlarge their intellectual powers, even as
" when I firft made them free." In this
fenfe only can the above phrafe be poffibly
underftood, for the following reafons: firft,
Mofes nowhere intimates, that the brute
creation

creation was made *for the ufe of man.* Secondly, the very fmall proportion of *the
whole* he has been able to reduce under his
dominion, and even that modicum not fubdued, but by the exertion, or rather perverfion of *thofe fuperior intellectual faculties*
into craft and violence, which were moft
certainly given him for very different purfuits. Thirdly, that, fo far from there being the fmalleft appearance that the animal
creation was fubjected either to the dominion or fervice of man, according to the
fenfe that he has wantonly and cruelly affumed, that the majority of them, almoft
to an infinite degree, are obnoxious to him,
and at enmity with him, and in no wife,
fhape, or form, under his rule and dominion. On the contrary, it may be juftly
faid, that " men are more flaves to man,
" than beafts to him." Fourthly, can it
poffibly be conceived, without doing violence to the juftice, goodnefs, and wifdom
of God, that he would inveft man with a
dominion to *drive out*, at his *caprice* and *pleafure*, that *breath of life*, which he had for
his wife purpofes fo bountifully *breathed* into all his animal creation? for although
Mofes particularly applies this fublime fentence to *Adam alone* in the 7th verfe of his
2d chapter, in thefe words, " And the Lord
" God created man of the duft of the

K   " ground,

" ground, and *breathed into his noftrils the*
" *breath of life, and man became a living foul;"*
yet it is felf-evident, that this operation
and divine infufion of a living foul or fpirit, muft have been, *a priori, general* to the
whole animal creation. Fifthly, what idea
muft we form of the wifdom and defigns of
God, if we fuppofe that, after his blefling
his animal creation, and laying a pofitive
injunction upon them to *increafe* and *multi-
ply* and *replenifh the earth*, he fhould, *at the
fame time*, give to man dominion and power
to counteract his purpofes, by *decreafing,
diminifhing*, and *deftroying them?*

105. Having fhewn above, that we cannot without violence to God and nature
conclude, that the brute creation was made
for the ufe of man, it follows, that his pre-
tended right of dominion is an ufurpation
over a race of intelligent beings, innocent,
at leaft, refpecting him; whofe lot in this
world is fufficiently painful and miferable,
without any additional load from man.
Here we will once more give our readers
the fentiments of the Rev. Mr. *Berrow*, as
ftrongly expreffive of our own, and apt to
our fubject. After a pathetic and truly Chri-
ftian-like apoftrophe on that noble animal
the horfe, which is equally applicable to
every other animal under man's tyranny,
he

he fubjoins,——" But wherefore all this
" wretchednefs ?—wherefore all thefe ago-
" nizing pains and miferies heaped on an
" helplefs offspring of divine providence?
" are they not flefh and blood?" *(Have
they not their* REAL *grievances and apprehenfions ?)* " Do *they* not, as well as *we,*
" know what forrow means? were they
" brought into a *fenfible exiftence* for nothing
" but *the fervice,* or rather to gratify the
" pride, the wantonnefs, the cruelty of
" man ? fhall one being be created, even
" under the bare poffibility of being made
" miferable, *folely for the ufe* or pleafure of
" another ?——Lord, what is man ? or
" rather, what are not brutes ?"——" The
" *Indians* afk, if brutes have not fouls? if
" not, then, fay they, *matter thinks. Ci-*
" *cero* fays, " That God himfelf is the foul
" of brutes;" therefore, fays the *Indian,*
" fhall they be found fuffering without a
" CAUSE, or without a *recompence ?"*——
Surely no; the doctrine of the Metempfychofis *alone points cut the caufe* for their fuffering *natural evils,* and at the fame time
fhews the promifed recompence.

106. Notwithftanding all that has been
faid, we fee it will be ftill objected to us,
that *Mofes,* in the controverted phrafe before us (" Let them have dominion"), muft

have

have meant thereby abfolute dominion and unaccountable rule, or he would not, in his law to the *Hebrews,* have devoted the animal creation to the fubjeꞓion of man, in the various facrifices *of them* inftituted by the law. To which we fay, that thofe cruel facrifices were fubfequently condemned and difcountenanced, as barbarous and inefficacious, both by GOD and CHRIST; and we may fairly lay it down as an inconteftable principle, that any aꞓ which GOD and CHRIST have at any one time pronounced *evil,* could never have been *good;* and therefore, that *Mofes,* in that inftitute, deviated from the commiffion he had received from GOD, as he did unwarily in other particulars, which drew on him the difpleafure of his Creator, and deprived him of the promifed felicity of fettling his people in the land to which he was appointed to conduꞓ them. Nor does it at all appear difficult to point out the caufes that led *Mofes* into this error : he knew that their appetites had for a long feries of ages been vitiated by the tafte of animal food; he hoped to reclaim them from it, by fhewing them, in the 29th verfe of the firft chapter of *Genefis* before recited, that that was not their originally deftined meat, and that by the ufe of animal food they had digreffed from their *primitive nature,* and had
tranf-

tranfgreffed againft *the very firft law* of their
Maker; but——very foon finding every admonition of the kind was loft upon them,
he weakly thought it might prove in fome
fort an extenuation of thefe *common murders*,
and a kind of fanctification of them, by introducing them as part of their religious
worfhip. To this he probably had a further
interefting and pious motive; he could not
but remark the depravity of, and the ftrong
bent in his people towards the fuperftitious
worfhip, facrifices and idolatries of the
Egyptians, Chaldeans, Tyrians, Canaanites,
&c. amongft whom he knew that *human facrifices* were as common as thofe of the brute
creation; therefore, to guard his people
againft *a greater evil*, he inftituted, as he
vainly imagined, *a lefs*; not adverting that
it belonged TO GOD ALONE, to *permit*
evil, that *good* may come of it. The vifion
of St. *Peter* may alfo be objected againft us,
and that *Chrift* himfelf winked at thefe mur-
derous practices, and even partook of them.
To this we anfwer, that *Chrift* knew too
well the total and confirmed depravity *of*
man to combat fo long-eftablifhed an enor-
mity; therefore the chief aim of his miffion was, *firft* to correct his morals, and, *if*
poffible, bring him to a ftate of *fenfibility* and
repentance; that once obtained, the aboli-

K 3   tion

tion *of that*, and many other enormities, he
knew, would follow of courfe.

107. Let us now hear the words of GOD
himfelf on this fubject by the mouth of his
infpired *Bramah:*——" The mortal forms,
" wherewith I fhall encompafs the *delin-*
" *quent debtah*, are *the work of my hand*;
" *they fhall not be deftroyed*, but left to their
" natural decay; therefore whichfoever of
" the *debtah* fhall by defigned violence bring
" about the diffolution of the mortal forms
" *animated by their delinquent brethren*——
" *thou, Sieb,* fhalt plunge the offending
" fpirit into the *onderah* for a fpace, and
" he fhall be doomed to pafs again the
" eighty-nine tranfmigrations, whatfoever
" ftage he may be arrived to at the time
" of fuch his offence."

108. Having thus, in a regular feries,
difcuffed the feveral events of the creation
and exiftence of angels, their rebellion and
fall; and having fhewn that the material
univerfe was conftructed for their habitation and fuftenance, and that mortal bodies
were formed for their more immediate punifhment and imprifonment; and having
alfo made it fufficiently clear, that man can
poffibly be no other than thofe identical
fallen

fallen angels; and laftly, that the brute creation could not have been made fubject to him, nor deftined for his ufe and fervice in the fenfe he has erroneoufly, not to fay wickedly, converted them to; it follows that we next take it into confideration to what other ufe or purpofe were they brought into exiftence?——The ancient doctrine of the Metempfychofis of *Bramah*, at once anfwers the matter in queftion, and would afford full fatisfaction to a *Gentoo*, a *Tartar*, or a *Chinefe*, but not to a Chriftian. (Here by-the-bye it is proper to note, that although the *Tartars* and *Chinefe* believe in the tranf-migration of the foul, yet they feem, as well as our ancient druids, to have totally loft fight of the fource, the root, the origi-nal principle from whence the doctrine of the Metempfychofis fprung, viz. the angelic fall and doom, which has been retained in its primitive purity only by the Gentoos.)
——The cafe ftanding thus, it remains to examine whether the ftate and predicament in which the brute creation appear and exift, can be accounted for upon any other rational fyftem. In order to which it will be neceffary to confider them under two points of view; firft, as *intelligent, ration-al beings, and free agents*; and fecondly, as *beings fubjected to mifery*.

K 4   109. The

189. The man who afferts his own rational intellectual faculties and free agency,
and denies them to the brutes, either thinks
not at all, or is actuated by pride and felf-
fufficient pre-eminence, or has been very
deficient in his obfervations and reflections
upon that numerous creation.——When
we fee a race of beings endued with the paffions of rage, revenge, dominion, ungovernable luft, jealoufy, hatred, envy, and
every other vice fimilar to our own, *except*
ingratitude; and when we behold them endued with the virtues (we had almoft faid
the Chriftian virtues) of love, fidelity, grati-
tude, friendfhip, courage, parental tendernefs, filial affection, patience, fubmiffion,
innocence and meeknefs, all in as high perfection, if not higher, than in ourfelves;
and when we further obferve them invefted
with the powers of happinefs, mifery, reflection, recollection, forefight, forecaft,
prodigies of art, without rule, line, fquare,
or compafs; fagacious in contriving, political in government; the amazing beauty of
fome, and ftupendous conftruction and animal œconomy of all!——All which *vices,*
virtues, powers and *properties,* are exempli-
fied in the various fpecies of the animal
creation.——When we daily fee, or may
fee, all this verified, and ftill appropriate
cogitation

cogitation and *reafon* to man alone, we fee
with the eyes of *folly* and *prejudice.*

110. That man is endued with higher
intellectual powers, and capable of carrying
his reafoning faculties to a more tranfcen-
dent pitch, we readily grant; but——why
will not human pride reft fatisfied with this
fuperiority, without aiming to diveft the
next great work of his Creator of the portion which he has gracioufly and evidently
beftowed upon it, as neceffary to their temporal exiftence?——If therefore the brute
foul, as fome (we will not call them philofophers) have taught, is material, and pe-
rifhes with the body, it is time to tremble
for the foul of man; for it is too true and
melancholy a fact, that it ftands not entitled
to a better lot:—the fpirituality and future
feparate exiftence of *the one*, refts on no
furer a foundation than *the other*; and all
appearances are as ftrong in favor of the
one as of the other.————Thus our pre-
judices and falfe reafoning, arifing from
ignorance of our real ftate and nature,
leads us into an uncomfortable dilemma,
and we are plunged into a labyrinth of confufion, from which nothing can difentangle
and extricate us, but—the doctrine of the
Metempfychofis, which elucidates and reconciles every difficulty by teaching, that
the foul of man and brute is one and the
fame

fame fpirit, firft in a ftate of greater degradation, a preparatory ftate of *punifhment* and *purgation*, previoufly neceffary to his paffing into his ftate of *probation*, in the fuperior and more enligh ened form of man. In further fupport of this conclufion, it remains that we confider the brute creation *as beings fubjeƈted to mifery.*

111. The juftice, the goodnefs of God ftands moft evidently impeached in the wild fuppofition that he could poffibly create a race of beings fubjeƈted to mifery, without fome caufe of offence on their parts.—Let us with a becoming indignation rejeƈt an opinion fo unworthy our God, and conclude there muft have been *a caufe*, and an efficient one, although no hypothefis hitherto produced has pointed it out to the fatisfaƈtion of a rational enquirer.——The ftate and exiftence of man ftands in the fame predicament, doomed through the progrefs of his life to a feries of natural and moral evils, without any *apparent caufe*, or without poffibly having been capable of deferving them by any tranfgreffion *here*; therefore our firm belief in God's juftice, and our reafon direƈted us to fearch for *that caufe of offence* in fome *former ftate* of the foul's exiftence, in which we happily fucceeded, at leaft to our full conviƈtion, and *we hope* to that of our candid readers. To that fource
we

we muſt again apply to ſolve the preſent difficulty reſpecting *the brute ſoul*, which muſt
undoubtedly have ſinned in a pre-exiſtent
ſtate, to reconcile its *many ſufferings here*
with the idea of a juſt and good GOD.——
The ſenſible reflections and ſentiments of
the ingenious Mr. *Dean* of *Middleton*, are
appoſite to our ſubject, and ſo pertinent to
what we have further to allege, that we
will take the freedom of tranſplanting them.
After pre-ſuppoſing that pains, diſeaſes,
death, &c. evils got entrance into the world
by ſin, he proceeds as follows : " Now brutes
" as well as men are ſubject to the ſame
" ſorts of pains and diſeaſes ; ſo far their
" caſes coincide. In all general deſolations
" they have ſuffered together ; in this they
" conform. They ſuffered with man *the*
" *injuries of the fall* (we wiſh he had ſaid
" *the angelic fall;* poſſibly he meant it).——
" They have periſhed with him in deluges,
" in conflagrations, in famines, in peſti-
" lences, in deſtructions of the ſword ; in
" ſhort, in all capital calamities they have
" had their ſhare, as well as man (to which
" he might have added, the many miſeries
" they endure from the tyranny of man).
" Now, if there is any reaſon to believe,
" that ſuch evils are of God's appointment,
" and occaſioned by ſin, muſt not brutes
" then in ſome reſpect or other be ſuppoſed
" to

" to be faulty ? We do not pretend to fay,
" or even to infinuate, that they are ca-
" pable of moral rules, and become crimi-
" nal after the manner of men ; but we al-
" lege, that they muft have fome kind of
" demerit, they muft have contracted de-
" filements fome way or other. *If we can-*
" *not fhew how this is, it is only an inftance,*
" *among ft many others, of our ignorance.*
" The facts infifted on are deducible
" from the preceding cafes, and the
" juftice of God.————God cannot pu-
" nifh his creatures without a caufe, and
" this caufe muft be guilt or demerit of
" fome kind or other; infinite juftice necef-
" farily fuppofes it." This Gentleman
ftops not here, but goes a ftep much higher
in his conclufion from the above premifes :
" that as brute animals have attended man
" in all great and capital calamities, fo they
" will alfo attend him in *his final deliver-*
" *ance,* and *be reftored with him."* How
he proves this from fcripture, we refer our
readers to his " Effay on the Future Life
" of Brutes," whilft we proceed on our
way.

112. Thus have we demonftrated, *the*
creation and ftate of man and beaft are utterly inexplicable upon any other hypothefis than the ancient doctrine of the Metempfychofis,

fychofis, which *alone* rationally accounts
for, and reconciles their exiftence, as intelligent free agents doomed to mifery, in
every ftage and circumftance of it, to be
ftrictly confiftent with the *goodnefs*, the *juftice*, and *mercy* of God; the ftate of the
brute creation, and the caufe of their fufferings no longer remains a matter of difficulty,
nor incompatible with divine juftice, but
conformable thereto; their mortal bodies
being formed for no other end or purpofe
but the punifhment and vehicles of convey-
ance for the *fame offending fpirit*, to a form,
which, although ftill a prifon for the foul,
was yet fo marveloufly fabricated (by a mo-
dus and conftruction imperceptible to us),
as to afford a greater fcope and latitude to
the exertion of thofe intellectual faculties
and free agency, which it was only capable
of exerting *in a limited degree*, whilft in its
ftate of deeper degradation; for, touching
the portion of *cogitation* and *confcientiouf-
nefs* the brute creation are poffeffed of, it
is impoffible for us to fay; it may, for aught
we know to the contrary, be equal to our
own: we are barely authorized in our conception drawn from vifible phenomena, that
their powers are under fome kind of reftraint, but of what nature we know not;
nor does it follow from the premifes, if
granted,

granted, that their cogitative faculties fhould be under any reftraint at all. We fee that they are in general miferable, without remedy or comfort; but that man is only fo by predilection, having refources within himfelf, if he pleafes to employ them, that are capable at all times of conftituting his felicity; and this privilege marks to us the fpecific difference and fuperiority of the *fame foul in brute and man*. In the *firft* it may be faid to be in *a clofe prifon*, and in the laft, a -prifoner more *at large*, and capable of working out its full and *final liberty*; a privilege it cannot obtain by iffuing from the mortal brute form, which is deftined to be its ftate of *punifhment* and *purgation*, as before obferved, and that of *man only*, its ftate of *trial* and *probation*; from which form alone it can poffibly emerge to its priftine celeftial ftate. It feems to have been the fentiments of *Lucian*, as well as of *Pythagoras*, and many others of the ancient philofophers, that what conftitutes the greateft punifhment of the brutes, is *their confcioufnefs* of having animated the *form of man*, and of not having benefited thereby; and that it is by their retaining the ideas of their former ftate of humanity, that many of their fpecies, by fmall training, fo readily comprehend his language and inftructions.

Chime-

Chimerical as this opinion may feem to fome, it appears in our judgment to have a good foundation.

113. From what has been faid, we have the pleafure of thinking the philofophic reafoning of the learned *Baxter* ftands confirmed and illuftrated; the fenfible fuggeftions of the Rev. Mr. *Berrow* enforced and verified; the doubts and perplexities of the Rev. Mr. *Dean*, touching the *caufe* for which the brutes are doomed to mifery, fully fatisfied; and the bold affertions of Mr. *John Ilive* well grounded, from whom we candidly confefs we took our firft hints, and became a thorough convert to his hypothefis, upon finding on enquiry, and the exertion of our own reafon, that it was built on the firft divine revelation that had been gracioufly delivered to man, to wit, THE CHARTAH BHADE OF BRAMAH; although it is very plain Mr. *Ilive* was ignorant of the doctrine of the Metempfychofis, by confining his conceptions only to the angelic fall, man's being the apoftate angels, and that this earth was the only hell; paffing over in filence the reft of the *animal creation*.

114. As

114. As the ancient doctrine of the Metempfychofis alone accounts, as has been faid, for the creation, nature, and ftate of man and beaft, fo it alfo clears up many difficulties and objections that have frequently been ftarted concerning the *true nature* of *Chrift*; fome conceiving him to be " *very God of very God*," that is, *God himfelf*, if they mean any thing: others conceive him to be *God and man*, but in what fenfe we believe infinite wifdom itfelf could not explain to the comprehenfion of a finite underftanding——Others conceive *Chrift* to have been *mere man*, enlightened or infpired by God to a *fuperlative degree*, and difavow the *pre-exiftent* ftate of his foul or fpirit. Touching the *two firft* of thefe opinions, we have already given *our conceptions*, efteeming them enthufiaftic, if not blafphemous ; but refpecting the fupporters of *the third*, they fhun (we fear) *Sylla*, and fall upon *Carybdis*.

115. A Treatife (which we never faw or heard of before we had clofed our Second General Head, although publifhed in 1767) intitled, " The true Doctrine of the New " Teftament concerning *Jefus Chrift* con- " fidered," contains a plaufible chain of objections to his fuppofed *pre-exiftence*. Although

though in that book, and the appendix, we have the fingular pleafure of finding our fentiments upon the evil tendency of the Athanafian doctrine, and the true meaning and reading of the firft chapter of St. *John's* Gofpel, fupported by fo learned and judicious an advocate *for truth*; yet—we cannot avoid thinking that this author hurts the caufe of Chriftianity in a moft tender part, by contefting the pre-exiftent ftate of *Chrift*, and thereby divefting him of his *original divinity*, the criterion, the *fine qua non* of his doctrines; for when he confiders him as only *mere enlightened man*, he moft certainly goes counter to the exprefs declarations of *Chrift*, in many places of the Gofpels touching himfelf, his pre-exiftency, and nature of his miffion, as being a delegate *immediately* from heaven; but more particularly in St. *John's* Gofpel, chap. iii. 16, 17, and 18th verfes. We concur in fentiment with this writer, and feel very diftinct ideas refpecting the DEITY of the Father, and the *divinity* of the Son; but when he could without fcruple admit, that *divinity* and *humanity may unite*, or rather, as the learned *Baxter* ftates it, that God, by his omnipotency, can unite a fpiritual being to any *material form* he pleafes; we cannot conceive why he fhould ftumble at allowing the pre-exiftence of the *divine Spirit of Chrift*. The

creation

creation and miferable exiftence of every mortal intelligent being, we have fully proved, can only be compatible with the juflice of God, upon the fuppofition of the pre-exiftent flate of their fpiritual part or *foul*; then where lies the difficulty of fuppofing the pre-exiftent nature of *Chrift?* as the *firft created, the firft begotten* of God of *all celeftial beings*, before all worlds, delegated by the Father to *unite for a time* with the mortal form of man, for the great purpofe of falvation to a race of offending intelligent beings——Thus *Chrift* may literally, with propriety, and without any myftery or confufion of ideas, be ftiled and acknowledged THE SON OF GOD AND MAN, as he himfelf occafionally ufes both thofe titles.——When this learned and ingenious writer gives an unprejudiced hearing, and full force to the doctrines of the Metempfychofis, and duly weighs the infufficiency of every other human hypothefis, to account for the *phenomena* of *our prefent exiftence*, and indeed of *all nature*; he will, we flatter ourfelves, receive full conviction that his doubts and difbelief of the pre-exiftent ftate and *original divinity* of *Chrift*, were ill-founded, and not *the true doctrine of the New Teftament.*

116. If

116. If *reafon* and *religion* are deemed
worthy a place in the argument, man has
now the fulleft conviction from *both*, of the
true relation in which he ftands to the whole
brute creation, and that he can lay no rational
claim to the power he has affumed for a
multitude of ages paft over fome of their
fpecies; nor has he any the fmalleft jufti-
fiable pretence for the ufes to which he has
converted others of them, murdering fome
for the gratification of his depraved unnatural appetites, fubjecting others to the
moft cruel labors without humanity or re-
morfe, devoting others for his wanton fport
to premeditated deaths, attended with all
the cruel and affecting circumftances of *protracted terror*; training, exafperating, aid-
ing, and abetting others to bloody combats
of death againft one another of the *fame fpecies*; fpiriting up and encouraging others of
them, *of different fpecies*, to difcord, contention, and battle, worrying each other,
fometimes to death itfelf, for man's inhuman diverfion; imprifoning and divefting
others of the fpecies of *that liberty* which
was originally given to them by their Creator, upon a tenure equal with man's own;
and this only for the fake of a *trifling amufement* and indulgence to the ear; exhaufting
the ftrength, and abridging the lives of multitudes of the moft noble of the brute crea-

tion

tion *in contentions of speed*, for the bafe purpofes of *iniquitous gain* and *worthlefs fame*,
acquired not without the application of many cruel ruthlefs ftripes, gaping wounds,
and languid fweats, that human pity, *if it
had exiftence*, would fhudder at.

117. The above catalogue *of evils*, which
man has hitherto, without fcruple or feeling, wantonly loaded the brute creation
with, we will fuppofe may be afcribed to
his having loft fight of *their original dignity*,
and the *rela'ion* they truly ftand in to himfelf; and therefore this ignorance may, in
fome degree, be pleaded in extenuation of
his guilt : but now he is fully evinced of
both, he in future remains without excufe,
if he does not recede from practices that
are neither warranted by reafon, religion,
juftice, or the common dictates of humanity. The further to induce him to this
worthy receffion, we beg leave to remind
him, that every brute is animated with *a
foul* identical to *his own*, advancing only *in
a progreffive ftate* TO MAN; and that he
has no right either to haften, or retard *that
progreffion*, that being an act which God
has referved to himfelf alone : GOD has
faid,——" *Thou fhalt do* NO *murder*," and
man has had the boldnefs, either totally to
difregard this commandment, or by putting
his

his own conftruction upon it, has infringed
it in every fenfe, where power gave him the
means : how could we then expect mercy
for the brute creation, when he has fhewn
none for his own fpecies ? But this is a kind
of murder we fhall not fpeak to here, in-
tending in this place further to examine his
pretenfions *not only to murder, but to eat the
animal beings*, and the fatal confequences of
this tranfgreffion to the world, requefting
our readers will have the goodnefs to advert
to what has been already prefented to them
on this fubject in our 103d and few following paragraphs. We know, that in this
difcuffion we fhall meet with potent enemies to contend with, no lefs than a moft
formidable train of all the fenfual appetites
and paffions, but that fhall not deter us ;
human reafon, although long debafed, and
fubjected to the dominion of *Circe*, is not
quite extinct, and only wants to be roufed
by application of the *celeftial Moly*, to fhine
forth in its native and original luftre.

118. Befides man's conceit of his right
of dominion over the brute creation (which
has been fufficiently refuted) he urges *two*
other pleas in fupport of his practice of *killing and eating his fellow-creatures* ; thefe he
thinks are unanfwerable——*The firft* is the
obvious courfe and deftination of Providence,

whereby

whereby we fee that every race of the animal
creation are in a perpetual ftate of war, and
doomed to be a prey, the one to nourifh
and fuftain the other *;—the fact, if laid
down as a *g neral* pofition, may be admitted, but with large exceptions, as many
tribes of quadrupeds are exempted from that
general law of nature, as the horfe, the
the cow, the deer, the goat, the fheep,
&c but allowing this plea to have its full
force refpecting the carnivorous tribes of
the brute creation, yet *man* cannot avail
himfelf of this law; *they* deviate not from
the line prefcribed them by the God of nature, but man, in becoming *a beaft of prey*,
acts not only in violation of his order and
rank in the fcale of beings, but alfo in oppofition to an exprefs interdict of God, as
promulged in the Bramanical and Mofaic
hiftory of his creation before cited ; and indeed, upon a furvey of the natural conftruction of his form, the quadrupeds above fpecified might gorge and regale their appetites
upon animal food with equal propriety as
man, who cannot plead *the law of neceffity*,
which carnivorous animals feem to be fubjected to for their daily fubfiftence.

119. Let us not, however, in our abundant zeal for the brute creation, be wanting

* Vide Part II. from page 77. to 86.

in

in our due applaufe to the amazing and unaccountable *moderation* and forbearance of
man, in that he has not in *Europe* yet arrived, to what moft certainly muft be the
higheft perfection of good eating, *the flefh
of his own fpecies*; which, from the nature
of its regimen, and the repletion of animal
falts and juices, muft yield a much more
exalted flavor, and higher enjoyment, than
any other kind of *brutal flefh* can poffibly
afford.—*Swift*, of ever witty and farcaftic
memory, was ludicrous on this fubject; but
we are quite ferious, and think man's abftinence from this *fupreme indulgence* the more
to be honored, and the more wonderful, as
he is not without precedents for the practice, on the authentic records of *America*,
and other *favage nations*; befides——his
virtue fhines brighter in this *great felf-de-
nial*, when he may with propriety urge
very cogent *political* reafons, that would
fully juftify his tranfplanting that *lufcious
delicacy* and fafhion into *Europe*, to wit, the
increafing fcarcity and *high price* of all animal food, both which evils would be effectually and fpeedily averted from us, by the
project of—KILLING AND EATING THE
CONSUMERS; from which practice, the too
great population of the human fpecies would
alfo be prevented. A confideration which

leads

leads us to man's *fecond plea* for killing and devouring the brute creation.

120. *The immenfe increafe of the animal creation*, which it has been fuppofed would over-run the world, and endanger man's fafety and exiftence, has been urged as an unanfwerable *plea of neceffity* for their de-ftruction;—to fay nothing of the wicked-nefs of this argument, which directly and openly arraigns the wifdom, goodnefs, and mercy of God, we will confider the force of it, and hope to prove it as ill-grounded as the former; for, in the firft place, fup-pofing (although not allowing) the fact, it can only give a fanction to man for kill-ing, *but not for eating:* nor can this argu-ment poffibly be applied, even with the femblance of propriety, againft any fpecies of the brutes, but thofe that are obvioufly obnoxious to him, and thefe fhun his fo-ciety.——Any fuperabundant increafe of the *finny race* cannot poffibly affect man's fafety or exiftence, yet he deftroys and de-vours them in common with their terreftrial and aerial brethren.——But to fhow the fallacy of this plea, we find it levelled only againft thofe unoffending animals which man has deftined *for his prey*, and no pre-tended inconvenience is felt from the in-creafe

creafe of thofe felected for our pleafure or our labor, as witnefs the elephant, the horfe, &c.——But to cut this plea fhort, and diveft it even of plaufibility, let us appeal to facts, which fet all reafoning at defiance;—let us caft our eyes back on the ancient extenfive empire of *Indoftan,* where, for a long fucceffion of ages, to the late period of their fubjection to *Tamerlane,* no animal was ever bereaved of life, but left to its natural decay and diffolution, and yet their increafe was never found, or objected to as an evil, or obnoxious to man.—On the contrary, it is moft evident, throughout the whole animal creation, man not excepted, that God has wifely adjufted the principles of decay in each, in a juft proportion to their increafe or prolific qualities, in fuch an equipoife, that the one fhall not exceed the other, to the confufion or detriment of his works.—If we admit, that fome parts may be overftocked, and that the increafe may exceed the means for their fupport, yet this affords no plea or fanction for flaughtering and eating them;—fince man has, without any authority from God or nature, doomed them to labor, to evade and fet at nought that part of his fentence which decreed " *that he fhould till the ground by the* " *fweat of his own brow,"* let him, in cafe of a fuperabundant increafe, *as the leaft fin-*
ful,

ful, export them to other regions that may ftand in need of them for fimilar purpofes, in place of devoting them to death, for the gratification of his unnatural appetites.——— There may be one fituation, and one only, wherein man can poffibly, with feeming juftice, deftroy the animal creation; and that is, when there fhould be fuch an increafe of thofe fpecies of fimilar conftruction with his own refpecting maftication, &c. that fhould rob or diveft him of that food which God and his own nature originally marked and pointed out for his fole fubfiftence; in fuch a cafe, provided he had no other means of freeing himfelf of them, he poffibly might ftand vindicated in killing, but *in no cafe* in eating them.———What has been above alledged refpecting the empire of *In- doftan*, may be as juftly applied to other regions and people of early times, as we fhall have occafion to fpecify below, where we purpofe to enquire, when the vice of flaughtering and devouring the brute creation began, and confider its fatal confequences, *as one of the great roots of phyfical and moral evil in the world.* But before we proceed to this enquiry, it is neceffary to obviate another plea in defence of this error, which jufts now ftarts up, and arrefts our intended courfe.

121. Man,

121. Man, when hard preffed, and at a lofs for rational argument (for he cannot eafily and with a good grace give up the favory flefh-pots of *Egypt*), has advanced a *third plea* in fupport of his practice, which he would alfo fanctify into *a plea of neceffi-ty*, which is, that without the ufe of animal food, and vinous and fpiritous potations, the human form could not be fuftained in full health and vigor.——Surely man cannot be in earneft, when he urges this as argument, for not only the experience of nations, but daily inftances in multitudes of individuals are againft him.——The fuperlatively wife and infpired DANIEL, in his firft chapter, exhibits to mankind a fine leffon, which comes in point to invalidate this futile plea.——The King of *Babylon*, defirous of having fome youths of the royal *Hebrew* line trained up in his court, " *to ftand* " *before the King,*" he appointed them a daily provifion of the *King's meat*, and *the wine* which he drank; but *Daniel*, anxious that neither himfelf nor the royal youths fhould be defiled, rejected *the meat and wine*, and making an intereft with the governor that was fet over them, " befeeched " him to give them *pulfe to eat; and water to* " *drink*;" the refult was, that at the expiration of the time prefixed by way of experiment, " *their countenances appeared fairer,*
" *and*

" *and fatter in flesh than all the children who*
" *had eat the portion of the King's meat.*"—
Thus we humbly conceive that we have
fairly driven man from every subterfuge,
every retrenchment, which he has cast up
in defence of the cruel and unnatural practice of *killing* and *eating* his fellow-brethren
of the animal creation, without *any necessi-
ty, or other rational plea, for so doing.*

122. When, or in what period of the
world, man fell into the fatal error of murdering and feeding upon his elder brethren
of the creation, is difficult to fix with any
precision, although we may with much probability conclude it had a very early rise;
as it has been observed, man grows not
wicked all at once, so we may rationally
conjecture this vice became not general, until within the space of three thousand years
back;—that copious fountain of wisdom
and knowledge, that inceffant advocate for
the rationality and morals of the brute
creation, the learned author of the Turkish
Spy, recites many authorities in proof, that
this vice was not practised in the *first times*,
but was an innovation on the primitive manners of mankind; he honors the Brachmans
of *India,* and feems to be a convert to the
doctrine of the Metempfychofis; he ftands
amazed at the fignal circumftances, pecu-

liar

liar only to the SANSCRIT, and the four
books of the law (*i. e. the Chartah Bhade
of Bramah*), written in that language; he
thinks it ſtrange that no hiſtory ſhould mention *ſo divine a ſpeech*, and draws his concluſion of the ſuperior antiquity of the Bramins, their language and books, to the reſt
of the world,—" *in regard that they fall not*
" *within any records, ſave their own.*"——
He then, with great truth, remarks, that
the people of *Indoſtan* are the only people
in the world who have, in all ages to this
day, paid a ſtrict obedience to that firſt injunction and law of GOD, *Thou ſhalt neither*
kill, nor eat thy fellow-creatures of the brute
creation. He alſo inſtances, that the primitive *Perſian* and *Egyptian* Magi abſtained
from and prohibited this vice to their followers, and this abſtinence remained inviolate ſo long as they retained the pure theology which had been communicated to them
by their neighbors the Bramins of *Indoſtan.*
——He alſo notes, that the ancient Druids
of *Gaul* and *Britain*, who taught the doctrine of the Metempſychoſis, abſtained from
killing and eating animal food, and remarks
likewiſe, that the firſt people of the world
made offerings to the gods only of the fruits
and flowers of the earth, which has been,
and is uniformly the practice of the people
of

of *Indoſtan* to this time.—He recites, that
the precepts of *Triptolemus* and *Draco*, the
firſt law-givers of the *Athenians*, comprehended the whole ſyſtem of virtue and piety
in practiſing theſe few following rules: " Let
" it be an eternal ſanction to the *Athenians*,
" to adore the immortal Gods, to revere the
" departed heroes, to celebrate their praiſe
" with ſongs, and the *firſt-fruits of the*
" *earth, and neither to kill man or beaſt.".

123. In whatſoever age this depravity
took its riſe, it is plain it obtained not generally all at once, but by ſlow degrees;
and as every *other* ſpecies of wickedneſs
gained footing and flouriſhed in the world,
ſo we may ſuppoſe this alſo grew to maturity with them, and became univerſal, except in the ſingle inſtance of a whole nation, marked above. The uſe of vinous, and
afterwards ſpiritous potations, we conceive
had a later riſe, and was a natural conſequent of an appetite previouſly vitiated by
the unnatural reliſh of animal food; and
we think it moſt probable, that both theſe
vices firſt took poſſeſſion of man in ſome
period of what *Bramah* calls the *Tirtah
Jogue*, or ſecond age, immediately ſucceeding the *Suttee Jogue*, or age of truth and
righteouſneſs; for it was in the *Tirtah*

3   *Jogue*

Jogue * (which may be properly ftiled the
firft age of evil) that the influence of *Moifafoor* or *Satan* brought about the *fecond* defection of one-third of the angelic fpirits;
and as his power increafed during the fuc-
ceeding *Duapaar* and *Kolee Jogues* †, fo
we may rationally couclude the *two vices*
under confideration became univerfal (excepting the *Gentoos*) about the middle of the
Kolee Jogue or age of corruption, that is,
about three thoufand years ago: how it
happened that the *Gentoos* alone, either never fell into the vice of killing and eating the
animal beings, or were reclaimed from it,
is eafily accounted for, from God's pofitive
injunctions againft it ‡, delivered by the
mouth and fcriptures of *Bramah*; for as to
the ufe of vinous and fpiritous liquors, it
fhould feem that was a vice not in being at
the period in which that infpired legiflator
revealed his *Chartah Bhade Shaftah* to the
Gentoos, to wit, 4870 years ago, for if it
had, it is moft probable it would not have
efcaped his notice and prohibition;—and
yet the *Gentoos* abftain as religioufly from
the one vice as the other, probably from
fome pofitive injunctions laid upon them

* Vide Part II. p. 68 and 69.
† Ibid, p. 70 and 71.
‡ Ibid, p. 51 and 52.

in

in the *Infoff Bhade*, or fourth book of *Bramah*'s Shaftah.

124. To give the devil his due, it muft in juftice be acknowledged, that the introduction of thefe two *firft-rate vices* was a mafter-piece of politics in *Moifafoor or Satan*, who alone was capable of working fo diabolical a change in rational intellectual beings. He had prefcience enough to forefee, by reafoning from caufes to effects, that if he fucceeded in the attempt, he fhould be able in time to counteract and utterly circumvent the merciful intentions of God towards the delinquent fpirits. To this he was ftimulated by feveral different motives, all tending to the fame end;—he confidered them, from their perfevering in penitence and holinefs throughout the *Suttee Jogue*, as in a ftate of rebellion againft himfelf, and with good reafon, as they had acknowledged him for their King and Leader in heaven;—he had alfo, with grief and indignation obferved, that during *that age* multitudes of them (on whofe fidelity he had depended) had efcaped out of his reach, and were advancing through the regions of purification towards their loft feats, and that probably the next age would leave him without any other fubjects but thofe of *his*

own tribe, whofe allegiance to him he knew was inviolable; therefore, effectually to guard againft a farther revolt of his old affociates, he meditated the infernal fcheme of tempting them to the ufe of animal food,. and intoxicating drinks, as an infallible expedient that would fully anfwer all his diabolical purpofes. For, *firft*, he knew he fhould thereby lead them into fin and difobedience, by a breach of an exprefs command and prohibition of their GoD. *Secondly*, he was fenfible that thofe unnatural aliments would inflame and exalt the defires *of the flefh*, above the rule and dominion *of the fpirit*. *Thirdly*, he knew alfo, that by natural confequence *difeafes* would enfue, that muft affuredly *abridge* their *term of probation* in the form *of man*, which would be no. inconfiderable point gained. *Fourthly*, his penetration made it obvious to him, that this *inflamed ftate of the human body* (from the continued acceffion of animal falts and juices, heated and fermented by the auxiliary force of fpiritous liquors) would be propagated through the fpecies; and that the fure effects would be, their *giving birth* amongft them to a train of monftrous, unnatural, violent, and confequently ungovernable paffions, as lufts of every kind and fpecies, ambition, avarice, envy, hatred, and malice, &c. that would regularly pro-

M   duce

duce *a progeny* of concomitant actions and effects; as, invasions of property, contentions, wars, battles, murders, and sudden deaths. *Fifthly*, he forefaw a farther favorable confequence from the indulgence of thefe paflions, as that they would, by the natural force of their operation, engage and confine their purfuits to the temporary fenfual enjoyments and acquifitions of *this world only*, and caufe them to lofe fight of *the next*, as well as of *the means* by which they were deftined to regain it. Thefe deviations from the path marked out for them, *Satan* knew would in the end eftrange their GOD from them, and that they and their pofterity would become *his own*, from generation to generation.

125. It is worth enquiry, by what fyftem of craft *Moifafoer, or Satan*, could poffibly induce rational beings fo widely to fwerve from their obedience, and from their original nature and dignity, into that of lions, tigers, wolves, &c. beafts of prey; nay, to exceed them in every kind of vicious refinement, and to leave them fo far behind in the race of luxurious, voluptuous gluttony, befides the *exalted invention* of either entirely divefting themfelves of their fenfes and reafon, or of turning them from their bias, by the licentious guzzle of wine and
fpirits;

an enchanting relifh and enjoyment, which
the brutes have not yet arrived to, one fpecies of them only excepted, which approach
in kind the neareft to our own, viz. the
Satyr, Oronootan, Baboon, and others of
the fame race, all of which (the firft excepted) we have feen fmoke and drink until they
became as completely beafts *as man himfelf*;
fo that man has not fo much caufe to plume
himfelf upon this glorious acquifition, as
he poffibly and vainly may have flattered
himfelf withal.—But, not to lofe fight of
our enquiry by any farther reflections on
thefe grievous truths, fo degrading to humanity,—we may fuppofe, that *Satan*, having had experience that the angelic fpirits,
in their fuperior and pre-exiftent ftate, had
not been proof againft his artful feductions,
began his operations, and exerted his influence, firft upon thofe who were appointed to prefide over the ceremonies of religious
worfhip, rightly judging, that if he could
corrupt thofe who had the lead on earth, the
reft would fall an eafy prey; he was aware,
that if he abruptly propofed the deftruction
of their fellow-creatures, without fome fpecious plea, human nature might ftart at the
propofition: he therefore cunningly fuggefted the fanctifying their murder by offering them up in facrifice, as a work that

would

would be moſt acceptable to the Deity; he doubtleſs likewiſe inſinuated, they would thereby not only do a thing pleaſing to GOD, but alſo render a ſignal ſervice to their delinquent brethren, who they knew were impriſoned in the brute forms, the ſhortening whoſe lives would expedite their progreſſive advance to that of man, from which form alone they could regain their loſt ſtations in the celeſtial regions. That this was an argument *Satan* laid no ſmall ſtreſs on, appears obvious from this, that it has been frequently made uſe of by ſeveral ancient prieſts and philoſophers, *his faithful deputies*, in juſtification of the inhuman practice.— This great point gained, *Satan* met with little difficulty in prevailing on them to taſte; and thus by degrees the killing and eating the moſt innocent ſpecies of theſe devoted miſerable beings, became an eſtabliſhed *religious cuſtom* all over the world; a practice, ſay the Bramins, which the devil himſelf could *only* have forged.——Yet *Satan* thought himſelf not quite ſecure of his votaries, without playing an after-game that would infallibly work out their future perdition; therefore his next ſtep was to influence them to extend their *religious ſacrifices* to their *own ſpecies:* to bring them to this ſupreme pitch of wicked ſuperſtition, he

he found fome difficulty, but at length prevailed, by infinuating, that they would
thereby not only more effectually deprecate
the difpleafure and vengeance of the gods,
but alfo free the fouls of thofe who were
thus devoted, from future tranfmigrations
through the mortal brute forms of punifhment and purgation.—If any of our readers
doubt the addrefs and fuccefs of *Satan* in
this arduous attempt, we have only to recommend them to the perufal of the hiftories of the ancient *Phenicians, Tyrians,* and
Carthaginians, who were all *fhoots* from the
Chaldean ftock, and alfo the hiftory of the
Canaanites in our Old Teftament.——*Satan*
ftill thinking his fcheme defective, gave the
finifhing ftroke to it, by fuggefting the practice of pouring out *libations* of wine to the
gods, without which the ceremonies of religious facrifices would be imperfect; this
obtained, he left them to themfelves, knowing, that as they had fo readily been induced to eat of the one, they would of courfe
make as licentious a ufe of the other; and
that he fhould, from the natural united effects of both, always find them in a proper
ftate to receive any diabolical impreffions he
fhould in future fuggeft to them, by his
own immediate operation on them, or by
thofe of his infernal agents:—and thus, al-

M 3   though

though he had failed of acquiring *supreme worship* in heaven, he at length effectually obtained it on earth.

126. We may with probability conclude, that some ages (although not many) might have elapsed before the laity came in either for a bit or a sup of those religious sacrifices; that these observing (by the instigation of *Satan*) how their priests *piously devoured them*, began to demur against supplying them with victims, unless they also came in for a share, which at last they obtained; the priests still referving the most delicious morsels for themselves.——And thus, in process of time, both priests and laity killed and eat the brute creation in common, without even *the pretence* of religious motives, or indeed any principle at all; a point which *Satan* forefaw they would in the end arrive at, and the event confirmed the sagacity of his judgment in forming a plan which at once afforded him a triumph over GOD *and man.*

127. Having above, we humbly conceive, made it manifestly appear, to the full conviction of every unprejudiced reader, that the *two vices* which we are combating have been, and still are, the pernicious

roots

roots from which all moral evils fprang, and continue to flourifh in the world; permit us next to repeat, that (according to the fhewing of the philofophers, moralifts, divines, and hiftorians of all nations) *there has been an utter depravity in mankind in every part of the known earth, from the earlieft records of time.* Let any cafuift affign any *other adequate caufe* for this univerfal depravity and corruption of the fpecies, that will account for this phenomenon, better than thofe which we have above attributed it to, and we will moft readily give up our fyftem;—*à caufe* there muft be fomewhere, and that a general one too, that could produce fuch *uniform effects.*——Divines point out no other caufe than that we are undoubtedly under *the influence of the devil.* This we know as well as they, but they feem not to know *how* it happened that we came under that direction; all the learned of the world concur in the opinion that *there was a time* when *primitive man* was not under his dominion: the angels *continued good* for a long fpace before they fell a facrifice to his feductions, and their own ambitious folly; and fo they did again for an age, when doomed to animate mortal forms on earth, for their firft tranfgreffion; and they perfevered in angelic virtue until *Satan* projected the introduction of thofe *two vices,*

M 4   which

which he was fenfible would infallibly
work fuch a change in the human body as
would of courfe impair it, and confequently
that the free ufe, exercife, and operation
of the *fpirit*'s intellectual powers of rectitude would be impeded, and liable to perverfion by foreign influence, which otherwife would have remained in full force and
vigor, as is verified by many inftances on
record, where man, by abftaining from
thefe *capital vices*, has kept his foul in fuch
a ftate as to refift every effort *of Satan* to
provoke him to fin.

12°. When the caufe of any difeafe is
difcovered, it amounts to more than half a
cure. Would man exert his intellectual
powers, he would foon pull down what *Satan* has been fo many ages erecting; his empire has acquired no ftability but from our
eafy fubmiffion to his diabolical fuggeftions;
and that in fuch wife, that we can now
hardly be faid to have any claim to that original free agency given to us, for the very
purpofe of withftanding his influence;
remove the caufe, the effect ceafes.
When man returns to his natural, primitive, fimple aliments, his inordinate defires, his paffions, and their direful iffue,
will as naturally fubfide, as they rofe; then
we may form a well-grounded hope of the
renewal

renewal and reftoration of the *primitive age*
of purity and holinefs; that *halcyon age*,
when man banqueted with innocence and
content upon the delicious produce of his
parent earth, without a thought of killing
and eating his fellow animals;—that age,
wherein the feathered tribe could in freedom and fecurity range in their proper element without dread or apprehenfion of the
cruel fowler;—when the roes and hinds,
with the timorous hares, might gambol
and fcamper at pleafure over the boundlefs
plains, without the rifk of being fcattered
and drove, in protracted terrors and difmay,
to the mountains, rocks, and brakes for
fanctuary againft the purfuit of the ruthlefs
hunter;—when the fcaly independent race
enjoyed at large their watery courfe, without moleftation, from the artful wiles of
the infidious angler;—when the fea remained yet unexplored, and COMMERCE,
that *bane* (falfely called the cement) of mankind, had not a being, and was not, as
now, an inftrument in the hands of *Satan*
to excite the fpecies to invafions, fraud, and
blood; the natural produce of the earth in
every region fupplied its offspring with all
that was ufeful and neceffary, becaufe men
were ftrangers to irregular defires, and we
have no *folid reafon* to imagine its inhabitants were lefs numerous then, than now.
                                                    As

As the wickednefs and unbounded violence of man brought on a rueful change on the face of the globe, fo we might rationally hope and expect, that on an univerfal return to his *primitive gocdnefs*, GOD would reftore to him his habitation, in all its original beauty and *natural fertility.*——This happy reftoration would man eafily accomplifh, if he prevailed with himfelf to abftain from thefe two capital vices, which were, as before obferved, the parents of every other fubfequent tranfgreffion on earth;—JUSTICE would then return in frefh luftre from her long banifhment, accompanied by the lovely train of *temperance, harmony, reciprocal benevolence,* and *lafting peace*; HAGGARD DISEASE would be drove into a longer banifhment than even *Juftice* fuffered, and (like her) only be known *by name.*——— DEATH would be commanded to ftand aloof, that man's happy term of probation on earth might be extended to a greater length, as a means for his future falvation. ——Then, and then only, may we hope to fee and feel the facred doctrines of *Chrift*'s gofpel operate *univerfally* on mankind, by producing a general rectitude of morals and piety.——We are not fo fanguine as to expect that this wondrous change would be brought about in *one generation,* but the *next* would moft fenfibly experience

its

its happy effects, and *Satan* would soon find himself repulsed and baffled in all his cuning and deep planned machinations, and be obliged to retreat with difgrace, and feek an empire in fome other region of the univerfe.

129. Now, as it appears beyond a controverfy, that the *depravity* herein lamented began in the priefthood, who firft unhappily fell under the influence of *Satan's* wicked fuggeftions; fo it is undoubtedly incumbent on popes, patriarchs, cardinals, archbifhops, bifhops, priefts, paftors, and rulers of every church on earth, to fet the pious example of beginning a general reformation of thefe two execrable evils, the killing and eating the rational brute creation, and guzzling vinous, &c. potations, ——They would do well to confider, that the perfevering in thefe vices themfelves, burdens *them* with a double weight of fin, as being the firft aggreffors, and as being fpecially commiffioned to guard the morals, and point out the right road of worfhipping the Deity to the laity; confiderations which, joined to their known affiduity and anxiety for the falvation of mankind, leaves us not the fmalleft room to fufpect, that they would hefitate a moment to fet fo laudable and effentially neceffary a precedent.

dent. To one unfkilled in the workings of
human nature, and the powerful fway of
the prince of the air, it may appear afto-
nifhing, that fo learned and holy a body of
men fhould continue fo long immerfed in
fuch grofs enormities;—but when we re-
flect, that the *(now human)* angelic fpirit
fell when it was more pure, and endued
with more fuperior and enlarged powers,
let us ceafe to wonder at its *errors* in its prefent degraded ftate, and aim only at the correction of *them*.—As an encouragement to
attempt and profecute this great work (we
may juftly fay) *of falvation*, we fhall remark, that as the laity too readily followed
the example of their ancient reverend teachers, fo it may be reafonably prefumed, they
will as readily, in thefe our times, joyfully
fubfcribe to and fupport their facerdotal
leaders in the pious reformation of thefe unnatural and impious practices, as it would
fo manifeftly infure to them their *prefent*, as
well as *future happy exiftence*.

130. Before we quit this our Third General Head, we will, to enforce our arguments, take leave to prefent our readers
with a lively picture of man's *primitive ftate*
in the age which we are laboring to reftore
him to; and alfo the progrefs of evil, fuperftition, and idolatry which *Satan* reduced

duced mankind to, after he had prepared
them, *as above*, to receive any impreffions
he was pleafed to meditate for their deſtruction.—Both thefe are drawn by an author
profoundly ſkilled in every fpecies of learning and wifdom.——" They went out and
" in, ſlept and waked, labored and reſted,
" in fafety and quiet. Avarice, envy, and
" injuſtice, had not as yet corrupted the
" minds of mortals. The earth brought
" forth corn, herbage, and fruits, without
" the huſbandman's or gardener's labor. All
" places abounded with plenty of *innocent*
" refreſhments, and. thofe primitive inha-
" bitants coveted no more. The cattle
" and the bees afforded them milk and
" honey, and the fountain-waters were ge-
" nerous as wine. This globe was a com-
" plete paradife, and no miſtaken zeal had
" taught men *religiouſly to invade another's*
" *rights, and in a pious fury to murder their*
" *neighbors, in hopes of meriting heaven*
" *hereafter.*——The law of nature was in
" univerfal force. Every man purfued the
" diɛtates of Reafon, without hearkening
" to religious fophiſtry, and facred fables."
——"But——when (at *Satan's* inſtigation)
" the lucre of gold had corrupted men's
" manners, and they, not contented with
" the riches and fweets which the furface
" of the earth daily afforded them, had
.   " found

" found a way to defcend into her bowels,
" ftung with an infatiable defire of hidden
" treafures; then began injuftice, oppref-
" fion, and cruelty to take place. Men
" made inclofures for themfelves, and en-
" compaffed a certain portion of land, with
" hedges, ditches, and pales, to fence them
" from the invafions of others; for the
" guilt of their own vicious inclinations
" filled them with fears, and made them
" jealous of one another. They built them-
" felves ftrong holds, fortreffes, caftles,
" and cities; and their terrors increafing
" with their criminal poffeffions, they per-
" fuaded themfelves that the very elements
" would prove their enemies, if not pacified
" by bribes and prefents. Hence fprang
" the firft invention of altars and facrifices,
" and from thefe pannic fears of mortals,
" the *gods* derived their pedigree; for one
" built a temple to the Sun, another to the
" Moon, a third to *Jupiter*, *Mars*, or the
" reft of the planets. Some adored the
" Fire, others the Water or Wind. Every
" one fet up to himfelf fuch a god as he
" fancied would be propitious to him.
" Thus error, being equally propagated
" with human nature, they created an infi-
" nite rabble of imaginary deities, paying
" to thofe idols the fupreme incommuni-
" cable

" cable honors due only to the Eternal
" Effence, Father, and Source of all things."

Fourth General Head.

131. With our readers permiffion, we
will open this head with the following texts
of *Bramah's* Chartah Bhade *,——" The
" Eternal One fpoke again and faid—
" I have not with-held my mercy from
" *Moifafoor, Rhaboon,* and the reft of the
" rebellious *debtah*;—but as they thirfted
" for power, *I will enlarge their powers of*
" *evil*;—they fhall have liberty to *pervade*
" *the eight boboons* of purgation and proba-
" tion, and the delinquent *debtah* fhall be
" expofed and open to the fame temptations
" that firft inftigated their revolt : but the
" exertion of thofe *enlarged powers* which
" I will give to the rebellious leaders fhall
" be *to them* the fource of aggravated guilt
" and punifhment; and the refiftance made
" to their temptations by the perverted
" *debtah*, fhall be to me *the great proof* of
" the fincerity of their forrow and repent-
" ance."——" The Eternal One ceaf-
" ed—And the faithful hoft fhouted forth
" fongs of praife and adoration, mixed with
" grief and lamentation for the fate of their

* Vide Part II. p. 57.

" lapfed

" lapfed brethren. —— They communed
" amongft themfelves, and with one voice,
" by the mouth of *Biſtnoo*, befought THE
" ETERNAL ONE, that they might have
" permiſſion to defcend occaſionally to the
" eight boboons of puniſhment, purgation,
" and probation, to aſſume the form of
" *Mhurd*, and by their prefence, council
" and example, guard the unhappy and
" perverted *debtah*, againſt the further
" temptations of *Moiſiſoor* and the rebel-
" lious leaders.—THE ETERNAL ONE af-
" fented, and the faithful heavenly bands
" ſhouted their fongs of gladnefs and thankf-
" giving."

132. Before we proceed, it may to fome
appear neceſſary that we clear up a feeming
contradiction in this part of Braman's fcriptures.——It may be objected, that GOD,
firſt by his fentence expofes the delinquent
angels to the fame temptations that in-
fluenced their revolt; and then, immediately
after, permits the faithful hoſt occaſionally
to defcend, and guard them from the artful wiles of the tempters,——or in other
words, to counteract his own decrees.—
To reconcile this feeming abfurdity, we
have only to conceive that the faithful hoſt
forefaw, that the delinquents might not of
themfelves be able to withſtand the fuperior
faculties

faculties of the revolted leaders; who, it may rationally be suppofed, were endued with higher powers in proportion to their original rank:—this circumftance premifed, we fay, it is eafy to imagine why God fhould relent at the warm and pious interceffion of his faithful angels, and affent to the auxiliary force petitioned for by the fame interceffion HE had before been prevailed upon to reverfe their firft doom, and emerge them from their place of *utter darknefs and anguifh*, into a *pleafing ftate* of probation, comparatively confidered; for, although they were fentenced to a ftate of degradation in their paffage through the brute forms, yet being confcious, from the fentence pronounced to them by *Birmah*, that through thefe they fhould arrive at a *form*, wherein they fhould have powers to work out their reftoration, their prefent ftate muft have appeared delectable to them, put in comparifon with the former, a ftate of eternal defpair and bitternefs. Now, as the faithful hoft had fucceeded in the *firft inftance*, why fhould they not in the fecond?—They did.—Thus the feeming contradiction in the text vanifhes, and at the fame time conveys to us a ufeful and comfortable moral, to wit, that the prayers and ardent folicitations of *good beings* are not without their effect with a merciful

N   deity.—

deity.——The apprehenfions too of the faithful hoft were well grounded; for even with their affiftance, *Satan* proved an over-match for them both, and fo continues to this day.

133. The vifible or invifible miniftration, or interpofition of angelic beings in the concerns of mortals, is a doctrine which carries with it the fanction of the three great divine revelations, the *Shaftah*, the *Old* and *New Teftament*, as well as the concurring opinion of all mankind; and therefore we may juftly rank it as one of the *primitive truths*, which had the moft undoubted evidence for its birth and propagation in the *firft times*.—From this doctrine (a relative of the Metempfychofis) flowed the firft principle of the Manichean fyftem originally breached by the *Perfian* Magi, amongft other mutilated tenets of the *Chartah Bhade*;—the firft principles of this *primitive truth* were fimple and intelligible, but (in common *with the reft of the primitive truths)* mankind in procefs of time loft fight of it; and being unable to account for the mixture of *good* and *evil* which appeared in their exiftence, they rafhly propagated the horrible doctrine of two abfolute and independent divinities that governed the univerfe, each of diametrically oppofite

6 ·   natures;

natures; not adverting, that a fingle confideration which prefented itfelf daily to
them, was fufficient to refute a doctrine
which at once wickedly deftroyed the very
exiftence of a Deity and Providence; whereas, had not *Satan* hoodwinked their underftanding, they might have feen, that as
no ftate whatfoever could poffibly be governed by two independent powers, without falling into anarchy and confufion; fo
much lefs could the univerfe :—but from
the caufes above and elfewhere affigned, it
is no wonder that mankind fell into a mil-
lion of abfurdities, not lefs iniquitous than
this.

134. The mixture of good and evil *in
this world* flowed naturally from the *fecond*
angelic defection in the human form, as
inevitable effects from adequate caufes; for
thefe beings were fo ftruck with the unexpected mercy of their Creator, in affording
them a trial and term of probation, in a
world replete with every beauty and accommodation beyond their defert; that they
continued truly fenfible of that grace *for a
fpace*, diftinguifhed by the ancient poets and
philofophers by the title of the golden age,
by *Bramah*, as the age of truth and holinefs; and it is reafonable to believe, that
during that period, many of them regained

their

their celestial habitations; and equally probable, that whilst they continued in this state of general contrition, neither natural or moral evil had a footing in this globe, but that the former commenced and kept pace with the latter; and it is a well grounded opinion of philosophers and divines, that during the *primitive age*, this globe was not subject to those convulsive vicissitudes of storms, earthquakes, deluges, &c. nor the animal forms to pestilential or other diseases, which moral evils produced at the beginning of the *second age*, when the second defection of the angelic beings under *mortal forms* took place as before noticed: then it was, that man began to kill and eat his brethren of the creation, the brute animals; and in process of time to kill and eat one another;—then began contentions for property and power, which produced invasions, murders, and every species of cruelty amongst themselves;—then began the contention between the elements by the designation of God, for the punishment of the ungrateful delinquents; and then also began the contention between the good and evil spiritual beings, the one laboring to recover them to their duty, the other to seduce them from it. Here we would strenuously recommend to our readers the perusal of the pious, forcible, and judicious

dicious reafoning of the Rev. Mr. *Dean*, (before cited) in the firſt volume of his éffay on the future lives of the brute creation, where he unanſwerably proves that moral tranſgreffions were the cauſes of phyſical evils, although he ſeems a ſtranger to the *true reaſon, a priori, why they ſhould be ſo.*

135. The learned *Baxter* concurs with the Bramins, touching the exiſtence of evil ſpirits; and reaſon, joined to the conſider-ation of the goodneſs of GOD, naturally leads us to conclude, that if evil ſpirits have exiſtence and power, there muſt alſo be good ones. —His words are theſe: " The " *eaſtern* philoſophers aſſert, that there are " living beings exiſting ſeparate from mat-" ter; that they act in that ſtate upon our " bodies, and provoke our ſleeping viſions." —And he cites *Plutarch* in the inſtances of *Brutus* and *Dion*, ſaying, " We muſt own " with *the old philoſophers*, that there are " bad ſpirits who envy good men, and en-" deavour to ſtumble them, left going on " in the ways of virtue, they ſhould enjoy " a better lot than themſelves." And our learned divine adds in another place, " That " theſe *bad ſpirits are permitted* to excite " dreams that frequently degenerate into " awaking poffeffions, madneſs, idiotiſm, " &c. and by ſuch an *aſcendance, miſlead*

N 3   " *the*

" *the foul:*"—From the fame eaftern fages, he might have known that there exift alfo *good fpirits* who voluntarily endeavor to counteract the bad.

136. During the *primitive age*, it fhould feem that *Satan* and his affociate leaders had fmall, if any influence in the world; he appears (like an able politician, only to wait for proper times and feafons to exert his abilities in:—he could not but know that the delinquents were now as much ftunned with the unhoped-for mercy of GOD, as they had been before by his vengeance, and therefore that this could be no favorable juncture to operate upon them:—But he alfo knew (as is the cafe with all rebels) that mercy would have no long effect upon them; that the embers of rebellion in them were only fmothered, but not extinguifhed; and that there was only wanting a proper period and occafion to blow them up, and make them blaze again with greater fury: he judged that they would in time (allured by the delicious enjoyments of their region of probation) forget both the torments and defpairing anguifh they had fuffered in the *region of utter darknefs*, as well as the mercy that had redeemed them from it; and he was perfectly 'right in his conclufion.——The

means

means this arch-traitor adopted to bring about his purpofes of evil, both *natural and moral*, we have developed in our fore-going General Head, omitting one circum-ftance of encouragement as more properly applicable here—*Satan* and his leaders, al-though fenfible that the powers of the faith-ful angelic beings they had to contend with, were equal with their own, yet they were not difmayed; knowing that the propen-fity to evil in the objects on whom their ef-forts were to be tried, would turn the ba-lance in their favor.

137. It is moft probable, that the earlieft records that we have of the world, and the tranfactions of it, may be properly termed *modern times*, when put in comparifon with thofe that preceded; at leaft we have no folid reafons, or certain guides, for our thinking otherwife. Howfoever the ancient records of the univerfe afferted to be in the poffeffion of the *Indians*, *Chinefe*, and *Egyp-tians*, ftand difcountenanced by the narrow and limited conjectures of the moderns, yet unprejudiced reafon (as before hinted) recoils at the fuppofition of the world's being in the *juvenile ftate* given to it by the chronologers of *Europe*; when, from all its interior and external phænomena, it ap-pears to ftand on its laft legs, or rather fup-

N 4 ported

ported only on its crutches ;— *Herodotus* was certainly a wife man, and although he recites many extravagant legends of the *Egyptian* priefts, yet it is eafy to diftinguifh by his manner of tranfmitting them to po-fterity, what he really had fufficient grounds to credit, and what to laugh at, as fabu-lous: amongft the former, is *the antiquity of their records*;———if thefe extended eighteen thoufand years back from the pe-riod in which he wrote, then who knows what revolutions in ftates, empires, learn-ing, arts and fciences may not have hap-pened in the times preceding *their records?* *all thofe phænomena, like birds of paffage*, taking their flight from one region to fettle for a time in another; or, to purfue our fimile in a different fpecies of thofe animals, diving and finking in one place to rife in another far diftant; as we have obferved to have happened *to them all*, within the pe-riod of our fcanty and imperfect chronicles : and yet, fcanty as they are, it is from *thefe alone*, we are enabled to form a rational fur-mife, or judge with any precifion of the paft; *from thefe* then we are fupported in faying, that *the foundation* of every known empire, kingdom, and ftate of the world, was *originally laid in blood and carnage*; and by thefe rofe to the fummit of their great-nefs, and by thefe fell to perdition.

138. On

138. On a retrofpect into authentic hiftory, we furvey the fatal and fanguinary
iffue of the civil wars of all nations; wherein thofe allied by the moft facred ties, en-
gaging on different parties, cut the throats
of each other, and gloried in the facrifice ——Let us next take a view of the lamentable effects of invafion, from the Pagan and idolatrous *Sefoftris*, to the Chriftian
Spaniard's invafion of *Peru* and *Mexico*, in
the profecution of which laft only, no lefs
than twenty millions of unoffending people
were flaughtered without mercy.——Let
us obferve the horrid concomitants of thofe
contentions, impioufly ftiled, *religious wars*;
wherein religion, intended to correct our
morals, and eftablifh peace on earth, has
been made the ftalking-horfe, to cover the
perpetration of the moft cruel and atrocious
crimes, dictated by ambition, and an infatiable thirft for dominion and property;
witnefs the progrefs of the *Koran*, eftablifhed by fire and fword throughout the
greateft part of the world, the crufades, (let
us not call them Chriftian) and the endlefs
contentions between the profeffors of Chriftianity themfelves, and the dire maffacres
they have been the caufe of;—religious wars
had no exiftence in the annals of antiquity;
this was a fpecies of wickednefs referved
for later, and more enlightened times, introduced

troduced by the perverfion of *Chrifts* gofpel.—Let us laftly confider the difmal effects of *all wars*, even to the prefent hour,
and the univerfal depravity of man; and
then fee if we can find any *adequate caufe*
for thofe horrible enormous *effects*, than
that above affigned, namely, *the influence of
Satan*, under which the whole race of angelic delinquent human beings unhappily
fell, at the clofe of the *primitive age*; a dominion he has preferved ever fince over the
fpecies, a very few individuals in every age
and every region excepted, who have nobly
withftood his wicked machinations, and
utmoft efforts, to pervert them; a confideration which amounts to proof, that *all might*
partake of this celeftial triumph *if they
would*, by joining the exertion of their *own
powers* with the faithful angelic beings, who
are ever at their call; for we have no more
caufe to doubt their exiftence and activity,
than we have to doubt thofe of the air and
wind, although invifible to us.

139. GOD, confcious that he has endow-
ed us with fufficient powers of refiftance,
abandons us to ourfelves; and it is by the
neglect of thofe powers that ftill *man goes on
as the devil drives him*, and muft neceffarily
fo continue, until he again, by the full exertion of his divine intellectual faculties, re-
covers

covers that purity he poffeffed in the primitive age; the full exertion of thofe powers he can only acquire, *by reftoring the body, and its plaftic juices, to their primitive natures*, thereby freeing the foul from thofe impeding chains which he himfelf has forged for her; the *fure means* for accomplifhing this great end, and fetting *Satan* at defiance, we have already pointed out; until then, we remain entangled in the fnares and nets of the devil, and, like other animals fo caught, fhall perfift in biting, fcratching, worrying and murdering one another to the end of time.——Here we beg leave to diffent from the too generally received opinion, that the ancient and modern heroes, conquerors, leaders of battles and invafion, allies of death and the devil, fo much celebrated in ftory (as your *Sefoftrifes, Semiramifes, Cyrufes, Crafufes, Cambyfes, Dariufes, Xerxes, Alexanders, Cafars, Mahommeds*, and a very long &c. &c. &c.), were or are inftruments, or a fcourge in the hands of GOD for the chaftifement of mankind, becaufe we think there appears *no neceffity* for fuch an interpofition ; nor can we bring ourfelves to believe that GOD ever did, or does confent, to thofe furious maffacres of the fpecies, recorded in the annals of the world, and perpetrated to this day: why fhould

we

we be driven to fo unneceffary a conclufion,
when we fee, that the genius of man, by
the guidance of *Satan*, is quite adequate to
the purpofe? nor have we a doubt, but that
he takes fpecial care, firft to infufe into his
hero a proper difpofition for blood and con-
queft, and then places a *prime leader of his.
own* at his elbow, to keep him fteady, and
proof againft the horrid and piercing groans,
fhrieks, and cries, of flaughtered parents,
hufbands, and brothers, ravifhed wives and
daughters, entertained at the fame time
with the heart-rending fcreams of their expiring infants; for howfoever heroes and
their blood-thirfty followers may, by cuftom and practice, be inured to thefe *glorious fcenes*, yet it might fometimes fo happen, that the feelings of humanity would
ftart up in their breaft, and were they not
immediately fuppreffed, *Satan*'s main purpofe would be defeated; for the greater
number of the fpecies cut off fhort *of their
term of probation*, the farther his iniquitous
end is anfwered; and therefore he never
fails to excite to murder upon every favorable occafion, no matter of what kind,
whether of man or brute;——we likewife
think it moft probable, that, upon extraordinary incidents, where he might have
doubts of the addrefs or influence of a *de-*

puty,

puty, he did some of the *first-rate heroes* the honor of accompanying them *himself* in their expeditions, particularly *Cyrus, Alexander, Cæsar, Mahommed,* and *Fernando Cortez,* with other captains both of ancient and modern date, needless to mention.——Respecting the destruction of *Babylon,* so minutely foretold by the prophets *Jeremiah* and *Isaiah,* where " their young men and " their host were to be utterly cut off by " the sword, their houses spoiled, their " wives and virgins ravished, those in the " womb not spared, and their children's " brains dashed out against the stones be- " fore their eyes;"——if we allow the prophets to have been justly inspired in the circumstances of this desolation, yet they certainly were mistaken as to the *first mover of it,* and, by some egregious error or other, deprived *Satan* of the honor of this glorious enterprize.

140. By what has been said, and with a reference to the Metempsychosis, it need not appear strange, that the world has at all times been equally populous, respecting both man and beast, or very nearly so ; for so few of the delinquent spirits in every age have transmigrated to heaven, that they have been hardly missed on earth.——Here, we know, will be objected to us *Moses's* account

of

of the deluge, and the new propagation of all the animal fpecies, from the ſtock which *Noah* faved in the ark.——To this we fay, that there have been many folid arguments urged againſt the uñiverfality of*Mofes's* deluge, which have never been refuted to the full fatisfaction of inquifitive reafon.—It is true, we have *Mofes's ipſe dixit* for the deſtruction of all, in whoſe noſtrils were the breath of life; but how came it to paſs, that a race of animals, as numerous, if not more fo, than thoſe of the earth, efcaped his notice fo far, as not even to be worthy the mention, namely, the fiſhes of the feas and rivers? in their noſtrils were furely the breath of life. But the caufe of *Mofes's* filence refpecting them is obvious; he knew the difficulty of conceiving how their deſtruction could be accompliſhed in their proper element, on which the moſt tremendous ſtorms and hurricanes are matters of ſport and paſtime to them; therefore he took the wifer part in paſſing them over in filence, as having no exiſtence in the fcale of beings. This confideration proves, that whatfoever the deluge might have been, the deſtruction of the animal creation *was not univerfal*; then fuffer us to aſk, in juſtice to the reſt of the devoted animals, what exemption this peculiar race was intitled to, that they did. not participate in the general wreck?

wreck ?—God's juftice, mercy, and providence are equal to all, " a fparrow falls not " to the ground unnoticed of him"—therefore it fhould feem, that the fpirits animating the inhabitants of the waters, fhould at that period have been *lefs guilty* than the other terreftrial fpecies; but that that might not have been the cafe, we fhall fhew prefently, and demonftrate, that the feeming partial favor of Providence for that race can be only accounted for from the doctrine of the Metempfychofis.

141. Let us fuppofe, for argument-fake only (making a large allowance for the liberal genius of travellers), that every nation in the world retains a tradition of a deluge, yet this by no means invalidates the opinion that that of *Mofes* was only local and partial.——Men had finned, although probably not in equal degree, nor at the fame period of time, in every region of the habitable world, and therefore all might merit the chaftifement of God, fome at one time, and fome at another; therefore why may we not fuppofe, that he was pleafed to make ufe of a fimilar mode of punifhment to them all at different periods :—thus, in our own times, we fee fome nations fuffer under earthquakes, ftorms, inundations, and peftilences,

ftilences, &c. at one time, and others at another; and thus all nations may have retained a tradition of a deluge; univerfal as to each particular, but ftrictly and properly fpeaking, local only.—On this probable furmife we need no longer puzzle ourfelves with the difficulty of peopling *America* either with man or beafts, or any of thofe numerous iflands which lie very far detached from any continent, and yet at their firft difcovery were found populous and flourifhing in both.———But leaving this difputed point of the univerfality of *Mofes*'s deluge, as many others have done before us, juft as we found it, and as one of thofe occult events in which mankind will never univerfally concur, we will fuppofe it to have been precifely and minutely as *Mofes* has defcribed it.

142. Then it follows, that the fouls of every being were oufted of their mortal habitation for a fpace, except thofe which animated the marine forms. Now, by *Mofes's* fhewing, God attributes no evil or wickednefs to any of the brute creation; *nor* to the myriads of *infant innocents* ftruggling under the bitter pangs of death in that dreadful cataftrophe; and yet *thefe* fuffered indiferiminately, and in common with *guilty man*.

Now,

Now, ye divines, philofophers, fages, and moralifts of the world! account for this general and undiftinguifhed ruin of animal life, confiftent with our ideas of *a juft* and *merciful* God, upon any other hypothefis than that of the *Metempfychofis of Bramah*, and ye fhall be to us more than our *Magnus Apollo*.—On the principles of this doctrine alone, thofe two divine attributes of the Deity ftand confeffed, and vindicated, whether applied to an univerfal, or partial deluge on the earth, or to any other marks of his difpleafure:—death, to which man was doomed at the deluge, was no more than he was fubject to before; but the deftruction being fo general, made it more fignal: the meafure of man's iniquity was more than full, it ran over; and God feemed determined, at one tremendous blow, to try if terror would not in future operate more powerfully upon them than his goodnefs had done. The brutes, animated by the fame delinquent fpirits, although under other mortal forms, had been equally guilty in their former tranfmigration of man, and therefore juftly fuffered; the infant human race were taken off, and the term of the fpirits probation, with that of their parents, cut fhort, as the fevereft ftroke of God's difpleafure to man.——The fifh, although exempted for the prefent from their fhare of

O the

the general calamity, yet partook of its confequences equal with the reft, in their future courfe of tranfmigration through other
mortal forms, from the dire change in the
nature of this habitable globe, whofe de-
lightful furface became rugged and inhofpi-
table; its pure circumambient atmofphere,
fo effential to health and longevity, became
vitiated; which, with other new and injurious phenomena in nature, contributed to
fhorten the date of animal life.——Then,
peftilence, famine, earthquakes, tempefts,
inundations, &c. became inftruments in
the hands of GOD for the chaftifement of
the delinquent fpirit's fecond apoftacy : and
thus man brought upon himfelf accumulated
natural evils, in confequence of his moral,
tranfgreffions; oppreffion, war, ambition,
and their cruel effects, in the hands of thofe
fpoilers of mankind *called heroes*, were inftigated, as before fhewn, by *another mover.*

143. We have faid above, that the cut-
ting fhort man's *term of probation* was the
fevereft ftroke of GOD's difpleafure; for he
alone knows how many direful viciffitudes,
and variety of irkfome forms the *delinquent
foul* muft pafs through, before it receives the
grace of re-entering the *human form*, for a
new combat betwixt vice and virtue.——
The *Egyptians*, according to *Herodotus*, fix
the

the precife term of three thoufand years between the *fpirit*'s banifhment from the human form, and its regaining that *ftate of*
probation, from which only they can hope to
tranfmigrate to heaven. In this opinion
they were followed by *Pythagoras*, who
averred his fpirit animated the mortal form
of *Euphorbus*, flain at the fiege of *Troy.*——
The Bramins affix no precife fpace of time
for the completion of this event; and teach
only, that the *delinquent fpirit* paffes through
eighty-eight mortal forms, *the fpecies* appointed by GoD alone; fo that, according
to this doctrine, the fpace may be long or
fhort, in proportion to the longevity or
quick decay (confiftent with the common
courfe of nature) of the mortal bodies it is
doomed to animate. That the determined
fpace affigned by the *Egyptians*, was void
of any folid foundation, and an innovation
on the original doctrine of the Metempfychofis, appears from the confideration of the
uncertain term between the diffolution of
the human form, and the fpirit's being allowed the grace of re-entering *any mortal*
form at all:——Thus THE ETERNAL
ONE, fpeaking in the text of *Bramah*, part
2d, p. 55.——" But it fhall be,——that if
" the rebellious *debtah* do not benefit of my
" favor in the eighty-ninth tranfmigration
" of *mhurd* (man) according to the powers·
" where-

" wherewith I will inveft them ;——thou,
" *Sieb*, fhalt return them *for a fpace* into the
" *onderah*, and from thence, after a time
" which *I fhall appoint, Biftnoo* fhall re-
" place them in the loweft *boboon* of punifh-
" ment and purgation *for a fecond trial:*—
" and in this wife *fhall they fuffer*, until, by
" their repentance and perfeverance in good
" works during their eighty-ninth tranfmi-
" gration of *mhurd*, they fhall attain the *ninth*
" *boboon*, even the firft of the feven boboons of
" *purification.*—For it is decreed, that the
" rebellious *debtah* fhall not enter the *mahah*
" *furgo*, nor behold my face, until they have
" paffed the eight *boboons* of *punifhment*, and
" the feven *boboons* of *purification.*"—Now
it is moft rational to conclude, that the term,
or fpace and degree of the fpirit's fufferings,
both before it is permitted to enter any mortal body, and during its imprifonment therein, are (conformable to infinite juftice and
mercy) proportioned to its greater or leffer
degree of guilt, in its *lapfed ftate of probation
in the human form.*——This being the cafe,
how greatly incumbent is it not on mankind, to exert with vigor that portion of
God's divine fpirit with which he is en-
dowed, that he may rife from this *gracious
ftate of trial*, to thofe manfions of blifs ftill
kept open for him ; the more efpecially as
he has a moral certainty, that fhould his own
powers

powers (from impeding caufes to which he ftands felf-fubjected) prove infufficient, there is *an invifible angelic aid* ready to fecond and fupport his pious endeavors.

FIFTH AND LAST GENERAL HEAD.

144. It may be remarked, that there are Fifth *two* points of *Bramah*'s doctrine, refpecting neral the ftate of the fpirit; after the diffolution of the human body; *the firft*, its refidence *for a fpace in the onderah*, the feat of dark- nefs and anguifh, before it is fuffered to animate any mortal form at all;—*The fecond*, its ftate of purification, when by a life of purity and virtue, during its previous ftate of *probation*, it ceafes from its mortal tranf- migrations.——We need not expatiate on the temporal pecuniary trade and advan- tages the church of *Rome* makes of *the firft* of thefe doctrines; the leaders of that church will anfwer before a fupreme and *infallible* judge, for that, and the multitude of other grofs and extravagant principles of faith, by which they pervert the pure doc- trines of Chrift, and miflead the people committed to their charge; from whom the true GOD, and his worfhip, are as effectual- ly obfcured, as ever they were from the *Canaanites, Egyptians*, and *Tyrians* of old.

O 3   —But

—But this by the bye; nor fhould we have been provoked to thefe reflections, had we not fo lately been an eye-witnefs of the corruptions, idolatries, vicious parade, and legerdemain of that mother-church of *Eu-rope.*——That there is an intermediate ftate of the fpirit's purification between its deliverance from the human body, and its admiffion to the prefence of God, is the opinion of all divines and philofophers; and countenanced by the Chriftian fyftem : no wonder then, that thefe two points of doctrine fhould have fo univerfally obtained, when it appears, that they hold a, rank amongft the *primitive truths,* revealed to the apoftate angels, when doomed to take the mortal forms upon them, and are confequently relative tenets of the Metempfychofis.

145. The doctrine of the fpirit's purification is evidently founded on the rational conclufion, that its various and many defilements contracted in the flefh, render it an object unworthy of admiffion to God, or of the fociety of thofe pure beings who had not known pollution, until it undergoes a perfect depuration ; to accomplifh which, it was neceffary it fhould pafs through *feven regions* or ftages of purification, according to the text of *Bramah :*

matter

matter, we know, when grofsly foiled, cannot be fufficiently cleanfed *at once*; but will
require the frequent reiteration of the fame
procefs; and thus we may conceive of the
foul : but why precifely *Seven* gradations of
cleanfings, we will not pretend to explain,
nor is it a matter of much importance.—
It is reafonable to imagine, that the fpirit's
paffage through thefe *feven* pure regions is
retarded, or expedited, in proportion to the
ftains it had contracted during its abode in
the flefh, and the degree of its *original*
tranfgreffion ; for we have no folid reafon
for thinking, that the apoftate angels all
equally finned; the *firft movers* to fedition
and rebellion being certainly *moft culpable.*
—That *feven* was a myftical number with
all antiquity appears beyond all doubt :
GOD refted on the *Seventh day* according to
Mofes ; the univerfe is divided by aftrono-
mers into *feven* primary planets ; the *feven*
angels, and the *feven* vials of the Revelations; the *feven* wife men ; the *feven* wonders of the world; the *feven* divifions, or
parts of the world, according to *Zoroafter*,
fpecified in the voyage of the curious, and
induftrious *Monfieur de Perron*; wherein
the reader, if he has nothing better to do,
may amufe himfelf with the rhapfodies,
and theological dreams of that legiflator of
the *Perfians*; and when he has done, we

O 4 dare

dare promife him he will not find either
his heart or his underftanding much enlightened:—The *feven* heavens, and the
heaven of heavens fo frequently mentioned
by the Jewifh *Rabbis*, and by *Mahommed*,
and the *Arabian* doctors, fo correfpondent
with *Bramah's feven celeftial regions of purification*, and the *mahah furgo*, or fupreme
heaven; and it is pretty plain, that *Mahommed*, whofe olio, or hodge-podge of religion, was compofed from every fyftem
then extant, borrowed his *feven* heavens,
and *heaven of heavens*, from the *Bramins*.

146. Refpecting the diffolution or deftruction of the univerfe, or fifteen boboons
of punifhment and purification, *Bramah's*
doctrine differs from all others; in that he
teaches, the deftruction of the *firft eight*
will *precede* that of the *laft feven*; at the
deftruction of the *firft*, he marks the final
day of judgment, but his text will fpeak
better for him than we can.——" When
" all was hufhed! THE ETERNAL ONE
" faid,—It fhall be—that, when the fpace
" of time, which I have decreed for the
" duration of the *Dunneahoudah*, and the
" fpace which my mercy has allotted for
" the probation of the *fallen debtah*, fhall
" be accomplifhed by the revolutions of
" the *four Joques*—in that day, fhould there
5   " be

" be any of them, who, *remaining repro-*
" *bate*, have not pafled the *eighth boboon*
" of punifhment and probation, and have
" not entered the *ninth boboon*, even the
" firft boboon of purification ;——— thou,
" *Sieb*, fhalt, armed with my power,
" CAST THEM INTO THE ONDERAH
" FOR EVER.———And thou fhalt then de-
" ftroy the eight boboons of punifhment,
" purgation and probation, and THEY
" SHALL BE NO MORE.—And thou, *Bifhnoo*,
" fhalt yet for a fpace preferve the *feven*
" *boboons of purification*, until the *debtah*,
" who have benefited of my grace and
" mercy, have *by thee* been purified from
" their fin :—and in the day when that fhall
" be accomplifhed, and they are reftored
" *to their ftate*, and admitted to my pre-
" fence,—*thou, Sieb*, fhalt then deftroy *the*
" *feven boboons of purification*, and—THEY
" SHALL BE NO MORE."———Thus, according to *Bramah*, as GOD has conftructed the
firft eight regions for the reception, punifhment, and probation of the apoftate
angels; fo, when the term allotted for *its*
duration, and *their* trial, expires, and the
remaining reprobates are plunged into the
place of darknefs and anguifh, thefe eight
regions becoming ufelefs, their form is deftined for deftruction, whilft the other feven
are yet to be preferved for the gracious purpofes expreffed in the text.

147. This

147. This partial deftruction of part of the univerfe carries nothing with it, incongruous to the wifdom and goodnefs of GOD, but rather exalts both.——Of all the numerous fpheres or fubdivifions of the fifteen primary boboons of *Bramah*, fabricated for the reception of the myriads of apoftate beings, no mortal can know how many ftill exift in their original form, or what changes they may not have undergone;—many of them fcattered through the vaft expanfe, may have been long (for aught we know to the contrary) reduced to their primitive *chaos*, without being miffed by us, notwithftanding our bufy, prying, artificial optics, to explore what does not belong to us; which refearches only afford us futile matter of conjecture, whereon to found imaginary planetary fyftems; the one exploded, as foon as birth is given to another with more plaufible appearances; thereby drawing off man's wifdom and attention from matters of more immediate and important concern to him.—Man has nothing to do in this world, if he keeps his talents properly employed, *but to explore himfelf*, and fecure his immortal part (at its exit from the body) from future mortal chains, either in the brute or human forms.——Had that profufion of wifdom, and divine powers in man, which has in

2   all

all ages been fquandered away in the purfuit of non-effentials, been applied to its
proper objects ; the *primitive truths* of his
falvation would not have lain fo long hid
from him, nor he fo long been a ftranger
to his real ftate and relative nature.

148. The ancient *Gentoos* celebrated the
aniverfary of their birth with folemn fafts
and thankfgiving, fucceeded by a feaft of
joy : this they did, upon the pious reflection, that the fpirit had ceafed from its
tranfmigrations through the brute forms,
and had attained to its ftate of probation in
man ; and upon this principle it was, that
they celebrated in like manner the birth
of their children.——We likewife celebrate
the birth of our children, and theirs, and
our own anniverfaries ; but alas ! in a very
different manner, and upon very different
confiderations ;—the man who celebrates a
birth-day, upon any other principle than
that of the Metempfychofis, does it either
from the incentives of folly, pride, felf-
love, and vanity, or from interefted views
of fucceffion ; motives, all moft unworthy
of a rational being : for man, *abftractedly
confidered*, has, GOD knows, little caufe for
pluming himfelf, or celebrating and rejoicing
for an event which introduces him into a
life fraught with many evils, inevitable, or

of

of his own procuring; fo that the beſt of us would more fenſibly commemorate the day of his nativity, as the poet *Dryden* makes *Marcus Antonius, in double pomp of ſadneſs*; but,—— when we conſider the ſame event with a retroſpect to the Metempſychoſis, and behold an *offending angelic being* freed from the brutal mortal chains, and entering into a ſtate wherein, by proꞬgreſſive degrees, he arrives to the full exꞬercife of his divine intellectual powers, and is enabled thereby to re-aſcend to thoſe reꞬgions of bliſs, which he had too juſtly forꞬfeited,——then he may with well-groundꞬed reaſon annually celebrate ſo gracious an incident with pious praiſe and thankſgivꞬing, and temperate ſocial joy and feſtivity; whether ourſelves, or any connected to us, are the objects :——otherwife, a cereꞬmonial of this kind muſt appear to every *thinking being*, an empty parade of vainꞬglory; and a mark of unaccountable inꞬfatuation, repugnant to common fenſe.

CON-

CONCLUSION.

149. We have now, candid reader, brought our five General Heads to a clofe; in the difcuffion of which, our chief aim has been the reftoring to mankind thofe effential PRIMITIVE TRUTHS, on which his real ftate and nature originally exifted, and ftill exifts; and on a due regard to which, his temporal and fpiritual happinefs ever did, and ever muft depend;—but yet, our tafk is not finifhed; it remains, that we difcipline the principal fubjects of our labor, and draw them together in one compact body, that they may thereby acquire more ftrength and influence than they poffibly can, fcattered as they are, at fuch a diftance from each other, as the nature of our difquifition required: it is alfo requifite that we obviate fome objections and difficulties attending our general fyftem, which have not yet been noticed, although we know they will ftart up againft us, in prejudiced, narrow, and felf-interefted minds;—but *thefe* are no lefs the objects of our benevolence, than the more enlarged and enlightened: we fhall

then

then conclude with a few perfuafive reflections, that will naturally rife from our fubject.

150. With all humility we conceive,
that we have proved beyond the power of
refutation, 1ſt, That *original ſin* took its rife
in heaven, and that we have no grounds to
look for it in the tranſgreſſions of *Adam*
and *Eve*, or any where elſe.——2dly, That
man and beaſt are either animated by the
apoſtate angels, or,—that they are nothing
—a mere vegetative portion of matter in
the creation, and that their exiſtence at all,
as intelligent beings, can only rationally be
accounted for, *from the pure doctrine of the*
Metempſychoſis.——3dly, That the brute
creation was not made either for the uſe or
dominion of man, in the ſenſe he has been
pleaſed to adopt and practiſe.—4thly, That
man, by murdering and eating the brute
animals, was guilty of a manifeſt violation
of his creator's commands, and of his own
original nature.——5thly, That thoſe unnatural violations, with the auxiliary force
of intoxicating potations, proved the ſource
on earth of all evil, both phyſical and moral ;
producing the ſecond defection from GOD
of the angelic delinquents in their mortal
form of probation in man, and thereby affording *Satan* an open field, and full ſcope,

for

for all his diabolical purpofes againft the fpecies.—6thly, That man has *no chance* for fetting Satan at defiance, and for fubduing the univerfal depravity of the fpecies, and reftoring piety and morals, and confequently *no chance* for falvation, but by putting a total ftop to thofe two (or rather three, including murder) primary vices:—cut off the root, and the branches will neceffarily perifh; hereby the *primitive age* would be reftored, and a reform in morals would probably reftore alfo the globe to its priftine beauty and natural fertility as before urged.—7thly, That it refts on *the Clergy* of all nations to begin this general reform, for reafons before given.

151. We are fenfible that there are many tribes amongft the inhabitants of every kingdom on the globe, who will be more deeply affeéted than others, fhould our general fyftem of reducing mankind to their primitive regimen take place. Upon the return of moral reétitude into the world, laws would become ufelefs, and confequently lawyers, and their mifchievous train of retainers, will have no employment.——— Phyficians and their coadjutors, upon the reftoration of the human body to its original nature, will, in the fecond generation

at

at leaft, have no friendly difeafe for their
fupport.--Wine-merchants, diftillers, brew-
ers, vintners, dealers in fpiritous liquors,
cooks, (thofe dangerous inftruments of
luxury, difeafe and death) and butchers,
&c. will all be turned a-drift, and be forced
to feek for other means of fubliftence.
When we become, *bona fide*, Chriftians, the
art and deftructive practice of war would
ceafe to be the bane of mankind, and the
inoffenfive brute creation ; and a numerous
race of able-bodied beings, who have hitherto been employed only to work out the
perdition of the fpecies, would contribute
to their fupport and maintenance, by being
employed in the cultivation of the lands of
the ftate they belong to ; a work they would
moft certainly prefer to the trade of fpil-
ling the blood of their fellow-creatures,
they know not why, or in fupport of the tyranny and wanton ambition of others.

152. Refpecting the firft of the two learned profeffions, it has long been the opinion
of wife men, *that laws*, which were at firft
intended for the fecurity of *property* and
peace, are, by a ftrange fatality in the courfe
of human affairs, become the greateft caufe
of manifold grievances to the fubjects of all
nations, and the great fomentors *of difcord:*
the

the caufe of this general perverfion is beft
known to the learned profeffors; whilft the
effects are felt only by their clients: and
yet we think it is no very difficult tafk to
account for, and explain this feeming para-
dox.——That there is a litigious, craving,
Satanic fpirit in man, that too generally
takes the rule and guidance of his actions,
we believe no one will be hardy enough to
difpute with us : this unhappy difpofition is
encouraged by the chicane of the laws, and
the addrefs of *making black appear white,
and white black*; but far be it from us to
impute thefe evils to the profeffors of the
law, or to any defect in the laws themfelves, which can only be juftly applied in
the firft inftance to the client's litigioufnefs,
who defervedly fuffers when *that fpirit* will
not allow him to fubmit the decifion of any
matters in difpute to two or three of his rational neighbors. The one half of mankind
fubfift and grow opulent by the ftupidity,
wickednefs, and folly of the other : man is
man's natural prey; and he that has the beft
talents will be beft fed.——Be this as it
may, we think, when our fyftem takes
place, mankind will not fuffer any great lofs
by the demolition of this learned tribe.——
It is faid of a wife Emperor, when on a vifit to this and a neighboring kingdom,

where he attended *the courts of juſtice,* "that " he declared he had but two lawyers in " his kingdom, and that he would *hang up* " *one of them as ſoon as he got home."* Our hiſtorians record one of our parliaments that obtained the title of *the holy parliament,* be-cauſe——*there was not one lawyer that had a ſeat in it.*——But theſe are ſentiments and ſuggeſtions moſt unworthy, and can be on-ly excuſed by the ſavageneſs and barbarity of thoſe times.

153. Touching the ſecond of the learned profeſſions, it has ever been a moot point, whether it has not, at all times, and in all nations, been rather injurious than benefi-cial to mankind; and it has been eſteemed a mark of the beſt regulated governments, where the feweſt of this tribe have been to-lerated : but this muſt have been in barba-rous times too.

154. With regard to the next ſix tribes upon the liſt, and their confederates, we, in Chriſtian charity, congratulate them up-on the inexpreſſible joy and comfort they muſt experience, upon the near proſpect of being freed from that daily load of guilt which muſt oppreſs and be a heavy weight upon their conſciences, *for poiſoning their fellow-*

fellow-fubjects: an unhappy neceffity this, which they labor under, in order to fuit their liquors and eatables to the vitiated tafte of their cuftomers.——As the profeffors of thefe *crafts* are generally men fkilled in *cunning devices,* we earneftly recommend them to turn their genius to the improvement of their country's manufactures and agriculture, in which neceffary branches hands are wanting: moving in thefe falutary fpheres, they would become an univerfal benefit and honor to their country; whereas hitherto they have only been the dangerous inftruments of deftruction to their fpecies.——But now, they will (fome of them at leaft) be the happy inftruments of increafe in every fpecies of grain, fo effential to the life of man; and thereby make fome atonement for the immenfe quantities confumed in fiery diftillations, compofitions, and potations, calculated for no other purpofe but to burn out, *with wicked fpeed,* the thread of human life.

155. Refpecting *the butchers,* who merit a paragraph to themfelves, as being a tribe for whom we find ourfelves more deeply concerned than for all the reft put together, becaufe——*humanity* and *tender feelings* being their peculiar characteriftic, what muft they not endure, at finding themfelves un-

der

der the fatal neceffity of daily, nay hourly,
fhedding torrents of innocent blood, to gratify the unnatural appetites of man ?——We
folemnly proteft, that we think there are
no fpecies of mankind more the objects of
commiferation ;——we have known many
of the moft confcientious among them
deeply and pioufly lament, that ever *the
trade* of killing and butchering the animal
creation was transferred from *the prieflhood,*
by whom it was firft fet up.——But we
truft the time is not far diftant, when we
fhall be able to felicitate their being relieved
from their *fanguinary tafk,* for which we
are moft fenfible they entertain a well-root-
ed and righteous averfion:——when that
happy day arrives, we warmly recommend
to them *to turn bakers,* for which *craft* an
increafe of profeffors will be much wanted;
and, to atone in fome degree for the deluges
of innocent blood they have fpilt, we earneftly intreat that they will put a ftop——
to the adulteration of bread, that neceffary
ftaff of life.——In recompence for the prefent difficulties and inconveniencies which
every one of thefe tribes will be liable to at
their firft fetting off from their old track,
we will ftart one fuggeftion of comfort,
which will be applicable to them all, and to
all mankind;——whatfoever property they
may be poffeffed of when our general fyftem
commences,

commences, it will be preferved to them for the noble purpofes of fupport for themfelves and families, and to diftribute in acts of charity and benevolence to their poor neighbors : for now they will no longer be under the temptation, nor be ftimulated to any defire of gormandizing and guzzling their fubftance away in what is too commonly, but erroneoufly, termed *good living* and *good fellowfhip* ; terms vague and unmeaning, as we hourly fee them the fource of the deepeft miferies to multitudes of individuals, whom we behold reduced from opulence to penury and want by this mode of *evil living* and *evil fellowfhip*,

156. Having thus obviated and removed, we hope to the fatisfaction of our readers, the few foregoing difficulties which feemed to obftruct our conclufion, we think it neceffary to add, *that woman, that great mover of man,* whofe *true* characteriftics are fobriety, mercy, delicacy, and tendernefs, will prove the ftrongeft fupport to the Reverend Clergy in the reform of thofe two (three we fhould fay again) deadly vices we are meditating to abolifh; and this for many other reafons than barely the confideration of thofe amiable qualities juft enumerated, although thefe cannot fail of their due influence.——On the principles of the Metempfychofis

tempfchofis they will have a purer enjoyment and amufement in their favorite animals, when it proceeds from, not only rational, but pious motives; an intellectual felicity they have never yet tafted——in this
way;——they will have the unfpeakable
pleafure of imagining, upon folid grounds,
that the fpirits which *now* animate their favorite lap-dogs, cats, parrots, fquirrels,
monkies, &c. &c. *heretofore* animated the
form of a beloved friend, tender 'parent,
hufband, brother, child, lover, &c. and
their extravagant (and now irrational) fond-
nefs for thefe animals will then appear to be
founded on principle:——mankind alfo,
by their humane example, will cherifh the
brute creation, and become their defenders,
in place of murdering them for fport and
paftime, and then devouring them; a fport
and paftime ftill *more inhuman*.

157. We have hitherto fpoken to mankind in general, but we now, with all humility and deference, addrefs ourfelves to
the inhabitants of GREAT BRITAIN and
IRELAND, but more particularly to their
clergy of every denomination.——As you,
Moft Reverend, Right Reverend, and Reverend Sirs, are juftly celebrated for your
profound learning and abilities; and (what
is much more to your honor and glory) di-
                                    ftinguifhed

ftinguifhed for the fanctity of your lives and
manners above any body of priefthood in the
known world ; fo it is the more incumbent on.
you *to ftand forth to that world,* as the firft
champions for the univerfal reftoration of
morals; and by your example to fupprefs
three capital vices, which are the only incentives to debauchery of every fpecies, in every
rank of mankind; the great fountain from
which the torrent of immorality overflows
all bounds, and muft foon overwhelm us
all, unlefs the timely check of fome powerful dam be erected againft it.———This has
been the language of all times ; divines have
preached, moralifts have wrote, for fucceffive ages, but all in vain : immorality ftill
acquired frefh force. Is not the reafon of
this failure moft obvious ?—the *direful caufes* of this general depravity have never been
attended to.———The foul (as before urged)
reafons, and moves in conformity to the prefent ftate of the organs and fluids of the body which it animates, and from which it
receives its powers of action : this is evident from frequent inftances of idiotifm and
infanity : when the organs and fluids are vitiated, and reduced to any unnatural ftate,
the foul lofes, in a proportionate degree, its
freedom and rational active powers; their
influence on each other is invariable and re-

ciprocal:

ciprocal: hence it is, that mankind by the
ufe of *unnatural aliment*, may be juftly faid
to have been in one uninterrupted *ftate of
delirium* from the expiration of *the primitive
age*; therefore it is no wonder that all reafoning is caft away upon beings whofe intellectual facultits are difordered, and in no
capacity of receiving it:——mankind muft
be firft brought to their fenfes, before reafon, or your pious exhortations, Reverend Sirs, can poffibly operate upon them;
but this once accomplifhed, they will then
be open to every falutary difcipline both of
divines and moralifts: but this moft defire-
able ftate can be only obtained by the immediate prohibition of all animal food, and intoxicating drinks, as before often (but not
too often) forcibly urged: until this is done,
the daily marks of Gop's difpleafure, in his
vifitations of peftilences, ftorms, inundations, famines, and earthquakes, brought
to our very doors, and your fpiritual re-
monftrances will have none effect.——This
being manifeftly the cafe, and as the indulgence of any fenfual appetites ought not to
ftand in competition with the prefent and
future falvation of the fouls committed to
your care and guidance, you will, Moft
Reverend, Right Reverend, and Reverend
Sirs, no longer give a fanction by your practice

tice to daily murders and vices, which have proved the bane of mankind in all ages, to the prefent hour; but nobly fuftain the fuperior character you have fo worthily acquired, by prefenting yourfelves as the firft great example of reformation.

158. As it has evidently been the general courfe of God's providence, *that a righteous nation fhall be happy*, it is no marvel that the inhabitants of the globe fhould have been, from the earlieft accounts of time to the prefent, plunged in diftractions, and vifited by dire calamities; for none have been righteous, no not one; at leaft to perfeverance.——The whole continued hiftory of the *Jews* affords a ftriking inftance in point: whilft they walked in righteoufnefs, *they profpered and were happy*; when they deviated from that path, they were punifhed, by God's withdrawing from them his immediate protection, and leaving them a prey to their enemies, which we conceive to be his ufual mode of punifhment; for, as to the portrait of him exhibited by *Mofes, Jeremiah, Ifaiah, Samuel*, and others of the prophets, who reprefent him as a being fubject to the paffions of *revenge, wrath, hatred*, and *violence*; we cannot help concluding. they exceeded their commiffions, and *humanized* their God to an unpardonable

able degree, to cover their own fanguinary
difpofitions and views: therefore we cannot
prevail on ourfelves to pay a compliment to
the veracity of thofe prophets, at the expence of our GOD ;————for we cannot confiftently conceive that GOD can be endued
with any paffions but thofe of *love* and *pity*,
without derogating from his *divine nature :*
when he finds it neceffary to punifh us for
our offences, in hopes of turning us to our
duty, it is not done from motives of *revenge*
and *wrath*, but thofe of *love*; accompanied
by commiferation for our blindnefs and
folly————whom the Lord loveth he chafti-
feth.————In the above predicament ftood
the *primitive Hindoos*, who fubfifted for a
long feries of ages in holinefs; peace, tran-
quillity, and happinefs ; but in procefs of
time, although they ftill kept themfelves
free from the ftains of murdering and eating their fellow-creatures, and the ufe of
fafcinating drinks ; yet, by blending idolatrous worfhip with that due only to the true
GOD, and their neglect of the *primitive
truths* bequeathed to them by their infpired
prophet and legiflator *Bramah*; they, in the
end loft the protection of GOD, who gave
them up a prey to inteftine divifions, and to
the Mahommedan invaders. Thus alfo it
is recorded of the primitive *Scythians*, whofe
extreme purity in morals and manners pro-
5   cured

cured them the protection of God, but a deviation from that ſtate of purity left them at laſt open to the ſucceſsful invaſions of many nations.——Theſe ſignal inſtances, with many more which might be cited to the ſame purpoſe, prove, that no nation can expect or hope to proſper, or be happy, but by *perſevering* in righteouſneſs; and that the ſtake, although great, may be eaſily won.

159. Piety and Virtue, with tears and loud laments, call out for a reform throughout all the earth !——Reformation muſt begin ſomewhere.——*Europe*, the moſt enlightened portion of it at preſent, preſumptuouſly uſurps the title of Christian, until ſhe exert all her powers to effect this great work :——the way is cleared for her,——the reign of ſuperſtition and fanaticiſm are nearly extinct,——the *curſed ſpirit* of religious perſecution (that wicked weapon in the hands of *Satan)* is *laid,*——philoſophy has enlarged the minds of the ſuperior ranks of people, and a dawn of unprejudiced reaſon begins to ſhine upon the inferior, leaving them open to the reception of truth, when conveyed to them free from unintelligible myſteries.——*Great Britain* ſtands in the firſt rank of religious reformers ; ſhe has now an opportunity of taking the lead to *Europe* in the reform and reſtoration of morals.

rals.——All reforms which men may meditate in matters of religion, are purely ideal and vague; and will prove, alas! no reform at all, but a mere pretence to one, without a reform in morals; as faith without works will affuredly ftand us in little ftead.—— *Great Britain* and her refpectable clergy have it now in their power to fhine forth in celeftial luftre, *a new ftar of guidance* and inftruction to *Europe*; and, by the reflection of her example, to enlighten the reft of the world:—in order to this, we moft anxioufly recommend the confideration of this moft important of all fubjects TO THE BEST OF KINGS AND MEN, and to the Legiflature and people of *Great Britain* and *Ireland* in general; but——our firft hope refts on the pious example and preaching of our Moft Reverend, Right Reverend, and Reverend Paftors: by their unwearied endeavors, we doubt not but we fhall foon fee effectually (although not literally) verified, the fpirit of that remarkable prophecy of the famous wandering *Jew*, recorded in the Turkifh Spy, which conveys a fuggeftion fo greatly honorable to the Britifh nation *.

160. As a reform in fpiritual matters (as above hinted) without a previous reform of

---

* Vide Turkifh Spy, vol. vii. p. 216.

morals,

morals, as the ſtate of human nature now
ſtands, is, as it were, beginning at the
wrong end of things; ſo, when our Reverend Clergy obſerve, that, by a return to
natural aliments, the return of reaſon and
morals make a rapid progreſs amongſt their
countrymen; then will be the happy time
to make a thorough reform in the ceremonials and principles of religious worſhip; for
then, and not before, will they be in a proper frame of mind to receive it; their bodies
being temperate and cool, their ſouls will
not be inflamed nor excited to irregular and
violent paſſions or deſires; but in their place
calm and unclouded reaſon and rectitude
will take the rule.——Our Reverend Paſ-
tors will then doubtleſs aboliſh, not only
the uſe of the *Athanaſian* Creed, but the
Nicene alſo, and correct that commonly called The Apoſtles.——They will pay ſome
regard to the injunctions of *Chriſt*, who
ſays, " But when ye pray, do not uſe *vain*
" *repetitions*, as the *Heathens do*, for they
" think they ſhall be heard *by much ſpeak-*
" *ing*," and cut ſhort the tedious tautology
and worrying of the Deity in the courſe of
the Liturgy, and leave not the ſmalleſt ſemblance of polytheiſm in any part of our
worſhip.——They will ſtudiouſly garble
the unintelligible *Thirty-nine Articles of*
Faith,

Faith, and correct the modes of *ordination* and *abfolution*; and no longer fwear to the belief and obfervance of tenets which they neither can, or do believe or obferve; nor prefume to be endued with *powers* which they know they have not, and which they alfo know belong to no being on earth.——— Thefe, and many more dregs of Paganifm and Popery, which we ftill erroneoufly retain, *they* will affuredly caft away from us; and thus—on the whole, we fhould become a new people: by quick gradations the pure fpirit of *Chrift*'s doctrines would' take root in our hearts; *power* would no longer conftitute the *rule of juftice*; the *primitive truths* and the *primitive age* would be reftored; mankind, who has from that period hitherto been, by nature, principle, and practice, *very devils*, would revert to a perfect fenfe of their original dignity and angelic fource, and no longer difgrace it; all jarring fects would be reconciled; peace and harmony would return to the earth; an effectual ftop would be put to the carnage of man and brute; and *all united*, would produce *a fure and happy tranfmigration to eternity*.———
GREAT BRITAIN AND IRELAND would blaze out as *the torch of righteoufnefs* to all the world; her.nations would profper; her people be happy; their *pious flame* would be
                                                    caught

caught by their neighboring ftates, and from thence be ſpread over the face of the whole earth; and THE KINGDOM OF SA-TAN WOULD BE NO MORE.

161. We are moſt ſenſible, that in this age of diffipation, infidelity, and ſenſuality, our labors and ſyſtem will be deemed by the diffolute and unthinking part of man-kind, utterly chimerical and impracticable: be it ſo; it is not from thoſe we expect a reform: our hopes reſt on the efforts of the many, who, although they ſwim with the current of vice, have yet *at heart* a reve-rence for the ſublime truths of religion and morality, and would gladly join in ſtem-ming the tide, howſoever they are, by a fatal complacence, borne down by the pre-vailing torrent of folly and faſhion: would *theſe* but exert their powers in the cauſe of virtue; *thoſe* would ſoon be aſhamed of be-ing out of *the mode.*——The marks of the divine diſpleaſure which hovers round us are tremendous! we know not how ſoon they may light upon us; therefore let us, by a general reform, effectually deprecate the " peſtilence that walketh in darkneſs," and thereby excite our GOD to " give his " angels charge over us."

162. Thus

162. Thus we have finifhed a Differtation, begun from no other motives *but the glory of God, and the prefent and future good of all mankind, and the reft of the animal intelligent beings :*——it muft be allowed that our attempt is laudable, howfoever imperfect the execution.——And now we take our final leave of the Public, to whom fome apology is due, for the tardy performance of our engagement, owing to unavoidable hindrances, as, bad health, a neceffity for change of climate, &c.

163. We could have fwelled the fize of our book with the addition of many more learned quotations and notes, from ancient and modern productions, to illuftrate and fupport our fyftem; but, as we benefit not ourfelves in any fhape by the fale of our publications, fo we have ftudioufly avoided taxing the Public for the emolument of our bookfeller.

164. Before we put an abfolute FINIS to our work, we think fome apology is alfo due to thofe individuals amongft our readers, who, either from a weak mind, hard head, or foft and tender confcience, may poffibly be offended with fome parts of our doctrines which bear a tendency fo diametrically oppofite to the fenfual paffions

and

and appetites of one clafs, and to others fo
repugnant to the *opinions* they have imbibed
in the early ftages of life, which they have
been taught to cherifh, and look upon as
orthodox and eftablifhed articles *of faith:*—
to fuch we only recommend, that they would
endeavor to enlarge their intellectuals, by
divefting their fouls of *all prejudice,* and
thinking for themfelves; and then we reft
affured that we fhall ftand exculpated from
all intention of offence.——We have already had occafion, more than once, to affert,
that our great and leading motive for this
Effay was the *revival* of the PRIMITIVE
TRUTHS, as the only fure bafis for the reftoration of morals and true religion; and
with this principle we clofe: conceiving,
at the fame time, that our laudable endeavors muft fhare the fame fate with thofe of
others (much more equal to a tafk of this
nature) and prove abortive of the end propofed, whilft a common error in the political inftitutes of all nations fubfifts, namely,
the provifion of penal laws for the public
punifhment OF VICE, without eftablifhing
laws for the encouragement and public reward of VIRTUE.——The principles of
fhame, and thirft of applaufe, fo firmly
implanted in every human breaft, feem to
have been utterly neglected, whilft they
might, in the hands of a wife legiflator or
adminiftration, be converted to the moft fa-

Q   lutary

lutary purpofes of every well-governed ftate.
——Some *univerfal caufes* there muft be,
why every age proves more depraved than
the laft: fome of the moft fatal we have
occafionally marked in the body of our
work, but the political error above noticed
is not amongft the leaft—The tendency of
all human laws feems calculated, not to
make mankind *better*, but to prevent their
growing *worfe:* how ineffectual all penal
laws have proved to anfwer this partial purpofe, every day's experience evinces; and
yet we perfevere without varying our fyftem,
although thereby we tacitly give up the
caufe of humanity; declaring in effect, that
human nature is incapable of amendment,
without trying whether in fact it is fo, or
not.——GOD himfelf has pointed out a
fhort inftitute of laws for man's example,
which man has never yet followed ; he has
decreed *punifhment* for fin, and *rewards* for
righteoufnefs: man punifhes evil actions,
but rewards not good ones, by any eftablifhed laws : herein GOD proves himfelf a *juft*
judge, and man fhews himfeif an *unjuft one,*
by leaving virtuous actions to their own reward in this life, in the breaft only of the
poffeffor, which, *in general,* proves but a
weak excitement to univerfal practice.—All
government is fuppofed to have taken its
rife from parental authority : although the
juft parent, in imitation of GOD, chaftifes

5   the

the faults of his children, yet he rewards
them for being good, notwithſtanding duty,
and their own intereſt, prompt them to be
ſo, for their own ſakes.—Hence it is moſt
obvious, that in the eſtabliſhed laws of all
nations, legiſlators have deviated from the
invariable œconomy of GOD, as well as
from the firſt maxims of human government in the world, in puniſhing crimes,
without eſtabliſhing laws, either *pecuniary*
or *honorary*, or both, for the reward and encouragement *of virtue*, in whatſoever objects or lights ſhe may appear.—Herein *alſo*,
we would ſtimulate the legiſlature of our
country *to take the lead* to *Europe:* let virtue be *honored* and *rewarded* by authority,
and vice would ſoon fall into difeſteem, as
unprofitable.

We make no apology to the Public for
the *matter* of our Eſſay, but as many inad-
vertencies may have eſcaped us in the execution, reſpecting want of ſtrict connec-
tion, diction, &c. for theſe we rely on the
good-nature and indulgence of the learned
world :—we have wrote from the full conviction of our heart and underſtanding;
therefore, ſhould our ſtile ſometimes appear
too dogmatic and dictatorial, we hope (the
cauſe conſidered) candor will kindly over-
look it.

Milford Haven, near Haverford Weſt,
.South Wales, 1ſt Nov. 1770.

F I N I S.

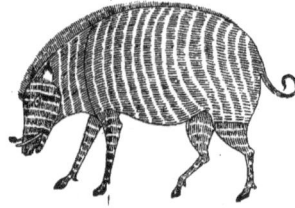

www.ingramcontent.com/pod-product-compliance
Lightning Source LLC
Chambersburg PA
CBHW030857270326

41929CB00008B/459